THE MICROSOFT EXCHANGE SERVER INTERNET MAIL CONNECTOR

Spyros Sakellariadis

A Division of
DUKE COMMUNICATIONS INTERNATIONAL
Loveland, Colorado

Library of Congress Cataloging-in-Publication Data

Sakellariadis, Spyros Steven.
  The Microsoft exchange server Internet mail connector / by Spyros
Sakellariadis. — 1st ed.
      p.   cm.
  Includes bibliographical references.
  ISBN 1-882419-60-X
  1. Electronic mail systems. 2. Microsoft Exchange server.
3. Internet (Computer network)   I. Title.
TK5105.73.S25 1997
005.7'13—dc21   96-51201
                                                CIP

Copyright © 1997 by DUKE PRESS
DUKE COMMUNICATIONS INTERNATIONAL
Loveland, Colorado

This book was printed and bound in the United States of America.

ISBN 1-882419-60-X

1 2 3 4 5 6 EB 9 8 7

Acknowledgments

I owe a debt of gratitude to many who made this book possible. Some helped actively, some passively, and some without even knowing it. To all of them, to my friends, to my colleagues at API, Microsoft, and Wang, I want to say thank you.

I am especially grateful to Salah for providing much-needed hardware, to PSINet for hosting my DNS servers, and to Internet Shopper, Ltd for providing a copy of its POP3 server. In addition, Dr. Eric Grossman of PSINet, Brian Dorricott of Internet Shopper, Jennifer Sides of Valinor, and Bettie Claxton and Mike Fitzmaurice of API all provided valuable insights on Exchange functionality.

My friends and family provided moral support, lending an ear when needed, and keeping out of my way when necessary. Many provided bogus email addresses for the book. In particular, I am indebted to Isken and Judith, Salah, Paul, Jill, Billy and Clair, Judy, Chris and Hilary, Lulu and George, and Spots.

Finally, I want to thank Joe Tucci, Neil Exter, Ron Cuneo, Bill Ryan, Dun Scott, Kevin Newman, and Sam Cottrell for providing a light at the end of the tunnel.

About the Author

Spyros Sakellariadis is Vice President, Information Technologies, of Advanced Paradigms, Inc., a subsidiary of Wang Laboratories, Inc. He is involved in implementing major Exchange messaging and Internet WWW systems and oversees the R&D and MIS functions at API. He has written numerous articles on Windows NT, Exchange, and SMS. His favorite job before API was as an independent computer consultant working from George's Cafe on a Greek beach.

TABLE OF CONTENTS at a glance

Table of Contents

CHAPTER 1

Introduction

This book tells you how to configure and use Microsoft's Exchange Server software to let Exchange clients communicate with e-mail users on the Internet. The Enterprise version of Exchange Server ships with the necessary software on a CD. In version 4.0 of Exchange Server, this software is called the Internet Mail Connector (IMC); in version 5.0, it is called the Internet Mail Service (IMS). However, because many of the references to the IMS in the Exchange 5.0 software (such as the services shown in the Control Panel) continue to refer to it as the Internet Mail Connector, in this book we will use the term *IMC* to refer to both the 4.0 and 5.0 versions. Appendix E outlines some of the differences between the IMC and the IMS.

The IMC is only a small part of Microsoft Exchange Server. We assume you know how to set up and use Exchange Server. In this book, we provide the background knowledge and procedures necessary for experienced Exchange administrators to connect their systems to the Internet. We will not cover important related topics, such as X.400 messaging and TCP/IP networking fundamentals, in any detail.

The book contains seven chapters.

1. Introduction
2. Simple Message Transfer Protocol (SMTP) Mail Basics
3. Internet Mail Connector Overview
4. Domain Name Service (DNS) Basics
5. Installing the Internet Mail Connector
6. IMC Reference Guide
7. Connector Models

Chapter 2, "Simple Message Transfer Protocol Mail Basics," is an elementary tutorial on SMTP mail. We include this chapter to ensure that you understand the environment to which you'll be connecting. Without a firm grasp of the concepts involved in SMTP mail, you'll have a difficult time customizing the IMC for your own needs and appreciating the function of some of the parameters you can adjust in the IMC's dialog boxes. We look at the standards for SMTP mail and trace the flow of a message through the system. If you're familiar with SMTP messaging you can skip Chapter 2, although you might find some of the details about tracing messages with the Microsoft Network Monitor valuable.

In Chapter 3, "Internet Mail Connector Overview," we give a high-level architectural overview of Exchange Server and the IMC. We discuss the functions of the Exchange servers and the IMC in a variety of configurations and organizations. We trace the flow of messages exchanged between users throughout an Exchange organization and those on remote SMTP hosts, and we relate this information to the concepts discussed in Chapter 2.

In Chapter 4, "Domain Name Service Basics," we discuss the concepts behind DNS and how they relate to the delivery of mail in an SMTP messaging environment. Many problems people have with the IMC arise from problems with DNS, not the facilities of the connector itself. Chapter 4 includes both a basic tutorial on DNS and instructions for setting up DNS name servers running on Windows NT 4.0 servers. We will use the name server configurations described in this chapter again in later chapters as we set up sample Exchange organizations.

Chapter 5, "Installing the Internet Mail Connector," takes you through the installation and configuration process. We discuss how to set up basic Internet connectivity and troubleshoot some of the more common installation problems.

Chapter 6, "IMC Reference Guide," goes through all the configuration parameters in the IMC's dialog boxes. This chapter builds on the concepts and functions described in the preceding chapters and gives examples of how to set up the IMC in different environments. In addition to describing how you could set up the IMC in a small lab with four computers, we discuss configuration details for larger installations. Where possible, we refer you to useful articles in the Exchange documentation or Microsoft Knowledge Base.

Chapter 7, "Connector Models," discusses four paradigms for Internet connectivity:

- Single-homed organization
- Multi-homed organization
- Multi-homed site
- Backboned organization

You can use many strategies to connect an Exchange messaging system to the Internet, and these four represent very different approaches to that end. We discuss the advantages and disadvantages of each approach and relate the configuration details to the discussions in previous chapters. After reading this chapter, you'll have the tools for planning Internet connectivity, and you'll understand some of the tradeoffs involved in each strategy.

The book includes five appendices:

- Appendix A. Connecting with an Internet Service Provider (ISP)
- Appendix B. Using Windows NT as a Router to Connect a Class C network to an ISP
- Appendix C. Monitoring the IMC with the Windows NT Performance Monitor
- Appendix D. Internet Shopper Ltd.'s NTMail
- Appendix E. Exchange Server 5.0

The appendices cover information that is not directly relevant to configuring the IMC but might be useful in specific environments.

Where appropriate, each chapter or section ends with a list of useful reference materials. Because many of these topics are changing rapidly, we also provide references to specific Internet newsgroups and discussion areas so you can have access to current opinions and solutions.

CHAPTER 2

Simple Message Transfer Protocol Mail Basics

Overview

Simple Message Transfer Protocol (SMTP) is a set of standards used for messaging applications. It is the *de facto* standard for all mail transferred over the Internet. In this chapter, we review the basic concepts of SMTP by examining the written standards that define the protocol. If you're already familiar with this material, you might to skip to Chapter 3, "IMC Overview."

An SMTP mail system operates at the application layer of the Open Systems Interconnect (OSI) stack, as shown in Figure 2.1. SMTP is a messaging protocol that runs only over TCP/IP networks and uses many of TCP/IP's features to discover routes by which to deliver mail. (We will discuss message routing and TCP/IP in Chapter 4, "DNS Basics.")

Figure 2.1

SMTP Messaging

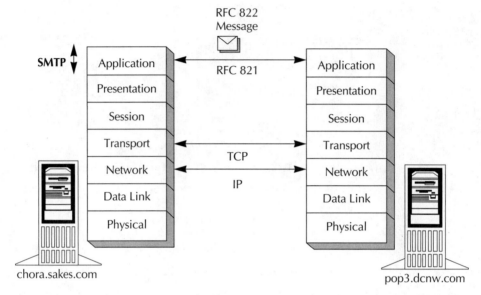

In Figure 2.1, a user on the host chora.sakes.com might use SMTP to send a message to a user on pop3.dcnw.com. To send the message, the following conditions must be met:

- The two hosts must be able to communicate over TCP/IP using port 25. (Any application or process using TCP for its transport is assigned a unique identification number called a TCP port; for a brief introduction to TCP ports, see "Supporting Microsoft Internet Information Server 2.0," Course 758, Microsoft Educational Services.)
- As long as the routers separating the two systems do not filter any of the IP ports, the two systems should also be able to ping each other.
- Both hosts must be running an SMTP messaging program.
  - They do not need to run the same SMTP messaging program; any application that complies with the SMTP specifications can send messages to any other SMTP-compliant program. For example, chora.sakes.com might be running Microsoft Exchange Server and pop3.dcnw.com might be a Unix system running Sendmail or a Windows NT system running Internet Shopper's NTMail.

○ Also, users don't have to run the same mail clients on their desktops — user Spyros could use the Microsoft Exchange client to communicate with chora.sakes.com and send mail to user Judy, who uses Eudora to access her mailbox on pop3.dcnw.com.

The procedures and standards for SMTP mail are defined in Requests For Comment (RFC) documents issued by the Internet Architecture Board (IAB), which is the body responsible for overall architectural considerations of the Internet. Once an RFC is published, it cannot be changed or deleted. If a change is needed, another RFC will be issued that extends or supersedes the previous one. More information about the RFC process can be obtained from the Internet Engineering Task Force (IETF), the protocol engineering, development, and standardization arm of the IAB, at http://www.ietf.org/.

Table 2.1 presents the primary RFCs relating to SMTP mail.

TABLE 2.1 SMTP MESSAGING RFCS		
RFC	Status	Title
821	Extended by 1425	Simple Mail Transfer Protocol
822	Extended by 1049	Format of ARPA Internet Text Messages
1049	Extended by 1154	Content-type Header Field for Internet Message
1154	Superseded by 1505	Encoding Header Field for Internet Messages
1225		Post Office Protocol - Version 3
1425		SMTP Service Extensions
1505		Encoding Header Field for Internet Messages
1341	Revised by 1521 1522	MIME (Multipurpose Internet Mail Extensions)
1521		MIME Part 1
1522		MIME Part 2

continued

RFC	Status	Title
TABLE 2.1 SMTP MESSAGING RFCS, CONTINUED		
1806	Supplements 1521	Communicating Presentation Information in Internet Messages: The Content-Disposition Header

In this chapter, we will look at several of these RFCs in detail, including

- RFC 821, which defines SMTP and governs how two SMTP implementations interact with each other to relay mail. An *SMTP implementation* is any vendor's SMTP mail program, such as Microsoft Exchange Server running the IMC. RFC 821 thus specifies the commands an SMTP mail system issues to another system to indicate that it is about to forward a mail message.
- RFC 822, which defines the structure of an SMTP mail message. An SMTP message is defined as a series of headers and a message body, consisting only of simple ASCII text. SMTP's dependence on ASCII text and its inability to handle complex body parts or attachments were addressed in subsequent RFCs, beginning in 1988.
- RFC 1225, which defines Post Office Protocol (POP) version 3. SMTP determines how hosts talk to each other; POP3 governs how users read their e-mail.
- RFC 1049, 1154, and 1505, which extend RFC 821, allowing binary code and documents to be attached to mail messages.
- RFC 1521 and 1522, which define multipurpose Internet mail extensions (MIME) that allow even more types of binary data in messages as well as multipart messages.

In addition, we will learn how to monitor SMTP traffic.

RFC 822 — Message Header and Body

RFC 822, Format of ARPA Internet Text Messages, was issued in August 1982. It defines the basic format for the message headers and the message body in all SMTP messages. Listing 2.1 shows a basic Internet mail message sent by a user Judy with e-mail address judy@dcnw.com.

This message is sent to Spyros Sakellariadis, with an e-mail address in the *domain* patmos.sakes.com (spyros@patmos.sakes.com). The header content is analyzed by the mail system receiving the message (in Figure 2.1, the

LISTING 2.1 BASIC INTERNET MAIL MESSAGE

```
TO: Spyros Sakellariadis <spyros@patmos.sakes.com>
FROM: Judy <judy@dcnw.com>
DATE: Sat 22 Jun 1996 12:11:11 -0400
SUBJECT: Basic SMTP message

Hello!
```

host chora.sakes.com, running Microsoft Exchange Server and the IMC), and the message is delivered to Spyros's mailbox. The message was sent by Judy in the e-mail *domain* dcnw.com (in Figure 2.1, from the *host* pop3.dcnw.com running Internet Shopper's NTMail software). The header in this message is very simple, and the body of the message is simpler still — Spyros will receive a message that says "Hello!"

Section 3.1 of RFC 822 defines the standard layout for the header and the body of messages transmitted over SMTP as consisting of "header fields and, optionally, a body."

The header contains information that lets the receiving SMTP host identify how to route the message and lets the recipient's SMTP mailer know how to read the message. The message header itself is a series of field names and values, followed by a single blank line. Section 3.1.1 of RFC 822 defines the header as follows:

> Each header field can be viewed as a single, logical line of ASCII characters, comprising a field-name and a field-body.

Where

> … a field … may be viewed as being composed of a field-name followed by a colon (":"), followed by a field-body, and terminated by a carriage return/line-feed. The field-name must be composed of printable ASCII characters (i.e., characters that have values between 33 and 126, decimal, except colon). The field-body may be composed of any ASCII characters except CR [Carriage Return] or LF [Line Feed].

The example in Listing 2.1 has four header fields: TO, FROM, DATE, and SUBJECT. The field names were supplied automatically by Judy's SMTP mailing system. The field bodies, supplied by Judy, are followed by a carriage return and line feed, and the four header fields are followed by a single blank line that separates them from the body of the message.

The minimum required header is three fields: DATE, FROM, and either a TO field or a BCC field. The example in Listing 2.1 clearly satisfies this minimum requirement. RFC 822 allows other header fields, including SUBJECT, CC, and COMMENT.

When the message in Listing 2.1 arrives at Spyros's mail server (chora.sakes.com), Judy's mail server (pop3.dcnw.com) will have added several headers, as shown in Listing 2.2.

LISTING 2.2 MESSAGE WITH ADDITIONAL HEADERS

```
TO: Spyros Sakellariadis <spyros@patmos.sakes.com>
FROM: Judy <judy@dcnw.com>
DATE: Sat 22 Jun 1996 12:11:11 -0400
SUBJECT: Basic SMTP message
X-Info: Evaluation version at pop3.dcnw.com
Message-Id: <18143885500034@dcnw.com>

Hello!
```

To the original headers, Judy's mail server added two more, the X-Info and the Message-Id headers. These headers comply with RFC 822 and are added by SMTP mailers to let the recipients trace the messages and know what type of systems handled the message along the way. In this case, the X-Info was added by the NTMail server based on a configuration parameter entered in the NTMail administrator, and the Message-Id was added automatically for identification purposes. (For a description of the NTMail program, see Appendix D.)

The specification for addresses is spelled out in RFC 822, Section 6.

A mailbox specification comprises a person, system or process name reference, a domain-dependent string, and a name-domain reference. The name reference is optional and is usually used to indicate the human name of a recipient. The name-domain reference specifies a sequence of sub-domains. The domain-dependent string is uninterpreted, except by the final sub-domain; the rest of the mail service merely transmits it as a literal string.

According to this passage, the sender or recipient of a message is specified as a mailbox, which has three parts:

- A person, system, or process name (optional)
- A domain-dependent string
- A name-domain reference

Table 2.2 shows the address structure of the mailbox "Spyros Sakellariadis <spyros@patmos.sakes.com>."

TABLE 2.2 ADDRESS STRUCTURE

Field	Value
Person, system, or process name	Spyros Sakellariadis
Domain-dependent string	spyros
Name-domain reference	patmos.sakes.com

The name "Spyros Sakellariadis" is optional on a mailbox and in the addressing string of an RFC 822 header; it is used to specify the given name of a recipient. The domain-dependent string "spyros" has meaning only to the mail system receiving the message. It is the object that most users of mail systems think of as their mailbox name. It has no meaning to any of the SMTP mail systems that transfer the message from the sender to the ultimate recipient, and it is passed along unchanged (the "literal string" specified in RFC 822, Section 6).

The name-domain object "patmos.sakes.com" refers to a sequence of subdomains. That is, "patmos" is a subdomain of "sakes.com," which is a subdomain of "com." This name-domain reference is used by the intermediary SMTP mail systems to route the messages to the mail system holding the "spyros" mailbox. Notice that the RFC says nothing about the names of the host systems in the domains. Thus, for example, the mail for the domain patmos.sakes.com may be handled by a host chora.sakes.com or another called campos.sakes.com. Similarly, mail for the domain dcnw.com could be handled by the system pop3.dcnw.com, or even one in an entirely different domain such as smtp.interramp.com. We will discuss mail routing and host names in Chapter 4, "DNS Basics."

Section 3.1 of RFC 822 defines the body of a message as follows:

The body is simply a sequence of lines containing ASCII characters. It is separated from the headers by a null line (i.e., a line with nothing preceding the CRLF).

The message shown in Listing 2.1 has a very simple message body that complied with this requirement — it consisted of the ASCII text "Hello!" Because messages can contain only ASCII text, mail systems such as MS Mail and Microsoft Exchange must ensure that any proprietary internal message format is translated into ASCII text before a message enters the SMTP system.

Problems arise when a message contains elements that cannot be expressed easily as ASCII text; for example, character formatting, colors, or bitmaps. RFC 822 has no solution for this. Users of mail systems have created utilities to convert nontext items into textual representation for inclusion in an SMTP message, but these conversions are very laborious and not user-friendly. The need for this capability led to a series of new RFCs that let SMTP mail accommodate complex body parts.

References

For more information about SMTP headers and message definitions, see

* **RFC 822, available at http://ds.internic.net/rfc/rfc822.txt**
* **"Implementing Microsoft Mail 3.2," Course 341, Microsoft Educational Services**
* **"Core Technologies of Microsoft Exchange Server," Course 632, Microsoft Educational Services**
* **"Supporting Microsoft Internet Information Server 2.0," Course 758, Microsoft Educational Services**

RFC 821 — SMTP Commands

RFC 821 defines how SMTP hosts on the Internet transfer mail. As we saw in Figure 2.1, SMTP operates at the application layer of the OSI model, and only over TCP/IP. To effect an SMTP transfer, one messaging system makes a connection to TCP port 25 of another messaging system and sends it a series of codes and data. For example, if judy@dcnw.com sends a message to spyros@patmos.sakes.com, then Judy's messaging server contacts Spyros's messaging server and sends it the information. SMTP refers to the interaction between the two messaging servers.

RFC 821, Section 2 defines the mail transfer procedure as follows:

Once the transmission channel is established, the SMTP-sender sends a MAIL command indicating the sender of the mail. If the SMTP-receiver can accept mail it responds with an OK reply. The SMTP-sender then sends a RCPT command identifying a recipient of the mail. If the SMTP-receiver can accept mail for that recipient it responds with an OK reply; if not, it responds with a reply rejecting that recipient (but not the whole mail transaction). The SMTP-sender and SMTP-receiver may negotiate several recipients. When the recipients have been negotiated the SMTP-sender sends the mail data, terminating with a special sequence. If the SMTP-receiver successfully processes the mail data it responds with an OK reply. The dialog is purposely lock-step, one-at-a-time.

This passage describes the "lock-step" of the SMTP process. Judy's messaging server contacts Spyros's server; Spyros's server replies. Judy's says it wants to send mail; Spyros's replies that it is ready to accept mail. Judy's indicates who the mail is from; Spyros's acknowledges, and so forth. The actual commands are defined in Section 4 of the RFC and include

```
HELO
MAIL FROM
RCPT TO
VRFY
DATA
QUIT
```

We will see how each of these commands is used shortly. (For a complete list of the commands, download the RFC from the Internet at the address given at the end of this section.)

Each dispatched command includes some sort of data. For example, the sender may issue the command

```
RCPT TO: Spyros <spyros@patmos.sakes.com>
```

This command tells the receiver that mail should be delivered to the mail server for the domain patmos.sakes.com. If the receiver is the correct system, it accepts the message and saves it to the mailbox for Spyros; otherwise, it may reject or forward the message.

The receiver acknowledges every command from the sender with a numeric code — called a result code — and, optionally, some text. The most common result codes are in Table 2.3.

TABLE 2.3 SMTP RESULT CODES	
Code	**Meaning**
220 <FQDN>	Service ready
250	Requested mail action OK, completed
354	Start mail input, end with <CRLF>.<CRLF>
500	Syntax error, command unrecognized
501	Syntax error in parameters or arguments

For example, the receiver might reply to the above RCPT TO command with

```
250 OK - Recipient Spyros <spyros@patmos.sakes.com>
```

This reply does not necessarily mean that the mailbox for Spyros is a valid one; it only indicates that the syntax of the sender's command was correct. Figure 2.2 shows a complete dialog between two SMTP hosts for a simple message from judy@dcnw.com to spyros@patmos.sakes.com.

Figure 2.2

SMTP Connection Between Two Mail Servers

pop3.dcnw.com

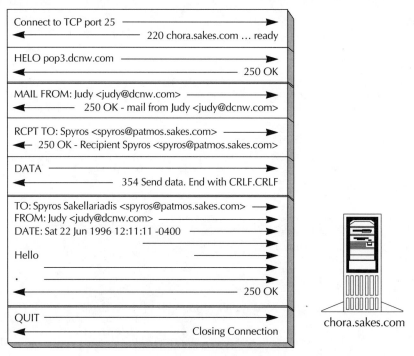

Connect to TCP port 25 ⟶
⟵ 220 chora.sakes.com ... ready

HELO pop3.dcnw.com ⟶
⟵ 250 OK

MAIL FROM: Judy <judy@dcnw.com> ⟶
⟵ 250 OK - mail from Judy <judy@dcnw.com>

RCPT TO: Spyros <spyros@patmos.sakes.com> ⟶
⟵ 250 OK - Recipient Spyros <spyros@patmos.sakes.com>

DATA ⟶
⟵ 354 Send data. End with CRLF.CRLF

TO: Spyros Sakellariadis <spyros@patmos.sakes.com> ⟶
FROM: Judy <judy@dcnw.com> ⟶
DATE: Sat 22 Jun 1996 12:11:11 -0400 ⟶
⟶

Hello ⟶

. ⟶
⟵ 250 OK

QUIT ⟶
⟵ Closing Connection

chora.sakes.com

Sending mail from one SMTP host to another entails seven simple steps.

1. The sending server (host pop3.dcnw.com) initiates a TCP connection to port 25 of the receiver (host chora.sakes.com). The receiving server sends back code 220 if it is ready to receive mail.

2. The sender requests an SMTP session by sending a HELO command, followed, optionally, by its name. The receiver returns an OK message if it accepts the session.

3. The sender forwards the identity of the user sending the message (judy@dcnw.com) using the MAIL FROM command. Note that the domain name (dcnw.com) is not the same as the specific host relaying the mail (pop3.dcnw.com). The receiver returns an OK message if the syntax is correct.

4. The sender sends a list of one or more recipients (spyros@patmos.sakes.com) of the message. If the message is addressed to multiple recipients (e.g., TO: Spots <spots@patmos.sakes.com>, Maria <maria@patmos.sakes.com>), the sender splits this address into multiple RCPT TO lines. Note again that the mail domain (patmos.sakes.com) does not have to be the same as the receiver's host name (chora.sakes.com).

5. The sender informs the receiver it is about to send the mail message by issuing the DATA command. The receiver confirms it can receive the data.

6. The sender transmits the data as an RFC 822 message in 7-bit ASCII characters. To signal the end of the message, the sender puts a single "." on a line by itself, and the receiver confirms receipt by sending an OK message.

7. After the data has been sent successfully, the sender repeats the process if it has another message to send; otherwise, the sender terminates the process by sending a QUIT message.

We can participate in the process directly by using Telnet to connect to an SMTP host and manually sending the commands as if they were from another SMTP message system. Figure 2.3 shows the start of an interactive Telnet session,

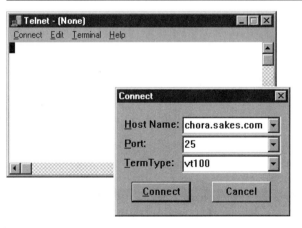

Figure 2.3
Interactive Telnet Session Logon

in which we are connecting to port 25 of the SMTP server chora.sakes.com.
This session will connect only if chora.sakes.com is running an SMTP service
— for example, Microsoft Exchange Server with the IMC installed, configured,
and running. In addition, a successful session requires that we have the host
name chora.sakes.com defined in the DNS or a local hosts table (for more
information about DNS, see Chapter 4). This connection lets us send mail to
chora.sakes.com just as if we were another server, such as pop3.dcnw.com.
Listing 2.3 shows the actual sequence of an interactive session.

LISTING 2.3 INTERACTIVE SMTP SESSION

```
220 chora.sakes.com Microsoft Exchange Internet Mail Connector ready
HELO pop3.dcnw.com
250 OK
MAIL FROM: Judy <judy@dcnw.com>
250 OK - mail from Judy <judy@dcnw.com>
RCPT TO: Spyros <spyros@patmos.sakes.com>
250 OK - Recipient Spyros <spyros@patmos.sakes.com>
DATA
354 Send data. End with CRLF.CRLF
TO: Spyros Sakellariadis <spyros@patmos.sakes.com>
FROM: Judy <judy@dcnw.com>
DATE: Sat 22 Jun 1996 12:11:11 -0400
SUBJECT: Basic SMTP message
X-Info: Evaluation version at pop3.dcnw.com
Message-Id: <18143885500034@dcnw.com>

Hello!


.
250 OK
QUIT
```

If chora.sakes.com is an SMTP host, it must be "listening" on port 25. If
chora.sakes.com is running Exchange Server, it listens on port 25 only when
the IMC service is running; if chora.sakes.com were a Unix host, it would
need to run a process such as Sendmail.

When we make a connection to that port by typing in the text in Figure 2.3, the server answers with an SMTP result code in compliance with RFC
821. The system must send a result code 220 if it is an SMTP host, and then it
can follow the result code with any text it chooses. Typically, implementors of
SMTP systems have the host reply with the name of the host and a description
of the type of software running on the host. In Listing 2.3, Line 1 shows
chora.sakes.com replying with its name, advising the sender (in this case,
advising us via the Telnet session) that it is a Microsoft Exchange Internet Mail
Connector process.

Once the sender has received the target host's confirmation, it starts an
SMTP conversation with the HELO command. This indicates that it plans to send

mail. The sender can append any information it wants to the HELO command; typically, the sender announces itself by sending along its host name. In line 2 of Listing 2.3, we typed "pop3.dcnw.com" after the HELO command to tell chora.sakes.com that we were the SMTP host pop3.dcnw.com. If we were really following convention, we would have typed something like "It's me, faking out another system!" In either case, if chora.sakes.com is ready for mail, it replies with a 250 command. It can ignore or acknowledge the optional text we included. In Line 3, the Microsoft Exchange Server IMC replies with a 250 OK and no further text; other systems say more.

The RFC 821 commands in Listing 2.3 form part of what is called the "envelope" of the message; they define who the message is for and who is it is from. In our case, the envelope starts with the HELO command and ends with the QUIT command. Inside the envelope is the message body, starting with the TO command and ending with the single line with a "." in it. The envelope gets the message to the SMTP host with the mailbox, and the message body — including the headers and the content of the message — is handed off to the recipient's mail client.

Although the envelope contains the RFC 821 command RCPT TO to deliver a message to a recipient, it is the RFC 822 command TO that contains the information that the recipient will see at the top of the message. On the other hand, if the user specified in the RCPT TO command is not found on the system, the sender of the message as specified by the RFC 821 MAIL FROM command will get a Nondelivery report, not the sender as specified by the RFC 822 FROM command. However, if the receiver of the message replies to the sender, it goes to the sender as specified by the RFC 822 FROM command. Confusing? Not really! All the interaction between servers is governed by the RFC 821 commands and the envelope. What the user sees, however, is determined by the contents of the message; that is, by the RFC 822 commands.

For more information, see

References

- **RFC 821 at http://ds.internic.net/rfc/rfc821.txt**
- **"Appendix A: Introduction to Messaging Standards," Microsoft Mail Resource Kit, Microsoft TechNet CD; the section entitled "SMTP"**
- **Microsoft TechNet CD; search for keyword SMTP**
- **the Web: search using Yahoo! or another search engine for keyword SMTP**
- **the following USENET newsgroups on the Internet:**
  - **microsoft.public.mail.connectivity**
  - **microsoft.public.exchange.connectivity**
  - **microsoft.public.messaging.misc**
  - **info.ietf.smtp**

RFC 1225 — POP3

SMTP defines only the way a mail host transfers mail to another host. It does not specify how users read their mail. Users of Unix systems can run a program (a User Agent, or UA) such as ELM or PINE to read their mail with the SMTP host. In addition, users can read their mail offline by downloading their mail from the SMTP host using a protocol known as the Post Office Protocol - Version 3 (POP3). This protocol is defined in RFC 1225 as follows:

> On certain types of smaller nodes in the Internet it is often impractical to maintain a message transport system (MTS). For example, a workstation may not have sufficient resources (cycles, disk space) in order to permit a SMTP server and associated local mail delivery system to be kept resident and continuously running. Similarly, it may be expensive (or impossible) to keep a personal computer interconnected to an IP-style network for long amounts of time (the node is lacking the resource known as "connectivity")....To solve this problem, a node which can support an MTS entity offers a mail-drop service to these less endowed nodes. The Post Office Protocol - Version 3 (POP3) is intended to permit a workstation to dynamically access a mail-drop on a server host in a useful fashion.

An SMTP host as defined by RFC 821 is a powerful server running a series of services or processes continuously. It stores incoming mail in a directory that can be accessed by an online client such as PINE. With RFC 1225, the IAB recognized that users may have "less endowed nodes" incapable of hosting SMTP, and that it may be too expensive to be connected to an SMTP host for sufficient time to read and respond to mail. The POP3 protocol was established so users of smaller systems could connect briefly to an SMTP server, download their mail, and then read it offline.

RFC 1225 defines the procedure for transferring mail between an SMTP host running the POP3 service and a POP3 client. The process is as follows:

> Initially, the server host starts the POP3 service by listening on TCP port 110. When a client host wishes to make use of the service, it establishes a TCP connection with the server host. When the connection is established, the POP3 server sends a greeting. The client and POP3 server then exchange commands and responses (respectively) until the connection is closed or aborted.

As with RFC 821, the two hosts communicate over TCP; an SMTP host listens on TCP port 25, while a POP3 host listens on port 110. Users wanting to download their mail run a POP3 mail client such as Eudora on their desktop and connect to the server over TCP/IP. After the server has acknowledged the connection, the POP3 client and the server follow a command-response sequence similar to the one used during an SMTP exchange.

Commands in the POP3 consist of a keyword possibly followed by an argument. All commands are terminated by a CRLF pair. Responses in the POP3 consist of a success indicator and a keyword possibly followed by additional information. All responses are terminated by a CRLF pair. There are currently two success indicators: positive ("+OK") and negative ("–ERR").

Just as RFC 821 defined a lock-step procedure for transferring mail between two SMTP hosts, RFC 1125 defines a similar procedure, depicted in Figure 2.4, for downloading mail.

Figure 2.4
POP3 Session

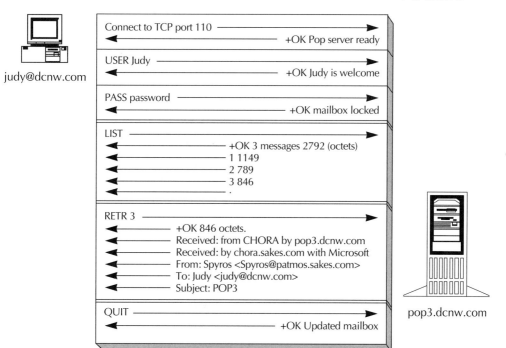

Retrieving mail from a POP3 server entails six steps.

1. The user (judy@dcnw.com) logs on to a workstation, loads a POP3 mail client, and asks to download mail. The POP3 client initiates a TCP connection to port 110 of the POP3 server (pop3.dcnw.com). The POP3 server sends back +OK if it is ready to download mail.

2. The client sends the user's account name. The server returns +OK if it recognizes the account.

3. The client sends the user's password, which is not encrypted. The server returns +OK if the password is correct.

4. The client then issues a LIST command to see if any mail is on the server to be downloaded. The server indicates the number of messages in the store, reports the total number of bytes, and shows a list of messages and their sizes.

5. The client then retrieves any message using the RETR <*msg*> command. Clients can issue as many or as few RETR commands as they please. Note that the entire message sent to the POP3 client is not encrypted. The client has the option of saving the messages sent to it.

6. To delete a message, the client issues a DELE <*msg*> command.

7. The POP3 client terminates a session by sending the QUIT message, and the server confirms the end of the session by sending a +OK message.

You download mail from a POP3 server, whereas you send mail to an SMTP server. The two use different protocols and the same host may or may not be configured with software that can run both. For example, you can configure NTMail Server and Sendmail as both SMTP and POP3 servers, whereas Microsoft Exchange Server version 4.0 is an SMTP server but not a POP3 server. Version 5.0 includes a POP3 server that must be configured separately. If you are configuring a POP3 client for use with an Internet Service Provider (ISP), you might have to enter different addresses for the SMTP server and the POP3 server.

You should also note that a mail client (UA) that can send and receive SMTP mail is not necessarily a POP3 client. As demonstrated in Table 2.4, you can purchase the Microsoft Exchange client in several ways, and only some of these give you SMTP or POP3 connectivity.

For example, the Exchange client that comes with Exchange Server can send mail only to an Exchange Server or to a Microsoft Mail Postoffice, depending upon how the delivery services are configured. If Exchange Server has the IMC configured, the Exchange client can send and receive SMTP mail via the Exchange Server; however, if the client is configured only with the Exchange Server service, it cannot connect directly to a POP3 server. Similarly, the

TABLE 2.4 MAIL CLIENTS

Source	Delivery Options Included	Remarks
Free with Windows 95	Microsoft Mail	MS Mail Client
Windows 95 Plus! Pack	Internet mail	POP3 client
Free with NT Server 3.51	Microsoft Mail	MS Mail Client
Free with NT Server 4.0	Internet mail Microsoft Mail	POP3 client MS Mail Client
Exchange Server CD	Exchange Server Microsoft Mail	Exchange Server client MS Mail Client

Microsoft Exchange client that comes with Windows 95 can send mail only to a Microsoft Mail Post Office; however, if you upgrade the client with the Windows 95 Plus! Pack, you can add the Internet Mail delivery service to the client, and it becomes a POP3 client that you can configure to connect directly with a POP3 server on the Internet. Finally, the Exchange client that comes with NT 4.0 includes an Internet mail delivery service that makes it a POP3 client.

We can use Telnet to effect a POP3 download as we did previously for the SMTP process. Listing 2.4 shows the sequence you use to do a POP3 download via Telnet.

In this example, the server pop3.dcnw.com is a POP3 server running Internet Shopper's NTMail (for more information about this product, see Appendix D). When we make a connection to port 110 of the server, it confirms that it is listening on that port by returning a +OK message. If the server were down, the Telnet session would be refused and we would have to try again later. Once the connection is made, we must identify ourselves, so we send the command "user" followed by the user's name, "judy." The server confirms that it has a mailbox for that user, and we send the command "pass" followed by the password for judy's mailbox. If the password is correct, the server locks the mailbox for exclusive access, and the client can retrieve and delete messages.

LISTING 2.4 INTERACTIVE POP3 SESSION

```
+OK Pop server ready.
user judy
+OK judy is welcome.
pass password
+OK mailbox locked
list
+OK 3 messages 2792 (octets)
1 1149
.
retr 3
+OK 846 octets.
Received from CHORA by pop3.dcnw.com (NTMail 3.01.03)id judy; Mon Aug.5
Received by chora.sakes.com with Microsoft Exchange (IMC 4.0.837.3) id
<01BB831f.D51441C0@chora.sakes.com>
From: Spyros <spyros@patmos.sakes.com>
To: Judy <judy@dcnw.com>
Subject: POP3
Date: Monday. 5 Aug 1996 22:45:39 -0400

Can you read this?
.
dele 3
+OK message 3 deleted.
quit
+OK Updated mailbox.
```

In Listing 2.4, we used the list command to find out how many messages judy has and then the command "retr 3" to retrieve the third message. After we download the message (saving the transfer to disk), we delete the message and quit the session. If we were to reconnect, we would find only the two previous messages still on the server.

The body of the message is a straightforward RFC 822 message. In addition to the headers and the message content entered by the UA of the message originator, we can see two headers appended by the mail systems through which the message passed, with message IDs, date stamps, and system identification information. The structure of the message body is consistent with the SMTP structure discussed previously.

References

For more information:

- **Download RFC 1225 from the Web site http://ds.internic.net/rfc/rfc1225.txt**
- **Search the Microsoft TechNet CD for keyword POP3**
- **Search the Web using Yahoo! or one of the other search engines for keyword POP3**

- **Monitor the following USENET newsgroups:**
  - **microsoft.public.mail.connectivity**
  - **microsoft.public.exchange.clients**
  - **microsoft.public.messaging.misc**
  - **info.ietf.smtp**

RFCs 1049, 1154, and 1505 — Headers and Attachments

As we discussed previously, RFC 822 defines the structure of an Internet mail message. This RFC has two major limitations: a 1,000-character-per-line limit, and a requirement that all data be in 7-bit ASCII format. The latter requirement made it difficult to include binary objects, such as pictures, in a mail message or to attach other objects, such as Microsoft Word documents, to the message. Attachments simply were not considered or defined in RFC 822.

RFC 1049 was issued to overcome these limitations. RFC 1049 added to the existing RFC 822 headers a "content-type" header that further describes the format of the message body, and specified a format for attachments. RFC 1049 was extended by RFC 1154 and updated again in RFC 1505. Although all messages must still be transmitted as 7-bit ASCII, the new headers allow the binary data to be encoded in such a way that the receiving host can decode them back into the original 8-bit binary code.

An RFC 822 message header contains only a few basic field types. Here's a simple one:

```
TO: Spyros <spyros@patmos.sakes.com>
FROM: Judy <judy@dcnw.com>
DATE: Sat 22 Jun 1996 14:15:10 -0400
SUBJECT: Fourth of July
```

The content of the message that follows the header must be transmitted in 7-bit ASCII text. However, according to RFC 1049, the original message can contain non-ASCII text and can be encoded by the mail system. When the mail system encodes a binary message, it adds an extra header to the message.

```
TO: Spyros <spyros@patmos.sakes.com>
FROM: Judy <judy@dcnw.com>
DATE: Sat 22 Jun 1996 14:15:10 -0400
SUBJECT: Fourth of July
Content-type: postscript
```

In this case, the originating mail system is telling the receiving host that the message contains binary postscript data. However, to send binary data using RFC 821, it must first be converted into 7-bit ASCII characters. The most commonly used method of converting the data is a program called Uuencode, which first appeared in BSD Unix version 4.0. Other less common methods are also available. RFC 1154 added another new header — called Encoding — that let the sender specify which method was used to convert the binary data into a 7-bit character stream.

```
TO: Spyros <spyros@patmos.sakes.com>
FROM: Judy <judy@dcnw.com>
DATE: Sat 22 Jun 1996 14:15:10 -0400
SUBJECT: Fourth of July
Content-type: postscript
Encoding: 1 text, 50 uuencode
```

This header tells the receiving host that the attached message is composed of two parts. The first is one line of text (7-bit ASCII), and the second is 50 lines of binary postscript data encoded in the uuencode format. With this information, the receiving host can convert the ASCII data into the original binary format.

How does uuencode translate 8-bit data into 7-bit ASCII format? The procedure follows these steps:

1. Read the binary data in groups of three bytes (24 bits) at a time

2. Separate the 24 bits into four groups of six bits

3. Add a space character (20h)

4. Add one or two leading zeros as needed to make the total 32 bits

5. Recast the 32 bits as four bytes of ASCII characters

It is difficult on paper to demonstrate representing binary data as ASCII because it is difficult to represent binary data on the printed page. However, we can demonstrate the uuencoding principle by converting regular ASCII data into uuencoded ASCII data. For example, if you run the line "Hello, World" through a uuencode program, the original 12 bytes would be converted to 16 bytes of uuencoded data, reading "2&5L;&\L(%====?\=O<FQD" (16 bytes). Table 2.5 shows the conversion of the first three bytes of the word "Hello."

The first three letters — H, e, and l — are represented by three bytes of eight bits each. These 24 bits are split into four groups of six bits. Next, the number 20h (1000000 binary) is added to offset the numbers, and one leading 0 is added (sometimes two are added) to get the groups of numbers up to eight bits each. Looking at the resultant 32 bits as four groups of 8-bit characters, they are "2&5L," the uuencoded value for "Hel."

In this case, we have uuencoded text that was already in 7-bit ASCII (it did not include any character above ASCII 127), so the value of the program is minimal. However, if you uuencode a file with nonprinting characters (below ASCII 32 or above ASCII 127), the program will convert them into printing characters.

TABLE 2.5 STEPS IN THE UUENCODING PROCESS	
Representation	**Value**
ANSI	Hel
Hex value	48 65 6C
Binary value	01001000 01100101 01101100
Binary, in 6-bit chunks	010010 000110 010101 101100
Adding 20h	110010 100110 110101 1001100
Padding with 0 as needed	00110010 00100110 00110101 01001100
ANSI	2&5L

When you run an entire binary file through a uuencode program, it creates an ASCII file. The block of uuencoded data is enclosed between a header line starting with the word "begin" and a trailer line starting with the word "end."

```
begin 644 hello.txt
M'@```!4```!3<'ER;W,@@4V4V%K96%L87))8861I<P`````%%0```%-%P>7)0<R
end
```

The second item in the header line is a number that represents a Unix permissions flag (in this case, giving the owner of the file full read, write, and execute permissions). The third part is the name of the encoded file. The body consists of a number of lines, each no longer than 62 characters (including the CRLF at the end of the line). The first character of every line is the letter M, followed by a character count, the encoded characters, and a Carriage Return and a Line Feed (0Dh 0Ah). The character count is a single printing character and represents the number of bytes in the line. This integer is always in the range from 0 to 63 and can be determined by subtracting the space character (20h) from the character shown. In the above example, M' therefore indicates that the line is 64 characters long — adding 20h to 64d (40h) gives you 60h, or the character " ' ".

You can find many programs that will uuencode a file manually. One popular shareware program is called WinCode, and one provided with the Windows NT Resource kit is called Ntuuencode. By following the uuencode specifications, files uuencoded by one vendor's program can be decoded by another vendor's program. Before RFC 1049 was issued, you had to uuencode binary files manually and insert them into the body of a text message to send it over the Internet. With the additional headers specified in RFC 1049 and 1154, however, the mail system encodes the information automatically, and the process is transparent to the user. Thus, a user of Microsoft Exchange can simply attach a binary graphic file to a message, and the server will automatically uuencode the image before sending it to a remote SMTP host.

References

For more information:

- **Download RFCs from the following Web sites:**
  http://ds.internic.net/rfc/rfc1049.txt
  http://ds.internic.net/rfc/rfc1154.txt
  http://ds.internic.net/rfc/rfc1505.txt

- **Search the Microsoft TechNet CD for keywords SMTP, uuencode**

- **Search the Web using Yahoo! or one of the other search engines for keywords SMTP, uuencode**

RFCs 1521 and 1522 — MIME

RFC 1521, MIME (Multipurpose Internet Mail Extensions), further extended the earlier definitions to provide for binary parts in the body of a message. It added the following five headers to the set defined in RFC 822:

```
MIME-Version
Content-type
Content-Transfer-Encoding
Content-ID
Content-Description
```

The MIME-Version header field indicates that the message conforms to the RFC. If a mail system supports MIME, it will use this header to process the message; if the system does not support MIME, it generates an error message. The content-type header precedes each body part in the message and indicates the type of the original message. Seven content types — each with numerous subtypes — were defined in RFC 1521. These content types are shown in Table 2.6.

Including the subtypes, RFC 1521 defined 14 message types, and you can define additional types and subtypes by registering them with the Internet Assigned Numbers Authority (IANA). The procedure for registering additional types is listed in Appendix E of RFC 1521. The latest list of registered MIME types is available from

ftp://ftp.isi.edu/in-notes/iana/assignments/media-types/media-types.

TABLE 2.6 RFC 1521 CONTENT TYPES

Content Type	Subtype	Encoding
Text	plain	Quoted-printable
Multipart	mixed alternative digest parallel	No content-transfer-encoding is permitted
Message	rfc822 partial external-body	7-bit for message/partial or message/external-body 7-bit, 8-bit, or binary for other
Application	octet-stream postscript	Base 64
Image	jpeg gif	Base 64
Audio	basic	Base 64
Video	mpeg	Base 64

As of August 1996, 78 message types had been defined, at least 13 of which had been registered by Microsoft. We will discuss how Exchange handles MIME types in Chapter 6. Many of these content types are likely to be formatted as 8-bit binary data. To send this data using SMTP in accordance with RFC 821, the data must be converted to 7-bit ASCII. RFC 1521 defines the five encoding methods for converting the data: 7-bit, 8-bit, base 64, binary, and quoted-printable.

In addition to the five types of encoding defined in the RFC, a sixth, x-token, lets vendors create proprietary encoding types of their own. Each of the specified encoding methods produces a different result. For example, the quoted-printable method replaces characters above ASCII 127 with an equals sign and the hex equivalent of the character. Occasionally, you will see messages that contain phrases of the form "=XX". Listing 2.5 contains an e-mail I received from an associate at Microsoft in this format.

LISTING 2.5 RAW MIME CONTENT

```
Topics of technical-breakout sessions will include:
=B7 Visual C++ 4.0 In-depth:New features will be highlighted,including =
how to quickly create fast, powerful database applications through new =
support for Data Access Objects.
=B7 Microsoft Foundation Class Library 4.0: Tips and tricks for =
programming with Data Access Object classes; enhancements in OLE and =
```

The headers in Listing 2.6 show that this message was encoded with the quoted-printable method.

LISTING 2.6 MIME HEADER INFORMATION

```
Received: from tide03.microsoft.com by smtpgate.paradigms.com
 with Microsoft Exchange (IMC 4.12.611) id AAYYJBLV; Thu, 18
 Jan 1996 09:33:59 -0500
X-MSMail-Message-ID: DC184EBA
X-MSMail-Conversation-ID: DC184EBA
From: Jack <jack@microsoft.com>
To: spyros@paradigms.com
Date: Thu, 18 Jan 96 06:19:22 PST
Subject: Satellite Telecast
X-MsXMTID: was-01-msg960118142809MTP[01.52.00]000000a4-12178
Message-Id: was-01-msg960118142809MTP[01.52.00]000000a4-12178
X-MSContent-Transfer-Encoding: Quoted-Printable
```

The quoted-printable method allows long lines, but they are wrapped for transmittal over SMTP using "=" as the continuation symbol. As a result, many of the lines in the message end in an "=" sign. In addition, the gateway found a bullet "•" (ASCII 183d or B7h), which it translated to the three characters "=B7", all under ASCII 127 (61d 66d 55d). Listing 2.7 shows what the text looked like before it was encoded.

LISTING 2.7 ORIGINAL MIME MESSAGE

```
Topics of technical-breakout sessions will include:

•  Visual C++ 4.0 In-depth:New features will be highlighted, including how to
   quickly create fast, powerful database applications through new support for
   Data Access Objects.

•  Microsoft Foundation Class Library 4.0: Tips and tricks for programming
   with Data Access Object classes; enhancements in OLE and
```

Similarly, the base 64 method encodes characters in a manner akin to uuencoding, using a different algorithm. Listing 2.8 presents an example of a message encoded in base 64.

LISTING 2.8 BASE 64 ENCODING

```
Content-Type: application/ms-tnef
Content-Transfer-Encoding: base64

eJ8+IgwTAQaQCAAEAAAAAABAAEAAQeQBgAIAAAA5AQAAAAAAADoAAEFgAMADgAAAMsHDAAHKwA-
IAAQAKgEBCYABACEAAABCNTRBNjg2NzE5MkJDRjExOUNGQjjAwMjBBRjMwRDVBMwAtBwEgDgAAAMsH-
DAAHAA4AKwALAAQALQEBCIAHABgAAABJUEQuTWljcm9zb2Z0IE1haWwuTm90ZQAxgAEAAQAAAAAA-
ENgAQAAgAAAAIAAgABA5AGANABAAASAAAACwAjAAAAAAALACkAAAAAAMA
```

One of the purposes of RFC 1521 is to allow multiple-part messages. An example is shown in Listing 2.9.

LISTING 2.9 MS-TNEF ENCODING

```
—— =_NextPart_000_01BAC4B2.54E6E1F0
Content-Type: text/plain; charset="us-ascii"
Content-Transfer-Encoding: 7 bit

join ms-back-office

—— =_NextPart_000_01BAC4B2.54E6E1F0
Content-Type: application/ms-tnef
        Content-Transfer-Encoding: base64

eJ8+IgwTAQaQCAAEAAAAAABAAEAAQeQBgAIAAAA5AQAAAAAAADoAAEFgAMADgAAAMsHDAAHKwA-
IAAQAKgEBCYABACEAAABCNTRBNjg2NzE5MkJDRjExOUNGQjjAwMjBBRjMwRDVBMwAtBwEgDgAAAMsH-
DAAHAA4AKwALAAQALQEBCIAHABgAAABJUEQuTWljcm9zb2Z0IE1haWwuTm90ZQAxgAEAAQAAAAAA-
ENgAQAAgAAAAIAAgABA5AGANABAAASAAAACwAjAAAAAAALACkAAAAAAMA
```

The message has two parts. The first is simply the text "join ms-back-office," which is included in the MIME message as plain text, 7-bit encoding. However, the message was composed with rich-text formatting (RTF), and the formatting of the text was included as an additional body part with type "ms-tnef" using base 64 encoding. We will discuss ms-tnef in more detail in Chapter 6.

For more information:

* **Download RFCs from the following Web sites:**
    http://ds.internic.net/rfc/rfc1521.txt
    http://ds.internic.net/rfc/rfc1522.txt
* **See "Appendix A: Introduction to Messaging Standards," Microsoft Mail Resource Kit, Microsoft TechNet CD, Section on MIME**
* **See *Internet E-Mail Services*, Electronic Messaging Association, 1994**
* **Search the Microsoft TechNet CD for keywords SMTP, MIME**

References

- **Search the Web using Yahoo! or one of the other search engines for keywords SMTP, MIME**
- **Check**
  http://www.cis.ohio-state.edu/text/faq/usenet/mail/mime-faq/part3/faq.html
- **Monitor the following USENET newsgroup:**
  - **comp.mail.mime**

Monitoring SMTP Traffic

In the previous sections, we saw how SMTP hosts send and receive mail, and we used Telnet to make a connection to port 25 of an SMTP receiver to emulate an SMTP sender. In the example shown in Listing 2.3, we typed the commands to the SMTP receiver in plain text. In a conversation between two SMTP hosts over the Internet, the dialog is also in plain text, and we can view this with any packet/protocol analyzer (generically called a *sniffer*).

In this section, we will use the Microsoft Network Monitor to view packets flowing from one SMTP host to another. The Network Monitor ships with Microsoft Systems Management Server (SMS), and a slightly stripped-down version ships with Windows NT 4.0; either is adequate for viewing the SMTP traffic. The purpose of this section is to demonstrate how to use this tool in a messaging environment and to show how the concepts we have been talking about in abstract terms relate to a real-life scenario.

For this setup, we have a Microsoft Exchange server running the IMC on a host called chora.sakes.com and Internet Shopper's NTMail server loaded on a host called pop3.dcnw.com. We set up Exchange clients on both servers: on the Exchange server the client is configured to use the Exchange Server service, and on the NTMail server the client is configured to use the Internet mail service (making it a POP3 client to the NTMail server).

To use the SMS Network Monitor, we first load the Windows NT Network Monitor Agent on chora.sakes.com and start the service. Next, we load the SMS Network Monitor on a desktop and configure it to monitor TCP/IP packets passing between the two servers, using the network interface card on chora.sakes.com as its probe on the network cable. We want to send a message from an Exchange user on chora.sakes.com to a POP3 user on pop3.dcnw.com. Figure 2.5 shows the message.

As the message travels over the wire to the target server, it is monitored by the sniffer. To aid in the analysis of the packets, we define a filter in the Network Monitor capture window, as shown in Figure 2.6.

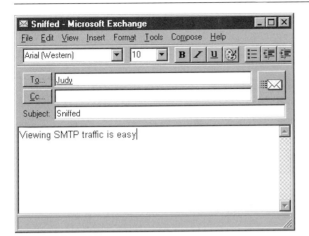

Figure 2.5
The Outbound SMTP Message Being Prepared

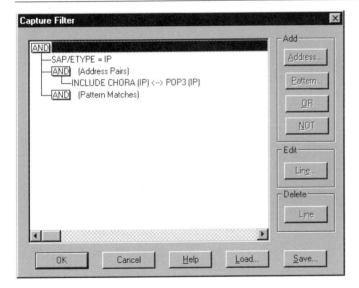

Figure 2.6
Capture Filter

By adding this filter, the Network Monitor will capture only those frames sent over IP between the servers chora.sakes.com and pop3.dcnw.com. This setup will greatly reduce the number of frames we will see and simplify the analysis of the information. (For a tutorial on using the SMS Network Monitor, see "Supporting Systems Management Server 1.1," Course 646, Microsoft Educational Services, and "Capacity Planning Microsoft Windows NT Server Networks," Course 635, Microsoft Educational Services.)

Almost immediately after sending the message shown in Figure 2.5, we can see the data in the sniffer. The first evidence of its presence is shown in the screen capture in Figure 2.7.

Figure 2.7

The SMTP Message in Transit

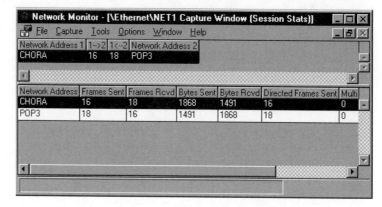

Displaying the frames in the summary window of the Network Monitor reveals about 20 frames associated with this message, as shown in Figure 2.8. When we view the detail of the frames, we see the Exchange server communicating according to RFC 821 with the NTMail server. For example, in Frame 7 we see the Exchange server IMC on chora.sakes.com making a connection over TCP to port 25 of pop3.dcnw.com. The hex detail in the Network Monitor, shown in Listing 2.10, conforms to the RFC 821 format (several lines have been removed for the sake of clarity).

Figure 2.8

The Frames in the SMTP Message

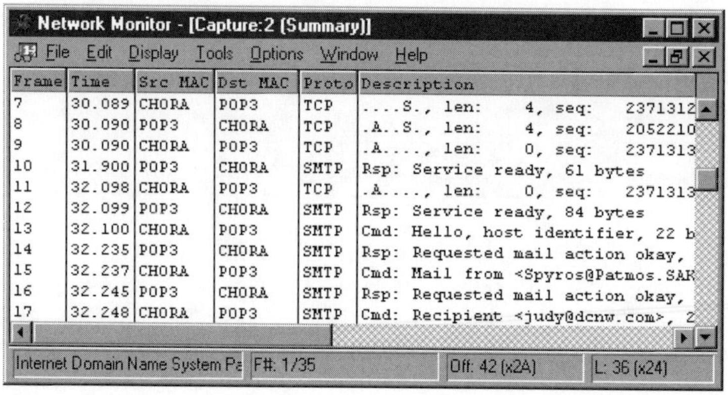

LISTING 2.10 FRAME 1 — SMTP CONNECTION

```
Frame   Time     Src MAC   Dst MAC A Protocol
7       30.089   CHORA     POP3      TCP

  FRAME: Base frame properties
  ETHERNET: ETYPE = 0x0800 : Protocol = IP:  DOD Internet Protocol
  IP: ID = 0xDE0F; Proto = TCP; Len: 44
      IP: Source Address = 206.247.73.110
      IP: Destination Address = 206.247.73.140
  TCP: ....S., len:4, seq:2371312, ack:0, win:8192, src:1350 dst:25 (SMTP)
      TCP: Source Port = 0x0546
      TCP: Destination Port = SMTP

00000:  00 80 C7 D7 68 7E 08 00 2B 3F D8 0D 08 00 45 00    ....h~..+?....E.
00010:  00 2C DE 0F 40 00 80 06 EB D2 CE F7 49 6E CE F7    .,..@.......In..
00020:  49 8C 05 46 00 19 00 24 2E F0 00 00 00 00 60 02    I..F...$......`.
00030:  20 00 12 CA 00 00 02 04 05 B4                       .........
```

At offset 1Ah of Frame 7, we see the IP address of chora.sakes.com (206.247.73.110, or CE F7 49 6E hex); at offset 1Eh we see the IP address of pop3.dcnw.com (206.247.73.140, or CE F7 49 8C); and at offset 24h we see the TCP port on pop3.dcnw.com (25d, or 00 19 hex).

Frames 8 through 12 contain incidental TCP/IP protocol information. Starting at Frame 13 we have the basic RFC 821 envelope, starting with the HELO statement.

```
00000:  00 80 C7 D7 68 7E 08 00 2B 3F D8 0D 08 00 45 00    ....h~..+?....E.
00010:  00 3E E1 0F 40 00 80 06 E8 C0 CE F7 49 6E CE F7    .>..@.......In..
00020:  49 8C 05 46 00 19 00 24 2E F1 00 1F 51 04 50 18    I..F...$....Q.P.
00030:  21 A7 A7 99 00 00 48 45 4C 4F 20 63 68 6F 72 61    !.....HELO chora
00040:  2E 73 61 6B 65 73 2E 63 6F 6D 0D 0A                .sakes.com..
```

Just as in Frame 7, the first few bytes contain the packet headers; the first 14 bytes of the frame contained the Ethernet header, the next 20 bytes contained the IP header, and the next 20 bytes the TCP header. The TCP data packet begins at 36h (54d), with the data "48 45 4C." Here, the SMTP sender has sent the string "HELO chora.sakes.com" to indicate that it is starting an RFC 821 dialog, and it identifies itself as the host chora.sakes.com. As we discussed previously, if the SMTP receiver is configured to accept messages from that host, it will respond with a "250" and a text message. You can see this in Frame 14, again at offset 36h after the Ethernet, IP, and TCP headers.

```
00030:  22 22 59 EC 00 00 32 35 30 20 70 6F 70 33 2E 64    ""Y...250 pop3.d
00040:  63 6E 77 2E 63 6F 6D 20 63 68 6F 72 61 2E 73 61    cnw.com chora.sa
00050:  6B 65 73 2E 63 6F 6D 0D 0A                         kes.com..
```

The SMTP receiver has identified itself as pop3.dcnw.com to chora.sakes.com. The SMTP sender continues to issue the remaining RFC 821 commands in sequence, identifying the sender and the recipients and sending the data, beginning in Frame 15.

```
00030:   21 84 1F 7E 00 00 4D 41 49 4C 20 46 52 4F 4D 3A   !..~..MAIL FROM:
00040:   3C 53 70 79 72 6F 73 40 50 61 74 6D 6F 73 2E 53   <Spyros@Patmos.S
00050:   41 4B 45 53 2E 63 6F 6D 3E 0D 0A                  AKES.com>..
```

The receiver follows with the OK response in Frame 16.

```
00030:   21 FD ED 19 00 00 32 35 30 20 4F 6B 2E 0D 0A      !.....250 Ok...
```

The command/response scenario continues as we discussed previously until the end of the RFC 821 envelope preamble at Frame 22, shown below.

```
00030:   21 DE 8E D8 00 00 33 35 34 20 53 74 61 72 74 20   !.....354 Start
00040:   6D 61 69 6C 20 69 6E 70 75 74 2C 20 65 6E 64 20   mail input, end
00050:   77 69 74 68 20 3C 43 52 4C 46 3E 2E 3C 43 52 4C   with <CRLF>.<CRL
00060:   46 3E 2E 0D 0A                                     F>...
```

After the end of the RFC 821 commands, the SMTP sender starts with the RFC 822 message. The message includes the headers and the message body. Listing 2.11 shows the entire RFC 822 message, starting with the headers added by the SMTP sender and receiver.

We will not analyze the entire message shown in Listing 2.11. You can tackle that as an exercise. You can see all the headers of the message, including the RFC 1049 and 1154 fields, and the body of the message. This example had no binary data to send, so the RFC 1154 header shows that the encoding is simply TEXT. After that header, at offset 001E0 the obligatory blank line, a Carriage Return-Line Feed pair (OA OD), is followed by the body of the message. As you can see, the entire RFC 822 message is in the clear, and anyone with a sniffer on the line can read the message that "Viewing SMTP traffic is easy!" We hear quite often that SMTP messaging is insecure, but it is important to realize just how easy it is for someone with physical access to any of the network traffic to view the data.

This plain-text transmittal of messages lets you create a customized sniffer that will alert you when certain events occur. For example, suppose you suspect that someone in your organization is sending out proprietary pricing information to your competition. You could create what is known as a *trigger* in the sniffer that monitors the wire for some tell-tale text string, such as "DMS Contract," captures the balance of the message, and issues an alert to the appropriate corporate authorities. Alternatively, you could create a trigger that monitors the wire for incoming strings containing the string ".gif" to determine whether employees are subscribing to some unauthorized "image-of-the-month" club. Procedures for creating basic triggers and traps are outlined in the Microsoft Systems Management Server Administrator's Guide. Of course, if the files are

LISTING 2.11 RFC 822 MESSAGE

```
00030:   21 43 1A 4C 00 00 52 65 63 65 69 76 65 64 3A 20   !C.L..Received:
00040:   62 79 20 63 68 6F 72 61 2E 73 61 6B 65 73 2E 63   by chora.sakes.c
00050:   6F 6D 20 77 69 74 68 20 53 4D 54 50 20 28 4D 69   om with SMTP (Mi
00060:   63 72 6F 73 6F 66 74 20 45 78 63 68 61 6E 67 65   crosoft Exchange
00070:   20 53 65 72 76 65 72 20 49 6E 74 65 72 6E 65 74    Server Internet
00080:   20 4D 61 69 6C 20 43 6F 6E 6E 65 63 74 6F 72 20    Mail Connector
00090:   56 65 72 73 69 6F 6E 20 34 2E 30 2E 39 39 33 2E   Version 4.0.993.
000A0:   35 29 0D 0A 09 69 64 20 3C 30 31 42 42 41 41 32   5)...id <01BBAA2
000B0:   31 2E 36 38 43 33 34 31 35 30 40 63 68 6F 72 61   1.68C34150@chora
000C0:   2E 73 61 6B 65 73 2E 63 6F 6D 3E 3B 20 54 75 65   .sakes.com>; Tue
000D0:   2C 20 32 34 20 53 65 70 20 31 39 39 36 20 31 34   , 24 Sep 1996 14
000E0:   3A 30 35 3A 31 35 20 2D 30 34 30 30 0D 0A 52 65   :05:15 -0400..Re
000F0:   63 65 69 76 65 64 3A 20 62 79 20 63 68 6F 72 61   ceived: by chora
00100:   2E 73 61 6B 65 73 2E 63 6F 6D 20 77 69 74 68 20   .sakes.com with
00110:   53 4D 54 50 20 28 4D 69 63 72 6F 73 6F 66 74 20   SMTP (Microsoft
00120:   45 78 63 68 61 6E 67 65 20 53 65 72 76 65 72 20   Exchange Server
00130:   49 6E 74 65 72 6E 65 74 20 4D 61 69 6C 20 43 6F   Internet Mail Co
00140:   6E 6E 65 63 74 6F 72 20 56 65 72 73 69 6F 6E 20   nnector Version
00150:   34 2E 30 2E 39 39 33 2E 35 29 0D 0A 09 69 64 20   4.0.993.5)...id
00160:   3C 30 31 42 42 41 41 32 30 2E 37 38 39 34 34 39   <01BBAA20.789449
00170:   34 30 40 63 68 6F 72 61 2E 73 61 6B 65 73 2E 63   40@chora.sakes.c
00180:   6F 6D 3E 3B 20 54 75 65 2C 20 32 34 20 53 65 70   om>; Tue, 24 Sep
00190:   20 31 39 39 36 20 31 33 3A 35 38 3A 33 32 20 2D    1996 13:58:32 -
001A0:   30 34 30 30 0D 0A 4D 65 73 73 61 67 65 2D 49 44   0400..Message-ID
001B0:   3A 20 3C 63 3D 55 53 25 61 3D 5F 25 70 3D 53 41   : <c=US%a=_%p=SA
001C0:   4B 45 53 25 6C 3D 43 48 4F 52 41 2D 39 36 30 39   KES%l=CHORA-9609
001D0:   32 34 31 38 30 35 31 33 5A 2D 32 40 63 68 6F 72   24180513Z-2@chor
001E0:   61 2E 73 61 6B 65 73 2E 63 6F 6D 3E 0D 0A 46 72   a.sakes.com>..Fr
001F0:   6F 6D 3A 20 53 70 79 72 6F 73 20 3C 53 70 79 72   om: Spyros <Spyr
00200:   6F 73 40 50 61 74 6D 6F 73 2E 53 41 4B 45 53 2E   os@Patmos.SAKES.
00210:   63 6F 6D 3E 0D 0A 54 6F 3A 20 27 4A 75 64 79 27   com>..To: 'Judy'
00220:   20 3C 6A 75 64 79 40 64 63 6E 77 2E 63 6F 6D 3E    <judy@dcnw.com>
00230:   0D 0A 53 75 62 6A 65 63 74 3A 20 53 6E 69 66 66   ..Subject: Sniff
00240:   65 64 0D 0A 44 61 74 65 3A 20 54 75 65 2C 20 32   ed..Date: Tue, 2
00250:   34 20 53 65 70 20 31 39 39 36 20 31 34 3A 30 35   4 Sep 1996 14:05
00260:   3A 31 33 20 2D 30 34 30 30 0D 0A 58 2D 4D 61 69   :13 -0400..X-Mai
00270:   6C 65 72 3A 20 20 4D 69 63 72 6F 73 6F 66 74 20   ler:  Microsoft
00280:   45 78 63 68 61 6E 67 65 20 53 65 72 76 65 72 20   Exchange Server
00290:   49 6E 74 65 72 6E 65 74 20 4D 61 69 6C 20 43 6F   Internet Mail Co
002A0:   6E 6E 65 63 74 6F 72 20 56 65 72 73 69 6F 6E 20   nnector Version
002B0:   34 2E 30 2E 39 39 33 2E 35 0D 0A 4D 49 4D 45 2D   4.0.993.5..MIME-
002C0:   56 65 72 73 69 6F 6E 3A 20 31 2E 30 0D 0A 43 6F   Version: 1.0..Co
002D0:   6E 74 65 6E 74 2D 54 79 70 65 3A 20 74 65 78 74   ntent-Type: text
002E0:   2F 70 6C 61 69 6E 3B 20 63 68 61 72 73 65 74 3D   /plain; charset=
002F0:   22 75 73 2D 61 73 63 69 69 22 0D 0A 43 6F 6E 74   "us-ascii"..Cont
00300:   65 6E 74 2D 54 72 61 6E 73 66 65 72 2D 45 6E 63   ent-Transfer-Enc
00310:   6F 64 69 6E 67 3A 20 37 62 69 74 0D 0A 0D 0A 56   oding: 7bit....V
00320:   69 65 77 69 6E 67 20 53 4D 54 50 20 74 72 61 66   iewing SMTP traf
00330:   66 69 63 20 69 73 20 65 61 73 79 21 0D 0A 2E 0D   fic is easy!...
```

encrypted manually, or even "zipped" with cryptic file names, then your trigger will need to be somewhat more sophisticated.

Because all messages are sent over the Internet unencrypted, all you need to do to monitor people's messages is tap the wire at an appropriate location. Internet newsgroups frequently speculate that certain organizations could monitor all traffic on the Internet if they had access to some of the larger DNS hosts. *Wired* magazine (May 1996) reports that those concerned with e-mail privacy try to confuse eavesdroppers by flooding their sniffers with irrelevant messages using "NSA sniffer bait" or "CDA bait." For example, you could end all correspondence to your mother with the signature in Listing 2.12.

LISTING 2.12 SNIFFER BAIT

```
Spyros
spyros@patmos.sakes.com
-----------------------------------------------------------------
I dislike terrorists, nuclear weapons, assassination, as well as
pornography, indecency, and republicans
-----------------------------------------------------------------
```

If certain organizations are using automatic triggers looking for key words, your correspondence with your mother would get archived and searched. The theory is that if enough people add sniffer bait to their messages, the sniffers will be rendered useless because of the volume of messages collected.

A second approach to protecting the privacy of mail messages transmitted over the Internet is to encrypt the data while in transmission. A popular program for encrypting data is Pretty Good Privacy (PGP), which was written and made publicly available on the Internet by Philip Zimmerman. Using PGP, however, requires significant additional actions by the sender and receiver, which is not currently practical. Microsoft Exchange Server ships with an encryption add-on, the Key Management Server, that lets users in the same organization easily encode messages sent to each other, even over the Internet. Procedures for setting up the Advanced Security features of Exchange Server are covered in the Exchange Administrator's Manual.

CHAPTER 3

Internet Mail Connector Overview

In the previous chapter, we discussed the basic concepts of Simple Message Transfer Protocol (SMTP) mail and how two SMTP hosts communicate. In this chapter we look at how Exchange Server operates in an SMTP environment. For illustrative purposes, we will examine

- the flow of messages from Exchange clients to recipients on the Internet
- how messages are routed between different servers and different sites in the same organization
- message formats you need to know to understand SMTP message routing.

IMC Architecture

Our examples for both Exchange Server-to-Internet communication and intra-organization communication will focus on a small organization with the topology shown in Figure 3.1. A single Exchange Organization called SAKES has two sites, Patmos and Athens. The Athens site has a single server, kifissia.sakes.com, and the Patmos site has two servers, chora.sakes.com and campos.sakes.com. The sites are joined by an X.400 connector and communicate with the Internet through the IMC running on chora.sakes.com. The Internet is represented by server pop3.dcnw.com. We will examine messages sent from users with mailboxes on each of the different servers to show you how Exchange handles SMTP mail.

Figure 3.1

Simple Exchange
Organization

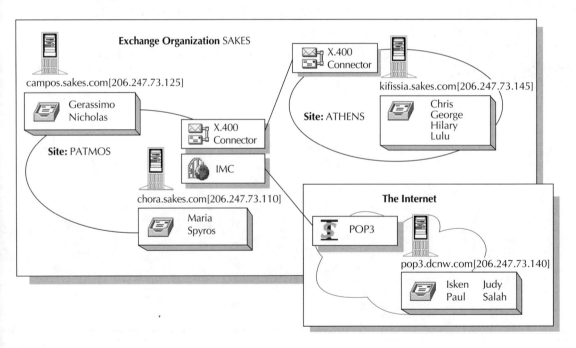

When you run Exchange Server and the IMC on a server, four or five basic services are running on the host. If you bring up the Control Panel Services applet, you'll see these services, as shown in Figure 3.2.

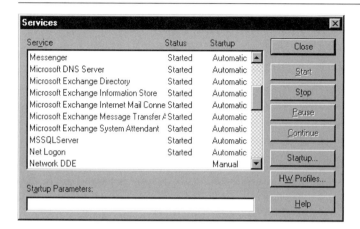

Figure 3.2

Control Panel — Exchange Services

The core Exchange services (the Directory, Information Store, Message Transfer Agent, and System Attendant) must always be present and running. Other services will appear depending on how you installed Exchange. In the organization shown in Figure 3.1, the server chora.sakes.com has the IMC installed, so it shows up in the Services listing in Figure 3.2. Other services, such as the Exchange Key Management Server, would appear if we had installed those on this host. The Exchange services shown in the Control Panel are Windows NT processes, as can be seen from the Windows NT Task Manager in Figure 3.3.

Table 3.1 shows how the five services shown in Figure 3.2 map to the individual processes shown in the task manager shown in Figure 3.3.

Exchange Server is a true multithreaded application, and each of its processes can spawn many threads. For example, during a period of medium activity the emsmta process on chora.sakes.com had about 70 threads, the msexcimc process had about 30 threads, and the store process had about 48 threads.

When a message is sent by an Exchange client to a recipient on the Internet, it is handled by multiple processes. A simple example of this sequence is a user sending a message to an Internet recipient from an Exchange server with the IMC on the local server. In Figure 3.1, user Spyros on chora.sakes.com could send a message to user Judy on pop3.dcnw.com. (Figure 3.4 shows the progress of this message from Spyros to Judy.)

TABLE 3.1 MAPPING SERVICES TO PROCESSES

Service	Process
Microsoft Exchange Directory	dsamain
Microsoft Exchange Information Store	store
Microsoft Exchange Internet Mail Connector	msexcimc
Microsoft Exchange Message Transfer Agent	emsmta
Microsoft Exchange System Attendant	mad

Figure 3.3

Windows NT Task Manager
— Exchange Processes

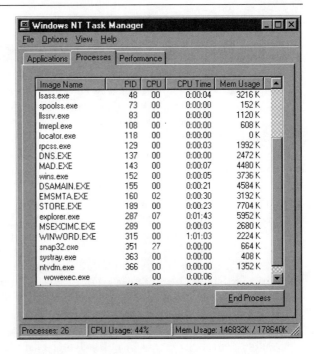

In Figure 3.4, user Spyros has a mailbox on the server chora.sakes.com and has an e-mail address of spyros@patmos.sakes.com. Judy has a mailbox on pop3.dcnw.com and has an e-mail address of judy@dcnw.com. When Spyros sends a message to Judy, it travels from his desktop to chora.sakes.com; from there it goes to pop3.dcnw.com and then on to Judy's desktop. In Chapter 2 we discussed much of what transpires between chora.sakes.com and

Figure 3.4

Basic Message Flow

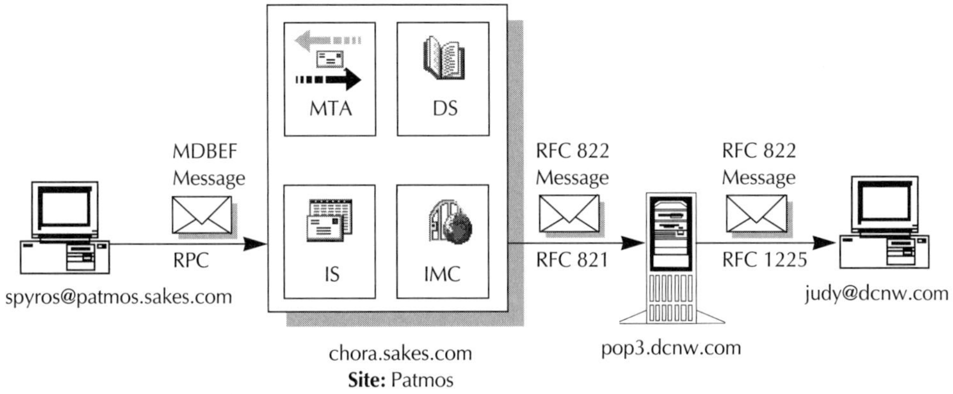

pop3.dcnw.com. To the outside world the Exchange server must look like a RFC 821-compliant server.

Now, we will look at the processes taking place within the Exchange server and examine its organization. The flow of a message through the local Exchange server is discussed in detail in Chapter 18 of the Microsoft Product Support Services course on Exchange Server, published on the monthly TechNet CD. Figure 3.5 is an expanded view of Figure 3.4, showing more details of the local message flow.

The Internet-bound message passes through a number of stages on the Exchange server. Let's briefly examine each of these stages.

In the first stage, the client prepares and sends the message. When the Exchange Server user sends a message to an Internet user, it is handed off by the client to the Information Store (IS) on the Exchange server. In our example, Spyros's Exchange client hands off the message to the IS on chora.sakes.com, and it is stored in the Spyros Outbox folder.

The next stage involves the Message Transfer Agent. Although Figure 3.5 does not show any direct interaction between the client and the MTA in this process, the MTA expedites the physical transfer. You can verify this involvement by pausing the MTA on the Exchange server — messages will never leave the Outbox of the Exchange client. If you install the basic version of Exchange Server, as opposed to the Enterprise edition, you will not see an MTA icon, but a hidden MTA is there all the same — otherwise messages would not leave the client.

Figure 3.5

Message Flow in an Exchange Server

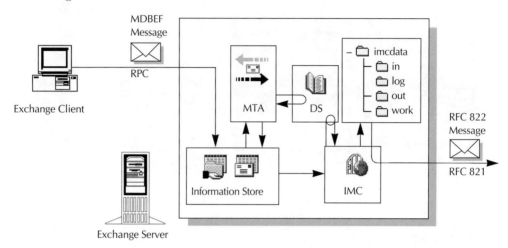

Because the recipient is not local to the IS, the MTA transfers the message to the appropriate location and service that handles the outbound mail. In this case, the MTA checks to see whether a properly configured IMC is running on the current server. If it is, the MTA puts the message in a queue for the IMC. You can view this queue from the Queues tab in the MTA Properties dialog box of the Administrator, shown in Figure 3.6.

The MTA queue has four messages destined for the IMC on chora.sakes.com. This queue is labeled "Internet Mail Connector (CHORA)" to indicate the server on which the connector is installed. Normally, the messages would pass through the queue very quickly, and you would not see them. If you do see messages in the queue, you might have a problem with the IMC. To get this screen shot, we stopped the IMC service from the Control Panel, simulating a problem with the connector or remote hosts and forcing messages to collect in the queue. If the IMC is not on the local server, but on remote server, the MTA will put the messages in a queue for that server.

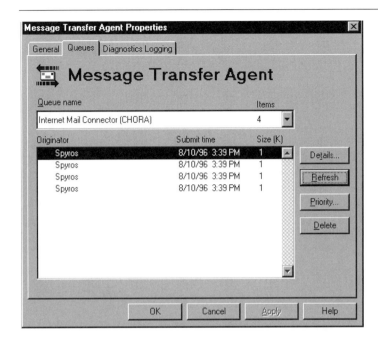

Figure 3.6

Messages in MTA Queue for the IMC

The messages go from the MTA's queue to a queue in the Internet Mail Connector labeled the MTS-Out queue. First, the MTA places the messages into the "Outbound messages awaiting conversion" queue. You can see more data about these queues using the Imcdump.exe utility on the Exchange Server CD. Figure 3.7 shows the Queues tab for the IMC on chora.sakes.com.

When the IMC receives a message in the MTS-Out queue, it contacts the Directory Service (DS) to verify the address, as shown in Figure 3.5. If the address is valid, the IMC converts the message and any attachments to RFC 822 format, placing temporary files in the \imcdata\work directory. When the conversion is finished, the files are placed in the \imcdata\out directory. They then appear in the "Outbound messages awaiting delivery" queue.

This queue is shown in Figure 3.7. Under normal circumstances, messages will reside in this queue for a very short time. If you find a number of messages here, it usually indicates a problem with the destination host. To get the screen shot shown in Figure 3.7, we restarted the IMC service on chora.sakes.com but shut down the SMTP service on pop3.dcnw.com. A real example of this sort happened the week of August 5, 1996, when America Online went offline for almost a whole day. The IMC queue at our office had nearly 100 messages stacked up for delivery to aol.com when the service came back online!

Figure 3.7

Messages in the IMC Queue for the Remote Host

At this stage, the messages are ready for transfer to an RFC 821-compliant host. In the example shown in Figure 3.4, the IMC on chora.sakes.com opens up one or more TCP/IP connections to port 25 of the SMTP host pop3.dcnw.com. From there, the process follows the protocols for communications between SMTP hosts, which are described in Chapter 2. The SMTP protocol log for the message, shown in Listing 3.1, verifies the process.

This data file is stored in the \imcdata\log directory, and it can be read with any ASCII editor, such as Notepad. The amount of data shown in the log file depends on parameters set in the Administrator program, which we'll discuss in Chapter 6. The example in Listing 3.1 shows an SMTP conversation identical to those discussed in Chapter 2. The process is as follows:

1. The Exchange server chora.sakes.com initiates a Transport Control Protocol (TCP) connection to port 25 of the server pop3.dcnw.com. The receiving server sends a code 220 to indicate that it is listening, and it also indicates that it is running an evaluation version of Internet Shopper's NTMail Server.

LISTING 3.1 LOG FILE

```
7/22/96 11:05:57 PM : A connection to 206.247.73.140 was established.7/22/96
11:06:31 PM : <<< IO: |220-Evaluation version of Internet Shopper's NT Mail
Server
7/22/96 11:06:31 PM : <<< IO: |220 pop3.dcnw.com NT SMTP Server v3.01.03
ready at Mon, 22 Jul 1996 22:59:36 -0400
7/22/96 11:06:31 PM : <<< 220 pop3.dcnw.com NT SMTP Server v3.01.03 ready at
Mon, 22 Jul 1996 22:59:36 -0400
7/22/96 11:06:31 PM : >>> HELO chora.sakes.com
7/22/96 11:06:31 PM : <<< IO: |250 pop3.dcnw.com chora.sakes.com
7/22/96 11:06:31 PM : <<< 250 pop3.dcnw.com chora.sakes.com
7/22/96 11:06:31 PM : >>> MAIL FROM:<Spyros@Patmos.SAKES.com>
7/22/96 11:06:31 PM : <<< IO: |250 Ok.
7/22/96 11:06:31 PM : <<< 250 Ok.
7/22/96 11:06:31 PM : >>> RCPT TO:<judy@dcnw.com>
7/22/96 11:06:31 PM : <<< IO: |250 Ok.
7/22/96 11:06:31 PM : <<< 250 Ok.
7/22/96 11:06:31 PM : >>> DATA
7/22/96 11:06:31 PM : <<< IO: |354 Start mail input, end with <CRLF>.<CRLF>.
7/22/96 11:06:31 PM : <<< 354 Start mail input, end with <CRLF>.<CRLF>.
7/22/96 11:06:31 PM : <<< IO: |250 Requested mail action Ok.
7/22/96 11:06:31 PM : <<< 250 Requested mail action Ok.
7/22/96 11:06:31 PM : >>> QUIT
7/22/96 11:06:31 PM : <<< IO: |221 Goodbye chora.sakes.com
7/22/96 11:06:31 PM : <<< 221 Goodbye chora.sakes.com
```

2. The Exchange server requests an SMTP session by sending a HELO command, followed by its name. The receiver returns an OK message and identifies itself.

3. The Exchange server indicates that it has mail from spyros@patmos.sakes.com, and the receiver returns an OK message.

4. The Exchange server indicates that it has mail for judy@dcnw.com, and the receiver returns an OK message.

5. The Exchange server informs the receiver it is about to send the mail message by issuing the DATA command. The receiver confirms it can receive the data by sending a command indicating it is OK to send.

6. The Exchange server transmits the data as an RFC 822 message, ending it with a ".", and the receiver confirms the receipt by sending an OK message.

7. The Exchange server terminates the process by sending a QUIT message.

Messages received from remote hosts and processed by the IMC are handled in a similar manner.

1. If the IMC has been configured to accept inbound messages, it listens on TCP port 25 for incoming connections from remote SMTP hosts.

2. Inbound messages are written to the \imcdata\work directory while they are being accepted, with the SMTP enveloped stripped.

3. Once the message has been received, the IMC moves it into the \imc-data\in directory.

4. The IMC will then contact the DS to verify that the recipient is valid. If it is, the IMC converts the message and any attachments into a native Exchange format and places it into the MTS-In queue. If the recipient is not valid, it returns a nondelivery report to the sender.

5. Finally, the MTA forwards the message to the recipient's information store. If the recipient is not local, the MTA routes the message to the MTA of the recipient's home server.

The progress of inbound messages can be tracked by looking at the IMC and MTA queues, just as we described for outbound messages, only in reverse as the message goes from the IMC queue to the MTA queue. It is simple to verify these steps by looking at the Exchange server logs and by setting up NT file I/O auditing on the \imcdata\ directories.

Despite compliance with most of the RFCs for SMTP mail, the IMC in Exchange Server 4.0 does not implement two commands specified in RFC 821. The first command, VRFY, is used to verify a recipient's address, as shown in the following example from the RFC documentation.

```
Sender:     VRFY Smith
Response:   250 Fred Smith <Smith@USC-ISIF.ARPA>
Sender:     VRFY Jones
Response:   550 String does not match anything.
```

If you attempt to send the VRFY command to Exchange Server, you get the response

```
502 Command not implemented
```

Although the VRFY command is implemented In Exchange Server 5.0, it is turned off by default. The administrator can enable it by setting the value of the REG_DWORD registry key EnableVRFY. The path to the key is

```
HKEY_LOCAL_MACHINE/System/Current Control Set/Services/MSExchangeIMC/
Parameters
```

If the key does not exist, VRFY is disabled by default. If it does exist and the value is 1, the VRFY command is enabled.

The EXPN command, used to expand a distribution list, is not implemented in Exchange Server. The following example comes from the RFC:

```
Sender:     EXPN Example-People
Response:   250-Jon Postel <Postel@USC-ISIF.ARPA>
Response:   250-Fred Fonebone <Fonebone@USC-ISIQ.ARPA>
Response:   250-Sam Q. Smith <SQSmith@USC-ISIQ.ARPA>
```

```
Response:   250-Quincy Smith <@USC-ISIF.ARPA:Q-Smith@ISI-VAXA.ARPA>
Response:   250-<joe@foo-unix.ARPA>
Response:   250 <xyz@bar-unix.ARPA>
```

Again, if you attempt to send the EXPN command to the Exchange server IMC, you get the 502 error message. The fact that the IMC does not support these two commands is mentioned in the *MS Exchange Server Support Instructor Guide*, on the Microsoft TechNet CD. (Note, however, that in an article on the same CD, entitled "MS Exchange and Mail Coexistence and Migration with LAN and Host Mail Systems," Brian Benjamin wrongly claims that the commands do work on version 4.0 of Exchange Server.)

References

For more information, see

- **RFC 821 at http://ds.internic.net/rfc/rfc821.txt**
- *Concepts and Planning Guide*, **Microsoft Exchange Server Documentation, Chapter 4**
- *MS Exchange Server Support Instructor Guide*, **Product Support Services Worldwide Training, January 2, 1996, Microsoft TechNet CD**

Message Routing within Exchange Organizations

In the previous section we discussed the flow of a message from an Exchange client to a single Exchange server on the way to the Internet. A more complex process, shown in Figure 3.8, involves a message traveling between a mail user on an Exchange server other than the server running the IMC and a user on the Internet.

The computers in Figure 3.8 are from the organization depicted in Figure 3.1. In this example, Nicholas is an Exchange user on server campos.sakes.com, and the IMC is installed on chora.sakes.com, both in the Patmos site. Because both Exchange servers are in the same site, the SMTP address for Nicholas — nicholas@patmos.sakes.com — is similar to that of Spyros. The addressing is configured in the Site Addressing object for the Site as a whole. In this example, Nicholas sends a message to judy@dcnw.com. The progress of the message is as follows:

1. Nicholas prepares the message and submits it to the IS on his home server, campos.sakes.com.

2. The MTA on campos.sakes.com transfers the message to the MTA on chora.sakes.com.

Figure 3.8
SMTP Messages within an Exchange Site

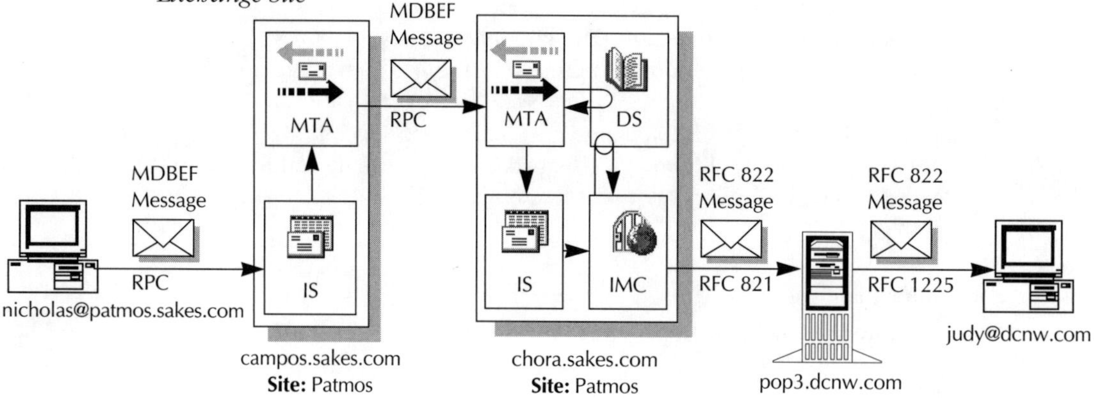

3. The IMC on chora.sakes.com opens up a TCP/IP connection to port 25 of Judy's server, pop3.dcnw.com, and delivers a message from nicholas@patmos.sakes.com to judy@dcnw.com.

4. Judy's POP3 client opens up a TCP/IP connection to port 110 of pop3.dcnw.com and downloads the message.

The main difference between this scenario and the previous one is that the message has to be transferred from Nicholas's server to the server running the IMC. Even though the message is ultimately converted into an RFC 822 format, it is not converted until it is about to leave the organization. In terms of tracking the message, it would go through the queues in the following order.

On campos.sakes.com

```
MTA queue:  CHORA
```

On chora.sakes.com

```
MTA queue: Internet Mail Connector (CHORA)
IMC queue: Outbound messages awaiting conversion
IMC queue: Outbound messages awaiting delivery
```

After Nicholas submits the message to his IS, you can track the message's progress by looking at each of these queues. For example, if Nicholas sends three messages to judy@dcnw.com, we'll see them first on campos.sakes.com in the MTA queue for chora.sakes.com.

Figure 3.9 shows the Queues tab for the MTA on campos.sakes.com. The messages from Nicholas are waiting for the MTA on chora.sakes.com to respond (we had to pause the MTA on chora.sakes.com to capture the screen in Figure 3.9), at which point the MTA on campos.sakes.com continues the delivery service. Once the messages reach chora.sakes.com, the passage through the various queues is the same as we discussed in the previous section. If Judy replies to Nicholas, it is received by the IMC on chora.sakes.com addressed to nicholas@patmos.sakes.com. After the IMC has processed this message, the MTA looks up nicholas@patmos.sakes.com in the directory, finds that Nicholas is a user on the server campos.sakes.com, and delivers the message there.

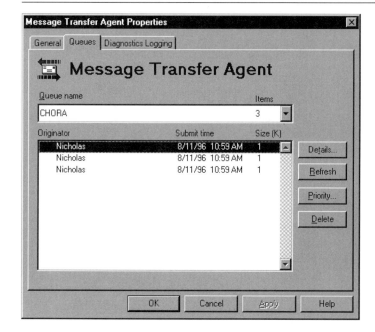

Figure 3.9
CHORA MTA Queue

Another scenario involves sending a message to an Internet recipient from an Exchange user on a server in a different site from the server running the IMC. Using the example from Figure 3.1, let's say that chris@athens.sakes.com is sending mail to judy@dcnw.com. This scenario is depicted in 3.10.

In this example, Chris is an Exchange user on the server kifissia.sakes.com. The server is in the Athens site, and it is not running the IMC, which is still running only on chora.sakes.com in the Patmos site. An X.400 connection exists between Athens and Patmos. The progress of the message is

Figure 3.10

Messages Between Exchange Sites

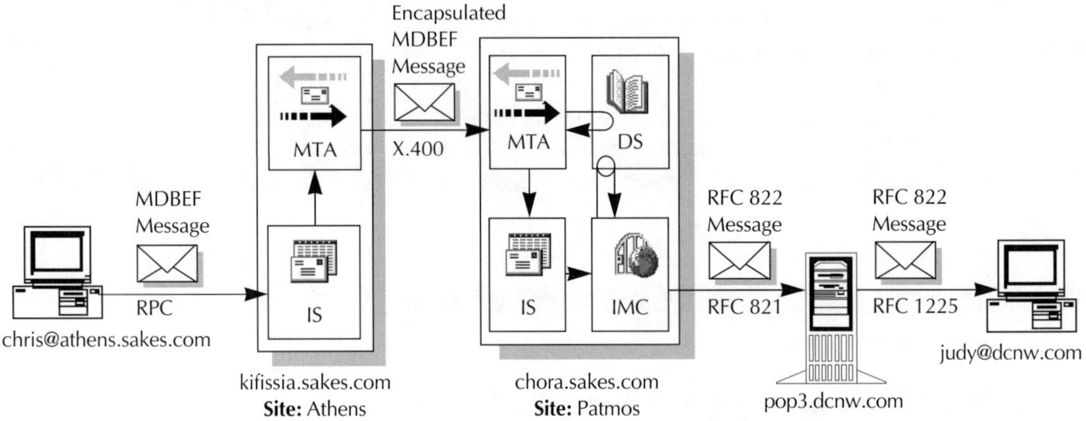

1. Chris prepares the message and submits it to the IS on his home server, kifissia.sakes.com.

2. The MTA on kifissia.sakes.com transfers the message to the MTA on chora.sakes.com.

3. The IMC on chora.sakes.com opens up a TCP/IP connection to port 25 of Judy's server, pop3.dcnw.com, and delivers the message from chris@athens.sakes.com to judy@dcnw.com.

4. Judy's POP3 client opens up a TCP/IP connection to port 110 of pop3.dcnw.com and downloads the message.

The primary difference between this scenario and the previous one is that the message has to be transferred from one site to another within the Exchange organization. The MTA on kifissia.sakes.com looks up the destination for the recipient of the message in the Gateway Address Routing Table (GWART) to determine through which connector the message should be routed. You can view this table in the Routing tab of the Site Addressing Properties dialog box on kifissia.sakes.com (see Figure 3.11).

Figure 3.11 shows the routing table in the Exchange Server Administrator on kifissia.sakes.com. The GWART is written to a text file on the disk, which is kept by each server in the Site in the *<install directory>*\mtadata directory. The file GWART0.MTA is the current routing table, and GWARTx.MTA is a copy of the routing table prior to the last change. In this case, we see that

Figure 3.11
The Gateway Address Routing Table

SMTP messages are to be sent through the connector it knows as the CHORA CONNECTOR. If we select the SMTP address type and click on Details, we get more information about the routing (see Figure 3.12).

Figure 3.12 shows the details of the route taken by the outbound SMTP message. First, it goes through the CHORA CONNECTOR, which is an X.400 connector that will get the message to the server chora.sakes.com in the Patmos site. Second, the message goes out from IMC (CHORA) installed on chora.sakes.com to the target SMTP host.

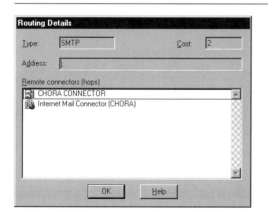

Figure 3.12
Details of the SMTP Routing

If Judy replies to Chris, the message is received by the IMC on chora.sakes.com and addressed to chris@athens.sakes.com. After the IMC has processed the message, the MTA looks up chris@athens.sakes.com in the directory, finds that Chris has a mailbox on the server kifissia.sakes.com in the Athens site, consults the GWART for how to get the message there, and forwards it to the CAMPOS connector.

Message Formats

You need to be familiar with two different message formats — the SMTP format and the Microsoft proprietary MDBEF format — to understand SMTP messaging in an Exchange environment. SMTP is the format for messages transmitted over the Internet. In this format, defined in RFC 821, the sender transmits the addressing information over TCP/IP in what is called an *envelope*. RFC 822 and its extensions define the body of the message, including both the headers and the message text. This message type is used by all messages between the IMC and remote SMTP hosts, and it was described fully in Chapter 2.

The second message type, MDBEF, is the proprietary format used by the Exchange IS and the MTA to transfer messages internally. MDBEF messages are translated by the IMC to RFC 822 messages for outgoing SMTP traffic. The message format is that of a Messaging Application Programming Interface (MAPI) object, and it is not limited to 7-bit ASCII format. It contains, for example, the rich-text formatting entered by a user, the digital signature of the user if the message is signed, and many other attributes that are accessible primarily through MAPI function calls. An MDBEF message is difficult to decode just by looking at the individual bytes of the message, and Microsoft has provided both a MAPI and an object linking and embedding (OLE) interface to help programmers create custom Exchange applications.

You can look at the data stream in a sniffer to see what an MDBEF message looks like. Figure 3.13, for example, shows a Network Monitor

Figure 3.13
Viewing the Server-Server Traffic in a Sniffer

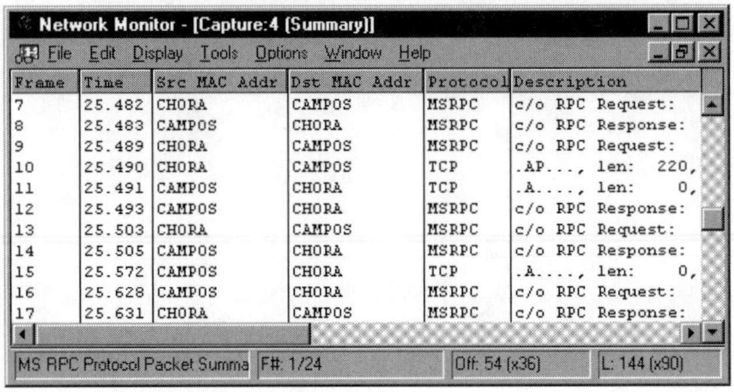

capture of a message sent from Spyros on chora.sakes.com to Nicholas on campos.sakes.com.

Two servers at a site communicate using Remote Procedure Calls (RPCs). When you view the data stream between two such servers, you see RPCs during the messaging process. To make an RPC, the RPC client must first obtain a handle to the RPC server application, which is shown in Figure 3.13 as the RPC Request and RPC Response. Once the sending computer, chora.sakes.com, has bound to the receiving computer, campos.sakes.com, the RPC communication can take place. When you look at the data captured by the Network Monitor, you cannot make out any ASCII text in either the envelope or the body of the message. Also, you won't find any of the text in either the message body or in the message header when you search the captured bit stream. In our example, we sent a message to Nicholas with the subject "Test" and body "hello," but you won't see "Nicholas," "Test," or "hello" anywhere in the captured data.

Although the format of an MDBEF message is not immediately obvious, MDBEF itself does not create an encrypted message. When an MDBEF message is sent over the wire between two servers, however, it is encrypted by default using a 40-bit key and RSA RC4 stream encryption. Between the client and a server, you can encrypt the message with a user-definable setting in the Exchange client. If security is an issue in your organization, you should require users to encrypt from client to server by going to the Tools menu, selecting Services and then Microsoft Exchange Server, clicking the Advanced tab, and selecting to encrypt "when using the network."

Also, you can install the Exchange Key Management Server and implement an encryption layer on top of the RPC encryption over the wire. This option encrypts the message in transit and while it's stored on the server.

The messaging between the servers in separate sites can be more revealing. Messages transmitted by the Exchange MTA over a site connector are still encrypted in an RC4 stream format, and the situation is essentially unchanged. However, messages transmitted by the Exchange MTA over an X.400 connector are encapsulated in a standard 1984 X.400 P1 envelope, and the body of the message can even be converted to the standard P2/P22 X.400 format (depending on how the administrator set up the X.400 connector). This P1 envelope is easily read. Listing 3.2 shows a Network Monitor capture of the data stream generated by a message going between Spyros, in the Patmos site, and Chris, in the Athens site.

You notice immediately that — compared to the data stream shown in Figure 3.13 — some of the header data is recognizable. To analyze the data in Listing 3.2 further, we need to break it down into individual bytes, which we do in Listing 3.3. The envelope starts at offset 55h.

LISTING 3.2 START OF X.400 P1 ENVELOPE

```
Frame Time Src MAC Addr Dst MAC Addr Protocol
9 3.191 CHORA KIFISSIA TCP
00050: 02 01 09 A0 80 A0 80 31 80 64 31 63 80 61 80 13  .......1.d1c.a..
00060: 02 55 53 00 00 62 80 13 01 20 00 00 13 05 53 41  .US..b... ....SA
00070: 4B 45 53 00 00 16 15 43 48 4F 52 41 2D 39 36 30  KES....CHORA-960
00080: 39 32 34 31 38 33 35 31 39 5A 2D 37 60 81 91 30  924183519Z-7`..0
00090: 80 61 80 13 02 55 53 00 00 62 80 13 01 20 00 00  .a...US..b... ..
000A0: A2 80 13 05 53 41 4B 45 53 00 00 83 06 50 61 74  ....SAKES....Pat
000B0: 6D 6F 73 A5 80 80 06 53 70 79 72 6F 73 00 00 00  mos....Spyros...
000C0: 00 A0 80 30 80 31 80 30 80 06 03 55 04 0A 13 05  ...0.1.0...U....
000D0: 53 41 4B 45 53 00 00 00 00 31 80 30 80 06 03 55  SAKES....1.0...U
000E0: 04 0B 13 06 50 41 54 4D 4F 53 00 00 00 00 31 80  ....PATMOS....1.
000F0: 30 80 06 03 55 04 03 13 0A 52 45 43 49 50 49 45  0...U....RECIPIE
00100: 4E 54 53 00 00 00 00 31 80 30 80 06 03 55 04 03  NTS....1.0...U..
00110: 13 06 53 50 59 52 4F 53 00 00 00 00 00 00 00 00  ..SPYROS........
```

LISTING 3.3 INTERPRETATION OF START OF X.400 P1 ENVELOPE

```
00055: A0 80 [context 0/constructor/length:indefinite | UserMPDU]
00057: 31 80 [set/constructor/length:indefinite | UMPDUEnvelope]
00059: 64 31 [application 4/constructor/length:indefinite | MPDUIdentifier]
0005B: 63 80 [application 3/constructor/length:indefinite |
             GlobalDomainIdentifier]
0005D: 61 80 [application 1/constructor/length:indefinite | CountryName]
0005F: 13 02 [PrintableString/primitive/length:2]
00061: 55 53 [US]
00063: 00 00 [End-of-contents for CountryName]
00065: 62 80 [application 2/constructor/length:indefinite | ADMD]
00067: 13 01 [PrintableString/primitive/length:1]
00069: 20 [ ] (blank space)
0006B: 00 00 [End-of-contents for ADMD]
0006D: 13 05 [PrintableString/primitive/length:5 | PRMD]
0006F: 53 41... [SAKES]
00073: 00 00 [End-of-contents for GlobalDomainIdentifier]
00075: 16 15 [ia5string/primitive/length:21 | Msg ID]
00077: 43 48... [CHORA-960702003853Z-1
...
00091: 61 80 [application 1/constructor/length:indefinite | CountryName]
00093: 13 02 [PrintableString/primitive/length:2]
00095: 55 53 [US]
00097: 00 00 [End-of-contents for CountryName]
00099: 62 80 [application 2/constructor/length:indefinite | ADMD]
0009B: 13 01 [PrintableString/primitive/length:1]
0009D: 20 [ ] (blank space)
0009E: 00 00 [End-of-contents for ADMD]
000A0: A2 80 [context 2/constructor/length:indefinite | PRMD]
000A2: 13 05 [PrintableString/primitive/length:5]
000A4: 53 41... [SAKES]
000A9: 00 00 [End-of-contents for PRMD]
000AB: 83 06 [context 3/primitive/length:6 |OrganizationName]
000AD: 50 61... [Patmos]
000B3: A5 80 [context 5/constructor/length:indefinite | PersonalName]
000B5: 80 06 [context 0/primitive/length:6 | Surname]
000B7: 53 70... [Spyros]
000BD: 00 00 [End-of-contents]
```

The message envelope is formatted using the 1984 X.400 P1 protocol, and it contains all the information required to deliver the message, including the address of the originator and recipient, the delivery priority, and any message trace information. A full analysis of the X.400 P1 envelope is out of the scope of this book; for more information about X.400, see *Introduction to X.400*, by Cemil Betanov, and the X.409 documentation.

You can also analyze the trace using a sniffer that can decode all the OSI layers, like ISO Transport, Session, Presentation, X.400 P1, P2, and ASN.1. The Microsoft Network Monitor cannot analyze the X.400 protocol; to do so, you'll need a more fully featured product like the Network General Ethernet Analyzer. For more information, see "How to Create X.400 Trace Using Network Monitor" in the Microsoft Knowledge Base (article Q152470). For now, we will limit our discussion to analyzing parts of the envelope that are relevant to the current topic.

In the data stream captured by the sniffer you can see both the X.400 address and the X.500 directory attributes of the sender (see Table 3.2).

TABLE 3.2 X.400 AND X.500 DATA IN THE P1 ENVELOPE

X.400 Envelope

Offset	Attribute	Value	Comment
00093	Country	US	
0009B	ADMD	" "	Single blank space
000A2	PRMD	SAKES	Exchange Organization
000A9	Organization Name	Patmos	Exchange Site

X.500 Directory Entry

Offset	Attribute	Value	Comment
000DB	Organization	SAKES	Exchange Organization
000ED	Organization Unit	Patmos	Exchange Site
00102	Common Name	Recipients	Recipients Container
0011B	Common Name	spyros	Mailbox

The X.400 address found starting at offset 00093 of the data stream shown in Listing 3.2 corresponds to the Site Addressing scheme shown in the Exchange Administrator. Figure 3.14 shows the X.400 properties for the Patmos site.

Figure 3.14

X.400 Address Space for Patmos

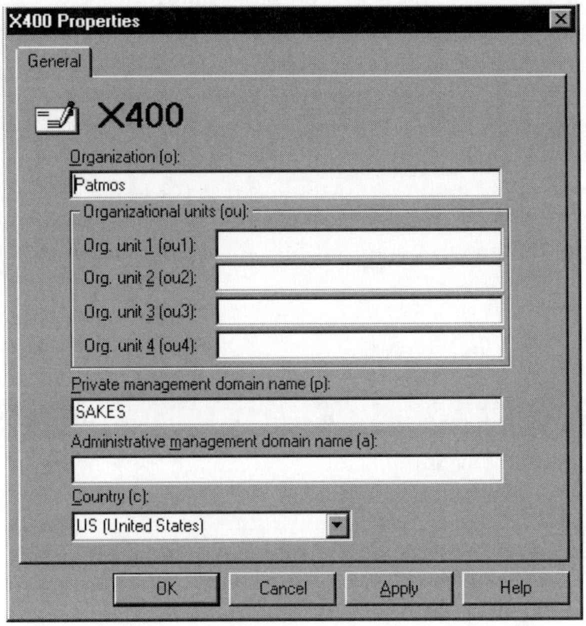

As you can see from Figure 3.14, the X.400 address space for the Patmos site is the same as that contained in the P1 envelope for messages traveling over the X.400 connector between Patmos and Athens.

Listing 3.2 contained both X.400 and X.500 information. You can easily confuse the two. The default mappings between Exchange, X.400, and X.500 are shown in Table 3.3.

Note that the message being sent to an Internet recipient is routed internally within the Exchange organization encapsulated in an X.400 P1 envelope. During this internal routing, the body of the message is preserved in MDBEF format. When the message arrives at the server running the IMC, the MDBEF message is converted to 7-bit ASCII by the IMC service for transmittal to the remote SMTP host.

TABLE 3.3 X.400 TO X.500 ADDRESS MAPPINGS

Exchange Server	X.400	X.500
Country	Country	Country
Organization	PRMD	Organization
Site name	Organization Name	Organizational Unit
Recipient Container		Common Name
Recipient Mailbox	Surname, Given Name	Common Name

For more information, see the following articles:

References

- "Appendix A: Introduction to Messaging Standards," Microsoft Mail Resource Kit, Microsoft TechNet CD; section on X.400

- "Appendix G: X.400 Concepts and Terminology," *Fundamentals of Microsoft Exchange Server 4.0,* Course 730, Microsoft Education and Certification

- "Appendix H: Use of Remote Procedure Calls (RPC) in Microsoft Exchange Server and Clients," *Fundamentals of Microsoft Exchange Server 4.0,* Course 730, Microsoft Education and Certification

- "MS Exchange Server: Using Industry Standards for Greater Compatibility," Microsoft TechNet CD, Technical Notes

- "MS Exchange Server Planning and Optimization Guide," Microsoft TechNet CD, Technical Notes

- "MS Exchange and Mail Coexistence and Migration with LAN and Host Mail Systems," by Brian Benjamin, Microsoft TechNet CD

- "X400: How MTAs Initiate and Communicate," *Microsoft Knowledge Base,* Article ID: Q86988, at
  http://www.microsoft.com/kb/bussys/mail/q86988.htm

- "How to Create X.400 Trace Using Network Monitor," *Microsoft Knowledge Base,* Article ID: Q152470, at
  http://www.microsoft.com/kb/bussys/mail/q152470.htm

- "X400: Documentation Index for X.400 and X.25 Protocols," *Microsoft Knowledge Base,* Article ID: Q86961

- *Introduction to X.400,* Cemil Betanov, Artech House Publishers, Boston, 1996
- *MAILbus400 Message Transfer Agent: Introduction and Glossary,* Digital Equipment Corporation, 1194. Order Number: AA-Q89LA-TE
- *MAILbus400 Message Transfer Agent: Planning and Setup,* Digital Equipment Corporation, 1194. Order Number: AA-Q89MB-TE
- *DEC X.500 Directory Service: Management,* Digital Equipment Corporation, 1194. Order Number: AA-QEVEB-TE
- *Externally Defined Body Parts (Body Part 15); Issues and Recommendations,* Electronic Messaging Association, 1994
- *Directory Attribute Mapping Guide,* Electronic Messaging Association, 1995
- *CCITT Recommendations X.400-X.430,* 1984 (commonly called the "Red Book")
- *CCITT/ISO Recommendations X.400-X.420,* 1988 ("Blue Book")

You can also check the Web sites and the newsgroup below.

- *Index to X.400 Web Pages,* http://domen.uninett.no/~hta/x400/
- *The X.400 Standards,* http://domen.uninett.no/~hta/x400/standards.html
- *ITU-TS. Series X Recommendations: X.200 to X.499,*
  http://www.itu.ch/itudoc/itu-t/rec/x/x200-499.html
- *X.400 Protocol Resources,*
  http://andrew2.andrew.cmu.edu/cyrus/email/standards-X400.html
- *Message Handling System,* http://www.to.icl.fi/mhstands.html
- comp.protocols.iso.x400 (USENET newsgroup)

CHAPTER 4

Domain Name Service Basics

In Chapter 3, we presented a high-level overview of Exchange Server's Simple Message Transfer Protocol (SMTP) architecture. In Chapter 2, we examined the basic features of SMTP and Transfer Control Protocol/Internet Protocol (TCP/IP) to provide a better understanding of the Exchange Internet Mail Connector (IMC).

In this chapter, we discuss the Domain Name Service (DNS), which is crucial for understanding how SMTP mail systems and the Exchange Server IMC route mail over the Internet. This chapter contains a basic tutorial on DNS; after a brief overview, we will discuss

- installing DNS, including DNS components
- configuring DNS, considering the many types of files
- monitoring DNS traffic

A note in the instructor's manual for the Microsoft Certified course on Exchange Server points out that "the vast majority of problems people will encounter configuring the Internet Mail Connector will be caused by a lack of understanding of DNS." This chapter should give you the understanding you need to avoid those problems.

Overview

As we discussed in Chapter 2, the procedures and standards for SMTP mail are defined in Requests For Comments (RFCs). The same is true for DNS. The primary RFCs relating to DNS are listed in Table 4.1.

TABLE 4.1 DNS RFCS		
RFC	**Status**	**Title**
791		Internet Protocol (IP)
793		Transmission Control Protocol (TCP)
1034		Domain Names - Concepts and Facilities
1035		Domain Names - Implementation and Specification
1348	Updates 1034, 1035	DNS NSAP Resource Records
1706	Supersedes 1348	DNS NSAP Resource Records

We learned in Chapter 2 that SMTP uses TCP to create a connection to a specific port on a destination host and to send mail data reliably over the connection. At the level of the network protocol, IP provides the means for one host to identify and send data to another host, using an IP address (for example, 206.247.73.140) to uniquely identify the remote host. This procedure is not adequate for SMTP functionality, however, because we do not want to send mail to users based on IP addresses.

DNS takes care of this problem by letting one host send data to another host using a host name (for example, pop3.dcnw.com) to uniquely identify the remote host, and it lets SMTP users send mail to each other using mailbox names instead of IP addresses.

Resolving Addresses with and without DNS

When you use a desktop client application, such as e-mail or a Web browser, to connect to a remote computer, your computer needs to resolve the addresses you have entered (spyros@patmos.sakes.com or www.microsoft.com) into the IP addresses it needs to connect to the remote server. DNS is a way to resolve addresses on a TCP/IP network.

Let's say, for example, you want to point your Web browser to a host such as http://www.microsoft.com. Without DNS, you would need to know that www.microsoft.com is a computer with IP address of 207.68.137.35. Similarly, consider the simple network introduced in Chapter 3, shown in Figure 4.1, that has the Microsoft Internet Information Server (IIS) Web server running on chora.sakes.com.

Figure 4.1
Simple Exchange Organization

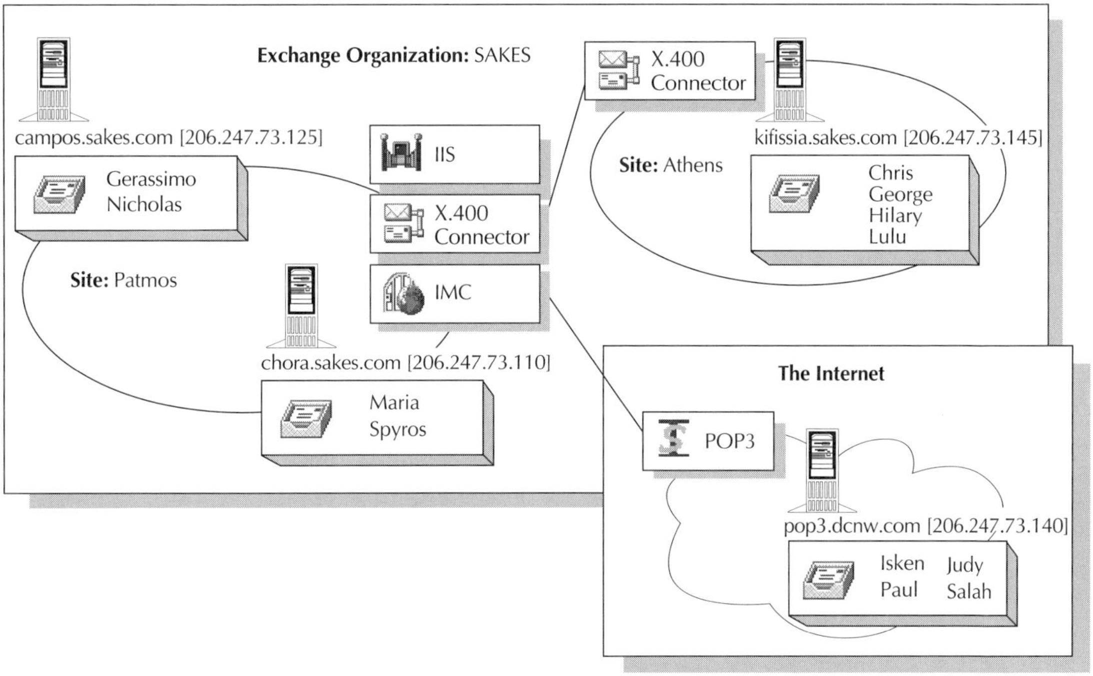

Without DNS or another method of name resolution, you could reach the Web server at chora.sakes.com only by entering its IP address into your browser. For example, to view the page patmo.htm, shown in Figure 4.2, you type **http://206.247.73.110/patmo.htm** into the address field of the Microsoft Internet Explorer.

You use the same procedure to exchange mail with a user on a POP3 server if you were using the Exchange client with the Internet service installed. In the examples used in Chapter 2, we needed to configure an Exchange client for Judy to be a POP3 client to the NTMail host pop3.dcnw.com. Without DNS,

Figure 4.2
WWW Server Resolution
Using IP Addresses

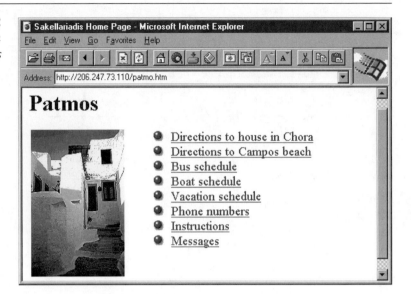

we would have had to enter the IP address of the server when we configured her mail profile.

To use the IP address in configuring the mail profile, you create a profile using the Mail and Fax applet in the Control Panel and then select Internet Mail as the delivery service for that profile. When you are asked to enter the location of the Internet Mail server, you can choose either a name or an IP address, and at this stage we would have had to enter the IP address of Judy's server. Figure 4.3 shows Internet Mail service for the profile.

In this screen we have entered the IP address of pop3.dcnw.com into the Internet Mail server field. When Judy composes and sends a mail message, her desktop will make a connection to port 25 of the server with this IP address and transfer the mail. When she wants to retrieve mail, her desktop will make a connection to port 110 of this server.

One alternative to memorizing these various addresses is to have a table on your desktop system that maps names to IP addresses. If your desktop is a Unix system, this local table is probably the file /etc/hosts or /etc/resolv.conf. If your desktop is a Windows NT system, the file is \system32\drivers\etc\hosts. Listing 4.1 shows the HOSTS file for Judy's desktop.

Figure 4.3
Configuring the Internet Mail Service

LISTING 4.1 HOSTS FILE ON JUDY'S DESKTOP

```
206.247.73.110   chora.sakes.com
206.247.73.125   campos.sakes.com
206.247.73.145   kifissia.sakes.com
206.247.73.140   pop3.dcnw.com
```

When Judy tries to access a remote host by name, her desktop system checks her local HOSTS table to resolve the name. The name chora.sakes.com is listed in this file, so she can use that name rather than the IP address in her browser, as shown in Figure 4.4.

Figure 4.4
WWW Server Resolution
Using Host Names

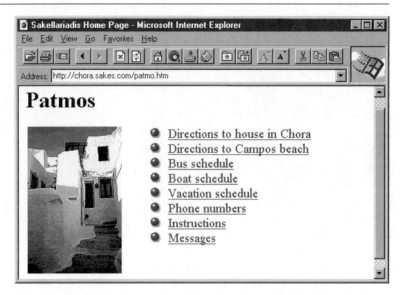

Notice that the IP address, shown in Figure 4.2, has been replaced with the name of the server in Figure 4.4. Names are easier to remember than IP numbers, so this system makes it easier to find remote servers. The problem with a local table strategy, however, is that your HOSTS file must have the IP address of every remote host you might want to contact. Also, every client in your network needs this HOSTS file.

Suppose, for example, we added a host felix.dcnw.com at 206.247.73.141 to the network shown in Figure 4.1. If Judy wants to reach felix.dcnw.com by name, we need to add the following entry to her HOSTS file:

```
206.247.73.141  felix.dcnw.com
```

Having added a record for felix.dcnw.com, Judy could now connect to felix.dcnw.com simply by entering the name of the remote computer. Unfortunately, updating Judy's HOSTS file doesn't help a user on chora.sakes.com, kifissia.sakes.com, or campos.sakes.com. To provide this function for those users, Judy needs to copy the updated HOSTS file from her desktop to the \system32\drivers\etc directory on each of the other users' systems.

The HOSTS file approach requires that you have — on every desktop — a correct HOSTS file that includes the IP address of every remote host you might want to contact. This arrangement may be practical in a small, stable network not connected to the Internet, but it is clearly not practical in a more global environment. Essentially, this approach makes finding computers on the Internet impossible.

The DNS approach was designed to solve this problem in an IP network. If you use DNS, you do not need to distribute files to the users' systems. At the desktop you configure TCP/IP to point permanently to another computer (either a local or a remote Internet host) that runs a database with the required information. That computer, the Domain Name Server, contains the addresses for some computers and knows who to ask for any other addresses.

To configure TCP/IP on a Windows NT server, select the Control Panel's Network applet, which is shown in Figure 4.5.

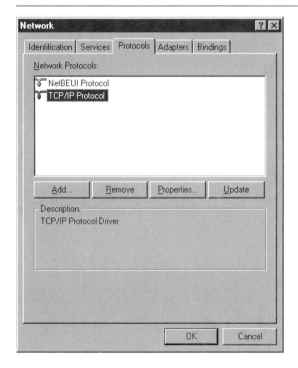

Figure 4.5
*Network Protocols—
TCP/IP*

To configure the DNS information, highlight TCP/IP Protocol in the box, click on Properties, and select the DNS tab of the TCP/IP Properties dialog box, which is shown in Figure 4.6.

Figure 4.6

TCP/IP Properties —
DNS Tab

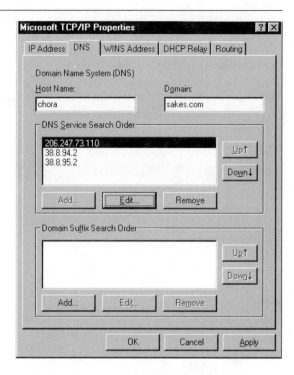

For Host Name and Domain, enter the name and domain of the desktop itself. Now enter IP addresses for up to three servers running DNS. Figure 4.6 shows DNS servers at 206.247.73.110, 38.8.94.2, and 38.8.95.2. The first address is chora.sakes.com, on which we have installed a Windows NT 4.0 DNS Server. The second two, shown in Table 4.2, are DNS servers for our Internet service provider (ISP), Performance Systems International (PSInet).

TABLE 4.2 PSINET NAME SERVERS

Host Name	IP Address
pri1.dns.psi.net	38.8.94.2
pri2.dns.psi.net	38.8.95.2

With the DNS service configured, when we try to reach any system by name, the TCP/IP protocol in our desktop will ask the servers listed in Table 4.2, in descending order, for the IP address of the remote system. Consequently, the only computers that need to be updated with host names are the DNS servers on the network or Internet — not the individual desktops.

We can summarize how a client resolves host names with a simple example. Suppose that a user logged on to a Windows NT server on the network configured as shown in Figure 4.6 and issued the command

```
ping pop3.dcnw.com
```

The system will use the sequence shown in Listing 4.2 to resolve the target host name.

LISTING 4.2 HOST NAME RESOLUTION

```
1. The system checks to see whether the target host name (pop3.dcnw.com) is
   the same as the local host name. In our case, it is not.
2. The system searches the HOSTS file. If an entry is found, it is used.
   Assuming that we did not add this entry into the HOSTS file, this check
   will fail.
3. The system sends a request to the first of the configured DNS servers,
   206.247.73.110. The host name resolution will succeed if that DNS service
   is online and has a record for pop3.dcnw.com or can query another DNS
   server for that information. If the DNS server at 206.247.73.110 cannot
   resolve the name, the user gets a bad IP address message, and the process
   ends. If the DNS server at 206.247.73.110 is offline, the resolution will
   also fail but the system will proceed to the next step.
4. A request is sent to the next of the configured DNS servers, 38.8.94.2.
   The results of this request depend on whether that server has information
   about the target host. If the DNS at 38.8.94.2 is offline, the system
   will proceed to the third DNS server, 38.8.95.2.
5. If all the DNS servers are unavailable, the name resolution fails.
```

For the purposes of setting up an Exchange Server IMC, step 3 is the most critical. The user's system can take other actions after step 5 but they are not germane to a discussion of SMTP. See the Microsoft TCP/IP manual that comes with Windows NT Server documentation for a more detailed discussion. For our purposes, the most important requirement is that the records in the DNS are correct, both for outgoing and for incoming mail.

In the past, you could only set up a Domain Name Server on a Unix — or larger — platform (though your desktops could be Windows- or Windows NT-based). Starting with the release of the Windows NT 3.51 Resource Kit and continuing with Windows NT 4.0, you can set up a Domain Name Server on Windows NT.

The rest of this chapter describes how to set up a Domain Name Server using Windows NT Server 4.0 and how to monitor DNS traffic.

Installing DNS

Installing DNS is very simple. For Windows NT 4.0, you install DNS from the Control Panel's Networks applet. From the Networks window, select the Services tab, click Add, and select Microsoft DNS Server from the list of services. After the files have been copied from the Windows NT Server CD-ROM, you will need to edit a number of configuration files and start the service. You can start the DNS service from the Control Panel's Services applet or by typing **NET START DNS** at a command prompt. Remember to configure each desktop to use the DNS when you set its TCP/IP protocol properties through the Control Panel's Network applet.

DNS Components

The major components of DNS are the Domain Name Space, Domain Name Servers and Resource Records (RR), and Domain Name Resolvers (DNRs).

The Domain Name Space is a tree-structured name space that contains the domain names and data associated with the names. For example, chora.sakes.com is a node within the sakes.com domain, which is a node in the com domain. Data associated with chora.sakes.com includes its IP address. When you use DNS to find a host address, you are querying the Domain Name Space to extract information.

The Domain Name Space for an entity is the name by which the entity is known on the Internet. For example, in the organization shown in Figure 4.1, we have two entities with two address spaces. The Exchange organization is known on the Internet as the sakes.com domain, and our sample Internet organization is known as the dcnw.com domain. Hosts at these organizations are known as a host name plus the domain name; for example, chora.sakes.com. Similarly, users in these domains can be found by their e-mail aliases; for example, judy@dcnw.com.

A Domain Name Server provides information about a subset of the Domain Name Space. There are two types of Domain Name Servers: primary and secondary. A primary server maintains a set of configuration files that contain information for the subset of the name space for which the server is authoritative. For example, the primary server for sakes.com contains IP addresses for all hosts in the sakes.com domain in configuration files. Resource Records are the entries in the configuration files that contain the actual data. A secondary server does not maintain any configuration files, but it copies the configuration files from the primary server in a process called a zone transfer. A secondary name server can respond to requests for name resolution, and it looks just like a primary name server from a user's perspective. Primary and secondary Domain Name Servers provide both performance and fault-tolerance benefits because you can split the workload between the servers, and if one goes down, the other can take over.

The Domain Name Server points to other Domain Name Servers that have information about other subsets of the Domain Name Space. When you query a Domain Name Server, it returns information if it is an authoritative server for that domain. If the Domain Name Server doesn't have the information, it refers you to a higher level Domain Name Server, which in turn can refer you to another Domain Name Server, until it locates the one with the requested information. In this way, no single server needs to have the all the information for every host you might need to contact.

A Domain Name Resolver extracts information from Domain Name Servers so you can use host addresses instead of IP addresses in clients such as a Web browser or a File Transfer Protocol (FTP) client, or with utilities such as ping, tracert, or finger. The DNR is typically built into the TCP/IP implementation on the desktop and needs to know only the IP address of the Domain Name Server. Configuring the DNR on the desktop is usually a matter of filling in the TCP/IP configuration data. Figures 4.5 and 4.6 show DNR configuration data in Windows NT 4.0.

Configuring DNS

When DNS starts, it reads a local boot configuration database. In Unix, it is usually the /etc/named.boot file. You can configure DNS in Windows NT Server 4.0 to use either the \system32\dns\boot file or a registry entry. This boot database points DNS to the configuration files (domain files, reverse look-up files, and a cache file) on the primary Domain Name Server, both for the database's Domain Name Space and for hosts in other domains.

For our discussion, we will assume DNS is running on both pop3.dcnw.com and on chora.sakes.com. Figure 4.7 shows the organization depicted in Figure 4.1 with the two DNS services added, as well as one of PSI's DNS servers.

The following sections describe how DNS is configured on the sakes.com and dcnw.com servers.

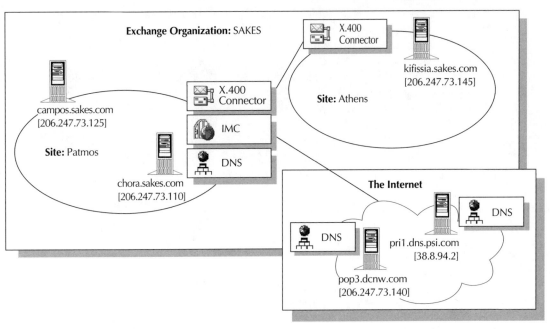

Figure 4.7
DNS Servers in the SAKES Organization

The Boot File

When DNS starts, it reads the boot file or registry entry to locate the database files. The boot file contains three main types of records, which are shown in the following fragment from a sample boot file (Listing 4.3).

LISTING 4.3 DNS BOOT FILE RECORDS

```
cache        .              <filename>
primary      <domain>       <filename>
secondary    <domain>       <hostlist>
```

In Windows NT Server 4.0, both the boot file and the configuration files must be stored in the \system32\dns directory. Listing 4.4 shows the boot file on pop3.dcnw.com.

The entries in Listing 4.4 indicate the names of the ASCII configuration files containing the Resource Records (RRs) for each of the domains shown. For example, the RRs for the sakes.com domain are in a file called sakes.com.dns; the RRs for the dcnw.com domain are in the dcnw.com.dns file. The same is true for the cache data, containing the addresses of root servers on the InterNIC, and the domains ending with "in-addr.arpa," which contain information that allow reverse IP lookups. We will examine each of these files in more detail in the sections that follow.

LISTING 4.4 DNS BOOT FILE ON POP3.DCNW.COM

```
primary      73.247.206.in-addr.arpa    73.247.206.in-addr.arpa.dns
primary      dcnw.com                   dcnw.com.dns
primary      sakes.com                  sakes.com.dns
cache        .                          cache.dns
```

Listing 4.5 shows a fragment of the boot file on chora.sakes.com.

LISTING 4.5 DNS BOOT FILE ON CHORA.SAKES.COM

```
secondary    dcnw.com      206.247.73.140    dcnw.com.dns
secondary    sakes.com     206.247.73.140    sakes.com.dns
cache        .                               cache.dns
```

Listing 4.4 shows that pop3.dcnw.com is the primary DNS for the domains dcnw.com and sakes.com. In Listing 4.5, we see that chora.sakes.com is shown as a secondary name server for these domains. Because pop3.dcnw.com is the primary DNS server for those domains, it maintains the sakes.com.dns and dcnw.com.dns configuration files with the IP addresses of the hosts in those domains. When the DNS on pop3.dcnw.com starts, pop3.dcnw.com responds to name query requests from any desktop. When the DNS service on chora.sakes.com starts, it reads the boot file, sees that it is secondary for those domains, and requests copies of the configuration files from pop3.dcnw.com.

A new graphical user interface (GUI) is available for administering the DNS in Windows NT 4.0; it is invoked from the Administrative Tools group. If you have already configured the DNS BOOT file and its associated database files, you will need to register the server in the GUI, much like registering a server in SQL Server Enterprise Manager. In our example, we have two DNS servers running, so we selected New Server from the DNS menu and entered the IP addresses for chora.sakes.com and pop3.dcnw.com. Figure 4.8 shows the servers in the DNS Manager.

Figure 4.8
DNS Manager

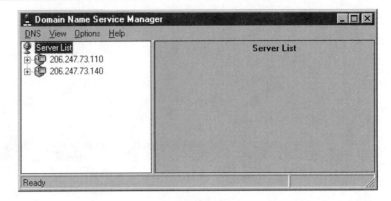

You can run the DNS Manager on any Windows NT server even if you do not have DNS running on that system. The graphical tool lets you manage DNS on servers on your network. Like the Exchange Server Administrator or the SQL Server Enterprise Manager, it is a remote procedure call (RPC)-based tool that requires a trusted connection to work. If we expand one of the servers shown in Figure 4.8 (for example, pop3.dcnw.com), we see a list of all the zones that it services, as shown in Figure 4.9.

Figure 4.9
DNS Zones Serviced by 206.247.73.140

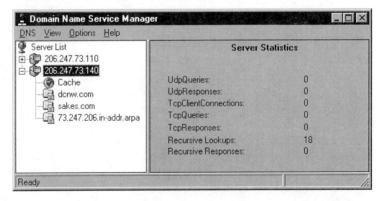

You can see that 206.247.73.140 (pop3.dcnw.com) is primary for three zones: sakes.com, dcnw.com, and one reverse-arpa domain. The left pane of the DNS Manager represents the boot file. The NT registry keeps the boot information in the System\Current Control Set\Services\DNS key, as shown in Figure 4.10.

Figure 4.10
Registry Entries for DNS

Both the database file name and a flag indicating the role of the name server are kept in the registry key. The parameter Type is a "1" for a primary server and a "2" for a secondary server.

To add a new zone, you could either edit the boot file directly with a tool such as Notepad, or you could select New Zone from the DNS menu (Figure 4.11).

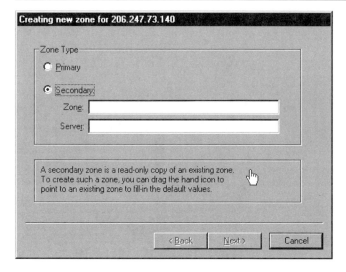

Figure 4.11
DNS New Zone

To create a new primary zone on a server, select the Primary option in Figure 4.11, click Next, and enter the zone name (e.g., dcnw.com) and a proposed name for the database file (e.g., dcnw.com.dns) in the next dialog box

(Figure 4.12). For our example, enter **dcnw.com** for the domain and **dcnw.com.dns** for the Zone File to complete creating a primary zone.

Figure 4.12

DNS New Primary Zone Data

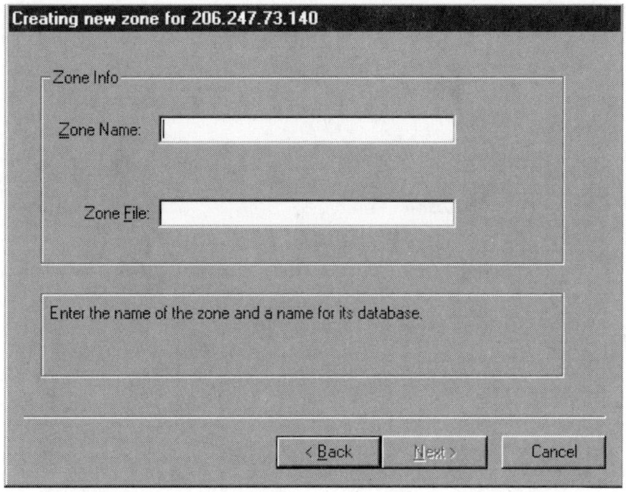

When the DNS service starts, it will read the boot file and see that it is supposed to be primary for the zone dcnw.com; it will then read the configuration data from the file dcnw.com.dns. At this point, it can respond to queries from clients requesting information about hosts in the dcnw.com domain — although it will not have any information to respond with, because we have not yet configured the dcnw.com.dns file.

If you look at the DNS entries in the System Log on the server, you see an entry for starting the DNS service similar to that in Table 4.3. Although the system log shows information about starting the DNS server, no further information is logged about zones for which the server is primary.

TABLE 4.3 SYSTEM LOG ENTRIES FOR PRIMARY DNS STARTUP

Date-Time	ID	Event Detail
12/9/96 7:01:10 AM	2	The DNS Server has started

As mentioned earlier, a DNS can be secondary for a zone. To create a secondary zone, select the Secondary option in Figure 4.11 and enter identification information for the zone's primary server in the zone and server fields. For example, you could create a secondary server for the domain sakes.com by entering in the name of the domain (sakes.com) and the name of the server that is primary for that zone (e.g. chora.sakes.com). You can also create a new secondary zone by dragging the hand icon in the dialog box into a primary zone in the DNS Manager's left panel.

When the DNS service on a secondary server starts, it queries the primary server for the configuration information. In our setup, when chora.sakes.com starts, it queries 206.247.73.140 (pop3.dcnw.com) for information about the sakes.com and dcnw.com domains, and it copies the configuration files from pop3.dcnw.com to its local \system32\dns directory. It can then respond to name queries for those domains just as well as pop3.dcnw.com can. The zone transfer to the secondary server begins when the DNS service starts and finishes after the files are copied.

The DNS entries in the System Log on chora.sakes.com, in Table 4.4, show the status of the zone transfers. These log entries demonstrate that when DNS started up on chora.sakes.com, it checked the version number on its local read-only copies of the configuration files for the domains for which it is secondary. It then checked the version number on the primary DNS, pop3.dcnw.com, determined that the files on pop3.dcnw.com were more recent, and copied them. Once this zone transfer was complete, the DNS server on chora.sakes.com started.

TABLE 4.4 SYSTEM LOG ENTRIES FOR DNS ZONE TRANSFER

Date-Time	ID	Event Detail
12/9/96 7:15:18 AM	702	New version 996062201 of zone sakes.com found at DNS server at 206.247.73.140. Zone transfer is in progress.
12/9/96 7:15:18 AM	702	New version 996062201 of zone dcnw.com found at DNS server at 206.247.73.140. Zone transfer is in progress.
12/9/96 7:15:18 AM	702	New version 996062201 of zone 247.206.in-addr.arpa found at DNS server at 206.247.73.140. Zone transfer is in progress.
12/9/96 7:15:19 AM	2	The DNS Server has started

The process of checking to see if files need to be updated is repeated regularly, based on parameters in some of the configuration files. We will examine those parameters shortly. If the administrator of the primary DNS modifies some data for dcnw.com, the next time chora.sakes.com rechecks version numbers, it will find a new version of the dcnw.com.dns file on pop3.dcnw.com and copy it. If the secondary checks again at a later time and finds no changes at the primary, it will not copy the file, but it will still log that information in the System Log. Table 4.5 shows that entry. In this case, the files are already synchronized, and there is no need to do a zone transfer.

TABLE 4.5 SYSTEM LOG ENTRY FOR "IN SYNC" DNS CONFIGURATION FILES		
Date-Time	**ID**	**Event Detail**
12/9/96 9:15:18 PM	701	Zone sakes.com in sync with version 996062201 at DNS server at 206.247.73.140.

Domain Files

As we said earlier, the boot file or registry entry points to domain files. The domain files contain RRs, which are defined in detail in RFC 1706. The main RR types used in configuring the IMC are

- Start of Authority (SOA) — identifies the authority for this domain data
- Name Server (NS) — lists a name server for this domain
- Address (A) — provides name-to-address mapping
- Alias (CNAME) — allows canonical names (aliases)
- Mail Exchanger (MX) — identifies the mail exchanger

In addition to these records, Microsoft Windows NT 4.0 DNS uses the following RR.

- Windows Internet Name Service (WINS) — directs DNS to use WINS for dynamic address mappings

We will examine each of these records in more detail. Even though the DNS Manager tool in Windows NT 4.0 makes it possible to set up a DNS without fully understanding the structure of the database configuration files, you should note that DNS must maintain files of the standard structure to stay in compliance with the Berkeley Internet Name Domain (BIND) software specification and to allow zone transfers to non-NT DNS servers.

Start of Authority (SOA) Records

The SOA record identifies which server has authority to define the hosts in its domain name space. When you create a new primary zone with the Windows NT 4.0 DNS Manager tool, an SOA record is created automatically. For example, when we created the zone for sakes.com on the server pop3.dcnw.com in the previous section, the DNS Manager software added an SOA record to the configuration file of sakes.com. You can see this record in the DNS Manager, as shown in Figure 4.13.

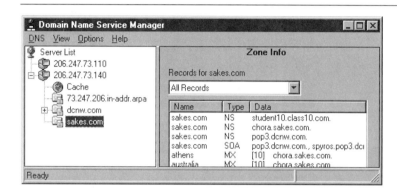

Figure 4.13

SOA Record Created by Setup

   The SOA record shows the current server, pop3.dcnw.com, as the authoritative server for the domain. Listing 4.6 shows the SOA record for the sakes.com domain on pop3.dcnw.com as it appears in the sakes.com.dns file.
   You can also see this record in the DNS Manager by double-clicking on the SOA entry in Figure 4.13. The dialog box shown in Figure 4.14 will appear.
   The SOA record is usually at the beginning of the domain file, which in this case is sakes.com.dns. The record indicates that the server pop3.dcnw.com has the authoritative records for that domain and that the mail administrator is spyros. It also lists various default parameters for the operation of the DNS. For example, Listing 4.6 and Figure 4.14 show a serial number of 23, which is the number the zone transfer process uses to determine whether the file on the

LISTING 4.6 SOA RECORD FOR POP3.DCNW.COM

```
@ IN SOA pop3.dcnw.com. spyros.pop3.dcnw.com.
      (23      ; serial
      3600              ; refresh after 1 hour
      600               ; retry after 10 minutes
      86400             ; expire after 1 day
      3600)             ; minimum TTL of 1 hour
```

Figure 4.14
DNS SOA Record

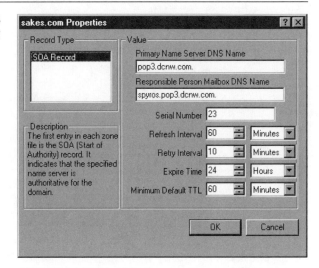

primary is more recent than the file on the secondary, and a refresh time of 3600 seconds, or 1 hour, which is the time after which the Domain Name Servers perform a zone transfer regardless of whether the domain files changed.

If a Domain Name Resolver — for example, Windows 95 running a utility such as NSLOOKUP — queries the DNS on either pop3.dcnw.com or chora.sakes.com, it will find that the authoritative server for sakes.com is pop3.dcnw.com. Also, because of the way DNS servers recursively pass queries to other DNS servers for remote domains, if the Windows 95 user queried the DNS on an Internet service provider (ISP) — for example, running on pri1.dns.psi.net — the answer would still be pop3.dcnw.com.

A handy utility for testing information in DNS servers is nslookup. Included with Windows NT 4.0, this utility can be invoked from a command line. When you type **nslookup**, you get a command prompt as shown in Figure 4.15.

Figure 4.15
Invoking Nslookup

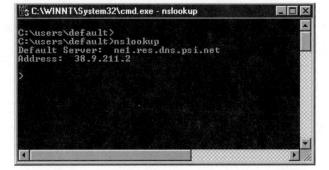

When you invoke nslookup, it automatically looks for the DNS server registered in your TCP/IP setup (as shown in Figure 4.5). In the example shown in Figure 4.15, the system is configured to use PSINet's DNS server at 38.9.211.2. If it finds the server, nslookup puts you at a > prompt, indicating that it is ready to search the DNS for information you input. To look for the SOA information, type **set type = SOA** and press Enter; another > prompt will be returned, as shown in Figure 4.16.

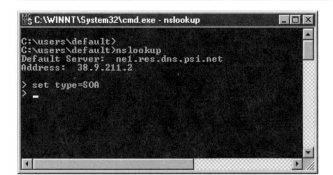

Figure 4.16
Looking for SOA Records

At this point, you have told nslookup that you are looking for SOA records, and the system is waiting for you to enter the name of a domain in which to search. If you enter a domain such as microsoft.com, you will get back the SOA information maintained in the DNS for Microsoft (Figure 4.17).

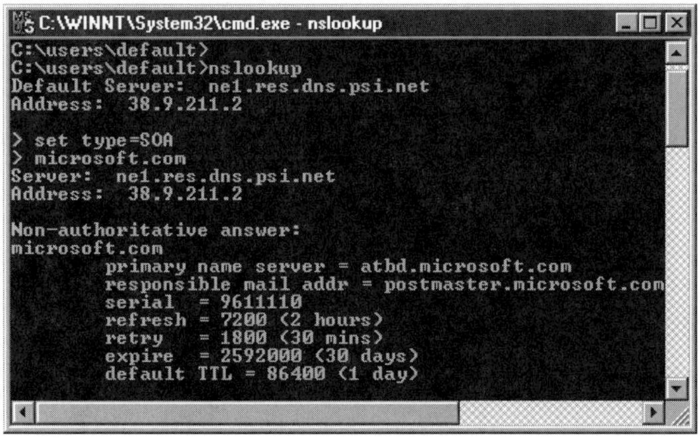

Figure 4.17
SOA Information for Microsoft

In this example, we see the details of the SOA record used by Microsoft. It is flagged as Non-authoritative because we queried PSINet's DNS, not Microsoft's.

If we enter **server atbd.microsoft.com** and then query the SOA record, we will receive the same data without the Non-authoritative qualifier. To get a full list of the syntax for nslookup, type **?** at the > prompt and press Enter.

Name Server (NS) Records

The NS record identifies each server running DNS in a domain. For example, we have two name servers in the sakes.com domain, pop3.dcnw.com and chora.sakes.com. When you create a new primary zone, the DNS Manager software automatically creates an NS record for the domain, just as it creates an SOA record, on the current server. You can create additional NS records by highlighting the domain and selecting New Record from the DNS menu. The New Resource Record dialog box will appear; select the record type and enter the name of the DNS Name Server. This procedure is shown in Figure 4.18.

Figure 4.18

Creating a New NS Record

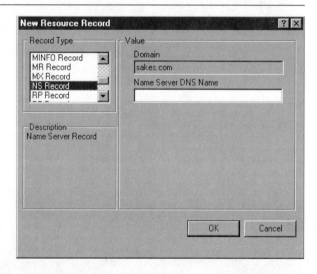

In our example, the two NS records in the configuration file would be

```
sakes.com.              IN NS   pop3.dcnw.com.
sakes.com.              IN NS   chora.sakes.com.
```

This file tells a Domain Name Resolver that pop3.dcnw.com and chora.sakes.com are running DNS for sakes.com. This information, as viewed in the DNS Manager, is shown in Figure 4.19.

We can query the DNS for NS records with nslookup in the same way we queried it for SOA records. In our example here, if we run nslookup against the server 206.247.73.140 and ask for the NS records for sakes.com, it returns

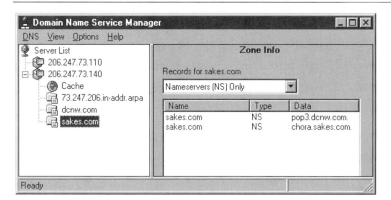

Figure 4.19
DNS NS Records

the information shown in Figure 4.19. Similarly, we can run nslookup against the PSINet Name Server 38.8.94.2, as we did in Figure 4.17, and ask for NS records for microsoft.com (Figure 4.20). In this case, nslookup shows you the name servers used by Microsoft (see Listing 4.7).

LISTING 4.7 MICROSOFT NAME SERVERS

```
microsoft.com    IN  NS        ATBD.microsoft.com
microsoft.com    IN  NS        DNS1.microsoft.com
microsoft.com    IN  NS        DNS1.NWNET.NET
microsoft.com    IN  NS        DNS2.NWNET.NET
```

Figure 4.20
DNS NS Records for Microsoft

```
C:\WINNT\System32\cmd.exe - nslookup

C:\users\default>nslookup
Default Server:  ne1.res.dns.psi.net
Address:  38.9.211.2

> set type=ns
> microsoft.com
Server:  ne1.res.dns.psi.net
Address:  38.9.211.2

Non-authoritative answer:
microsoft.com    nameserver = DNS1.microsoft.com
microsoft.com    nameserver = DNS1.NWNET.NET
microsoft.com    nameserver = DNS2.NWNET.NET
microsoft.com    nameserver = ATBD.microsoft.com

DNS1.microsoft.com    internet address = 131.107.1.240
DNS1.NWNET.NET  internet address = 192.220.250.1
DNS2.NWNET.NET  internet address = 192.220.251.1
ATBD.microsoft.com    internet address = 131.107.1.7
>
```

Microsoft is using two name servers at Microsoft and two at NorthWest-Net. The Domain Name Resolvers do not know or care which name server is authoritative for any domain, and nothing in the NS record identifies which server is the primary Domain Name Server and which secondary. To find out, you must query the SOA record.

Address (A) and Alias (CNAME) Records

The Address (A) record, or Host record, and Alias (CNAME) record provide the name-to-address mappings that a Domain Name Resolver uses to find systems by name. For example, Listing 4.8 shows the name-to-address mappings for the sakes.com domain.

```
LISTING 4.8 DNS ADDRESS RECORDS

campos.sakes.com        IN      A       206.247.73.125
chora.sakes.com         IN      A       206.247.73.110
kifissia.sakes.com      IN      A       206.247.73.145

ftp.sakes.com           IN      CNAME   chora.sakes.com.
www.sakes.com           IN      CNAME   chora.sakes.com.
```

The IN specifies the class record and stands for Internet; other classes such as CHAOS exist but you rarely see them. The A specifies the IP address of the host. After you define a host, you can specify aliases (CNAME records) for it. For example, ftp.sakes.com and www.sakes.com are aliases for chora.sakes.com. Thus, if you point your Web browser to www.sakes.com, the DNS will actually connect you to the host chora.sakes.com at 206.247.73.110.

To create a new A record in the DNS, highlight the domain in the DNS Manager and select New Record from the DNS menu. The New Resource Record dialog box (Figure 4.21) appears; select an A record from the list of record types and enter the appropriate information. You can also see this data in the DNS Manager, as shown in Figure 4.22.

You can use the list box at the top of the right pane of Figure 4.22 to select a specific record type. Figure 4.22 shows only the A records for the sakes.com domain, corresponding to the entries in the database file shown in Listing 4.8. If a user who tries to contact chora.sakes.com by name has his or her TCP/IP set up to query the DNS Name Server at 206.247.73.140, the name resolution will return chora.sakes.com's IP address of 206.247.73.110. In Chapter 6 we'll discuss a number of important configurations in the IMC that rely on setting up the correct A records in DNS.

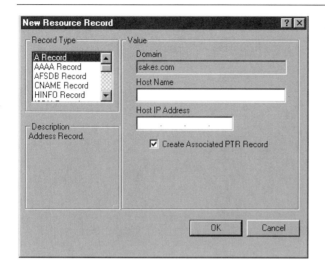

Figure 4.21

Creating an A Record

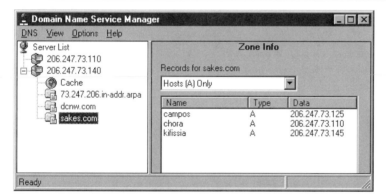

Figure 4.22

DNS A Records

Mail Exchanger (MX) Records

To resolve queries about mail recipients, DNS uses a Mail Exchanger (MX) record. Listing 4.9 shows the MX records for the sakes.com domain.

To add an MX record using the DNS Manager, highlight the zone, select New Record from the DNS menu, and choose MX Record from the Record Type (Figure 4.23).

Figure 4.23

Creating an MX Record

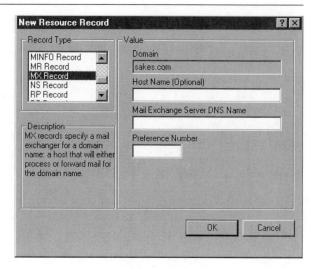

If you use the data in Listing 4.9 to fill in this dialog box, you can see the same data in the DNS Manager, as shown in Figure 4.24.

LISTING 4.9 DNS MX RECORDS

```
sakes.com.              IN  MX    10 chora.sakes.com.
athens.sakes.com        IN  MX    10 chora.sakes.com.
patmos.sakes.com.       IN  MX    10 chora.sakes.com.
patmos.sakes.com.       IN  MX    20 mx.smtp.psi.net.
```

Figure 4.24

DNS MX Records

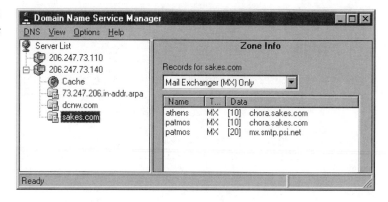

The MX record points to the host running the domain's SMTP mail service. In the example from Figure 3.1 discussed at length in Chapter 3, only the Exchange server chora.sakes.com has a configured the IMC and it receives inbound SMTP mail for users in both the patmos.sakes.com and athens.sakes.com e-mail domains. Patmos.sakes.com is the address space for all users in Exchange site Patmos; that is, all the mailboxes on chora.sakes.com and campos.sakes.com. Athens.sakes.com is the address space for all users in Exchange site Athens; that is, all the mailboxes on kifissia.sakes.com. SMTP mail for both domains is forwarded to chora.sakes.com by the originating SMTP hosts because a DNS query resolves those e-mail addresses into that host name.

For example, when judy@dcnw.com sends mail to spyros@patmos.sakes.com, her SMTP host forwards the message to the SMTP host for patmos.sakes.com. The MX record in the DNS shown in Figure 4.24 indicates that the server chora.sakes.com is handling mail for the domain patmos.sakes.com, so Judy's mailer forwards the mail there. Mail for chris@athens.sakes.com also gets forwarded to the Exchange server chora.sakes.com. If we installed the IMC on kifissia.sakes.com, we would change the MX record in the DNS so that inbound mail for a user in the athens.sakes.com domain would be forwarded to kifissia.sakes.com.

The number shown after the letters MX in Figure 4.24 indicates a priority level. If the originating mailer can not find a working SMTP host on the server with the highest priority level (the lowest number), it attempts to deliver the mail to the server with the next highest priority level (the second-lowest number). In this example, mail for spyros@patmos.sakes.com will first be sent to chora.sakes.com, which has a priority level of 10. If that server is inaccessible, the originating mailer then tries to deliver to mx.smtp.psi.net, a mail server at PSINet that temporarily handles mail while chora.sakes.com is unavailable. Normally, a number of Exchange servers in your network would handle incoming mail and you would set up your MX records to deliver to them. If you have an ISP willing to be a secondary mail host (known as *secondary MX'ng*) you can have mail delivered to the ISP if your server cannot be accessed, as we just discussed. You should then make sure that the ISP regularly tries to forward that mail to you.

We will discuss the use of MX records and the IMC in Chapter 6.

Windows Internet Name Service (WINS) Records

DNS has a couple of well-known problems. The first problem occurs when clients try to reach a server in a network where the DNS administrator is behind schedule in making changes to the DNS configurations. Suppose, as we discussed previously, a user on the network tries to ping felix.dcnw.com and is relying on the DNS to resolve the name. If the DNS administrator has not yet manually updated the DNS to include an A record for felix.dcnw.com, the name query request will fail. This problem occurs because DNS name registration is not dynamically updated — it relies on manual intervention.

The second problem occurs in environments where network administrators are using dynamic host configuration protocol (DHCP) to manage IP addresses. If felix.dcnw.com has a static IP address, the DNS administrator could create an A record and a client could resolve the name. However, if the network administrator assigns IP addresses dynamically using DHCP, the IP address of felix.dcnw.com could change at any moment without the DNS being aware of the change, and clients could no longer resolve the name. This problem also occurs because the DNS name registration relies upon manual intervention.

Microsoft has included a WINS look-up record in the DNS that ships with Windows NT 4.0. This record is specific to Windows NT, and it addresses these problems directly. In addition to the basic record types supported in the configuration files (A, PTR, NS, SOA, CNAME, MX, MB, MR, MG, HINFO, TXT, MINFO, RT, RP, X25, ISDN, WKS, and AFSDB), Microsoft has added the WINS lookup record

```
@       IN      WINS              206.247.73.120
```

This record instructs the DNS to query the WINS server at the IP address shown if no A record exists for the host in question.

To add a WINS record using the DNS Manager, you follow a different procedure than that for creating MX, A, SOA, and NS records. In the Server List, right-click the primary zone icon, and select Properties to bring up the Zone Properties window. Click the WINS Lookup tab, as shown in Figure 4.25.

Select the Use WINS Resolution check box, and enter the IP addresses of your WINS Servers in the edit box shown.

The place.dns sample file provided by Microsoft with the DNS setup files, excerpted below, explains the use of this record.

> [The] presence of a WINS record at the zone root instructs the name server to use WINS to look up any request for A (address) records for names which are DIRECT children of zone root, and which do NOT have A records in the zone file.

This record has a major impact on the process shown in Listing 4.2. Imagine a client trying to resolve the name pop3.dcnw.com, and an A record exists for it in the DNS. The WINS record lets the DNS query the WINS database for pop3.dcnw.com and return a successful name query response to the resolver. Even though DNS is updated only manually, it can now recursively

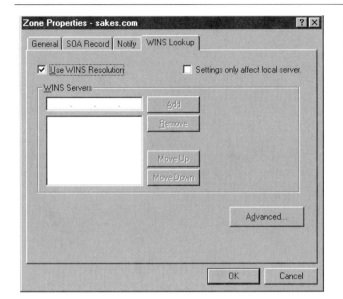

Figure 4.25
*Adding a
DNS WINS Record*

query a dynamically updated WINS server for information. Essentially, the
Microsoft DNS server is now dynamically updated.

Reverse Look-Up Files

Whereas domain files let a DNR use a host name to find a host's IP address,
some programs require the reverse — resolving IP addresses into host names.
For example, some mailer programs will not accept messages from systems
with IP addresses that do not resolve to host names, and some firewalls will
not pass data from similar systems. The Reverse Look-Up files in the DNS provide a means for this IP-to-address-lookup.

You need one reverse look-up file for each network you administer.
Reverse look-up files refer to domains by reversing the IP address octets; the
filenames are usually similar. The boot file on pop3.dcnw.com has entries for
the domains sakes.com and dcnw.com, with hosts in the class C subnet
206.247.73.0. In addition, the boot file has the entry

```
primary 73.247.206.in-addr.arpa        73.247.206.in-addr.arpa.dns
```

This entry shows that the RRs for the domain 73.247.206.in-addr.arpa are
in the 73.247.206.in-addr.arpa.dns configuration file, which has the entries
shown in Listing 4.10.

LISTING 4.10 DNS PTR (POINTER) RECORDS

```
110     IN PTR   chora.sakes.com
125     IN PTR   campos.sakes.com
145     IN PTR   kifissia.sakes.com
140     IN PTR   pop3.dcnw.com
```

To read this file, append the octets in the domain name, in reverse order, to the octet in the first column. For example, the first line in the in-addr.arpa file specifies that the number 110 points to the host chora.sakes.com. This file holds records for the 73.247.206 domain, so the first line really indicates that the IP address 206.247.73.110 refers to the host chora.sakes.com. Note that this information is the *reverse* of the configuration file sakes.com.dns, which states that chora.sakes.com is at 206.247.73.110. The in-addr.arpa files give you address-to-name mappings, whereas the regular domain files give you name-to-address mappings.

You can add a pointer (PTR) record using the DNS Manager in two ways. The more manual and purer manner is to create the PTR record just as you would any other record. First, create the Reverse Lookup zone and associated domain file the way you create any other primary zone. In the example in Figure 4.26, we have created a zone 73.247.206.in-addr.arpa, which will maintain the addresses for all hosts in the class C network 206.247.73.0.

Figure 4.26

Adding a Reverse Lookup Zone

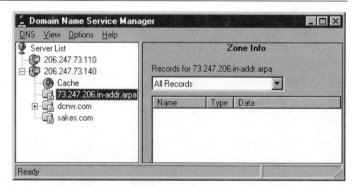

Now, to add the PTR records, highlight the zone, select New Record from the DNS menu, and choose a PTR Record from the Record Type, as shown in Figure 4.27.

Notice that this time not all the same Record Types are available as when you created A, NS, or SOA records. The DNS Manager recognizes that the new zone is a reverse-lookup zone and displays only the appropriate types. Once you select PTR record, enter the IP address for the host and its name.

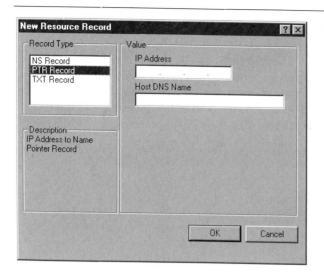

Figure 4.27
Adding a Reverse Lookup Record

An easier way to create the PTR record is to create it when you create the A record for a host. Assuming you already have the reverse lookup zone created, go to create an A record in the normal way, as shown in Figure 4.21. At that point, make sure the check box Create Associated PTR Record is checked, and the PTR record will be created in the reverse lookup domain at the same time as the A record is created in the regular domain.

Once the information in Listing 4.10 is entered into the DNS Manager, you can see the information in the DNS Manager (Figure 4.28).

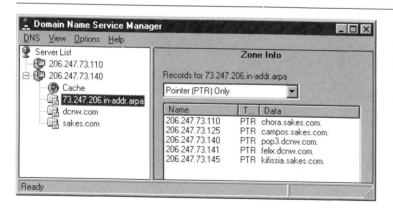

Figure 4.28
PTR Records in the DNS Manager

In this case, the DNS Manager shows the entire IP address rather than the last octet (Listing 4.10), which is much more intuitive.

Cache File

The cache file resolves names outside the authoritative domain of the current DNS. If a DNR queries your DNS and finds that the name is not within the zone of your server, DNS refers the query to any server listed higher in the hierarchy cache file. The sample file provided with Windows NT will probably be sufficient for setting up your DNS; this file contains the entries of the top-level Domain Name Servers. Listing 4.11 shows a fragment of the sample file.

LISTING 4.11 A PORTION OF THE SAMPLE CACHE FILE

```
A.ROOT-SERVERS.NET.       2163095040       IN       A        198.41.0.4
                          2163095040       IN       NS       B.ROOT-SERVERS.NET.
B.ROOT-SERVERS.NET.       2163095040       IN       A        128.9.0.107
                          2163095040       IN       NS       C.ROOT-SERVERS.NET.
C.ROOT-SERVERS.NET.       2163095040       IN       A        192.33.4.12
                          2163095040       IN       NS       D.ROOT-SERVERS.NET.
D.ROOT-SERVERS.NET.       2163095040       IN       A        128.8.10.90
                          2163095040       IN       NS       E.ROOT-SERVERS.NET.
```

Note that the cache file includes both the A and NS records for the root servers. The root servers are named currently A.ROOT-SERVERS.NET through I.ROOT-SERVERS.NET; until recently they had names like NS.INTERNIC.NET, NIC.NORDU.NET, and TERP.UMD.EDU, but the Internet Advisory Board renamed them to accommodate the structure and growth of the Internet better. Figure 4.29 shows the cache file in the DNS Manager.

Figure 4.29
DNS Cache File

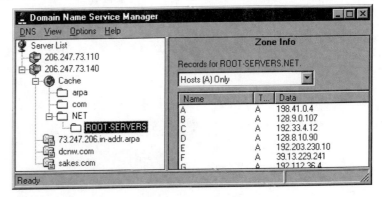

Monitoring DNS Traffic

In the previous sections, we saw how TCP/IP clients resolve host names using DNS. We can view the DNS resolution using the system management software

(SMS) Network Monitor, as we did in Chapter 2 for SMTP traffic. If you look at the organization shown in Figure 4.1, the Microsoft Internet Information Server (IIS) Web server is running on chora.sakes.com, and we have DNS running as the primary server for the sakes.com domain on pop3.dcnw.com. We will bring up the Internet Explorer on kifissia.sakes.com and point it to the Web page shown in Figure 4.4, http://chora.sakes.com/patmo.htm. If we load the Network Monitor on chora.sakes.com and monitor IP packets between the servers on the network, we can see the information shown in Figure 4.30.

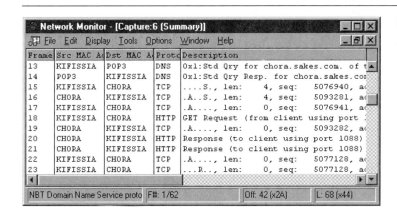

Figure 4.30
DNS and HTTP Packets

The first thing that the Network Monitor picks up is a DNS query from kifissia.sakes.com to pop3.dcnw.com, shown in Frame 13 of Figure 4.30. Listing 4.12 shows the frame details.

LISTING 4.12 NETWORK MONITOR VIEW OF DNS QUERY

```
Frame  Src MAC Ad Dst MAC Ad Protoc
13     KIFISSIA   POP3       DNS     0x1:Std Qry for chora.sakes.com.

  IP: ID = 0x5503; Proto = UDP; Len: 61
     IP: Source Address = 206.247.73.145
     IP: Destination Address = 206.247.73.140
  UDP: Src Port: Unknown, (1087); Dst Port: DNS (53); Length = 41 (0x29)
     UDP: Destination Port = DNS
  DNS: 0x1:Std Qry for chora.sakes.com. of type Host Addr on class INET
     addr.
       DNS: Question Section: chora.sakes.com. of type Host Addr on class
          INET addr.
          DNS: Question Name: chora.sakes.com.
          DNS: Question Type = Host Address

00000:   00 80 C7 D7 68 7E 00 A0 24 21 07 BF 08 00 45 00    ....h~..$!....E.
00010:   00 3D 55 03 00 00 80 11 B4 A0 CE F7 49 91 CE F7    .=U.........I...
00020:   49 8C 04 3F 00 35 00 29 A7 C3 00 01 01 00 00 01    I..?.5.)........
00030:   00 00 00 00 00 00 05 63 68 6F 72 61 05 73 61 6B    .......chora.sak
00040:   65 73 03 63 6F 6D 00 00 01 00 01                   es.com.....
```

The client, kifissia.sakes.com, starts by making a connection to port 53 of its DNS server at 206.247.73.140 (pop3.dcnw.com); it then sends a query for a Host Address record for target Web server chora.sakes.com. The response from the DNS server is in Frame 14, the details of which are shown in Listing 4.13. At address 055h we see the IP address for host chora.sakes.com is 206.247.73.110 (CE F7 49 6E), as we expected. At this point, we can also see the statistics in the DNS Manager (Figure 4.31).

```
LISTING 4.13 NETWORK MONITOR VIEW OF DNS RESPONSE

Frame  Src MAC Ad Dst MAC Ad Protoc
14     POP3       KIFISSIA   DNS     0x1:Std Qry Resp. for chora.sakes.com.

  IP: ID = 0xBD05; Proto = UDP; Len: 77
     IP: Source Address = 206.247.73.140
     IP: Destination Address = 206.247.73.145
 UDP: Src Port: DNS, (53); Dst Port: Unknown (1087); Length = 57 (0x39)
     UDP: Source Port = DNS
 DNS: 0x1:Std Qry Resp. for chora.sakes.com. of type Host Addr on class
     INET addr.
     DNS: Answer section: chora.sakes.com. of type Host Addr on class INET
        addr.
        DNS: Resource Name: chora.sakes.com.
        DNS: Resource Type = Host Address
        DNS: Resource Class = Internet address class
        DNS: Time To Live = 3600 (0xE10)
        DNS: Resource Data Length = 4 (0x4)
        DNS: IP address = 206.247.73.110

00000:  00 A0 24 21 07 BF 00 80 C7 D7 68 7E 08 00 45 00    ..$!......h~..E.
00010:  00 4D BD 05 00 00 80 11 4C 8E CE F7 49 8C CE F7    .M......L...I...
00020:  49 91 00 35 04 3F 00 39 9A 3B 00 01 85 80 00 01    I..5.?.9.;.....
00030:  00 01 00 00 00 00 05 63 68 6F 72 61 05 73 61 6B    .......chora.sak
00040:  65 73 03 63 6F 6D 00 00 01 00 01 C0 0C 00 01 00    es.com..........
00050:  01 00 00 0E 10 00 04 CE F7 49 6E                   .........In
```

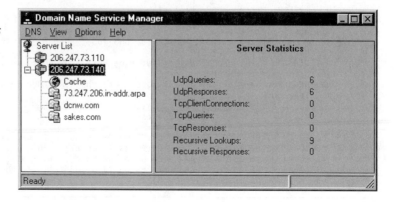

Figure 4.31
DNS Statistics

The DNS UDP query from kifissia.sakes.com to pop3.dcnw.com shows as a single integer increment on the line UdpQueries. Before the query from kifissia.sakes.com, that number was 5; after the query it was 6. Also, the response from the DNS server is shown in the UdpResponses counter, which increased from 5 to 6 after the query from kifissia.sakes.com.

Once kifissia.sakes.com has resolved the name using DNS, it queries the IIS for the home page of the Web server. It connects to port 80 (50h) of chora.sakes.com and retrieves the requested page patmo.htm. This process is in Frame 18 of the Network Monitor capture, the details of which are shown in Listing 4.14.

LISTING 4.14 HTTP REQUEST

```
Frame   Src MAC Ad Dst MAC Ad Protoc
18      KIFISSIA   CHORA       HTTP    GET Request (from client using port 1088)

   IP:  ID = 0x5803; Proto = TCP; Len: 227
        IP: Source Address = 206.247.73.145
        IP: Destination Address = 206.247.73.110
   TCP: .AP..., len:  187, seq:   5076941, ack:    5093282, win: 8760, src: 1088
        dst:    80
        TCP: Source Port = 0x0440
        TCP: Destination Port = Hypertext Transfer Protocol
   HTTP: GET Request (from client using port 1088)
        HTTP: Request Method = GET
        HTTP: Uniform Resource Identifier = /patmo.htm
        HTTP: Protocol Version = HTTP/1.0

00000:   08 00 2B 3F D8 0D 00 A0 24 21 07 BF 08 00 45 00    ..+?....$!....E.
00010:   00 E3 58 03 40 00 80 06 71 23 CE F7 49 91 CE F7    ..X.@...q#..I...
00020:   49 6E 04 40 00 50 00 4D 77 CD 00 4D B7 A2 50 18    In.@.P.Mw..M..P.
00030:   22 38 AB 16 00 00 47 45 54 20 2F 70 61 74 6D 6F    "8....GET /patmo
00040:   2E 68 74 6D 20 48 54 54 50 2F 31 2E 30 0D 0A 41    .htm HTTP/1.0..A
```

Listing 4.14 shows the client, kifissia.sakes.com, going now to the IP address of the target Web server and requesting the HTML page /patmo.htm over the Hypertext Transfer Protocol (HTTP). When the Web server on chora.sakes.com sends the data, the Internet Explorer on kifissia.sakes.com finally displays it.

The example just discussed represents a very simple case of name resolution. In a slightly more complex case from Figure 3.1 (page 38), for example, the Exchange user Spyros sends a mail message to judy@dcnw.com. When Spyros submits his message to the Exchange server for delivery, we will get several DNS queries in the Network Monitor, which is shown in Figure 4.32.

Figure 4.32
DNS and SMTP Packets

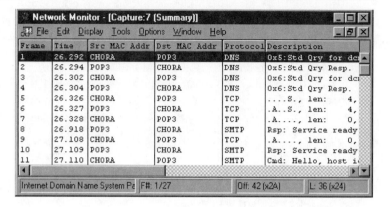

Frames 1 to 4 contain the DNS queries, and the standard RFC 821 SMTP conversation starts in Frame 5 with a TCP connection to port 25 of the SMTP host. The DNS MX query is shown in Listing 4.15.

```
LISTING 4.15 DNS MX QUERY

Frame   Time      Src MAC Addr   Dst MAC Addr   Protocol
3       26.302    CHORA          POP3           DNS        0x6:Std Qry for dcnw.com.

   IP: ID = 0xC113; Proto = UDP; Len: 54
      IP: Source Address = 206.247.73.110
      IP: Destination Address = 206.247.73.140
  UDP: Src Port: Unknown, (1382); Dst Port: DNS (53); Length = 34 (0x22)
      UDP: Destination Port = DNS
  DNS: 0x6:Std Qry for dcnw.com. of type Mail Xchg on class INET addr.
           DNS: 0............... = Query
           DNS: .0000.......... = Standard Query
           DNS: .....0......... = Server not authority for domain
           DNS: ......0........ = Message complete
           DNS: .......1....... = Recursive query desired
           DNS: ........0...... = No recursive queries
           DNS: .........000... = Reserved
           DNS: ............0000 = No error
  DNS: Question Section: dcnw.com. of type Mail Xchg on class INET addr.
           DNS: Question Name: dcnw.com.
           DNS: Question Type = Mail exchange
           DNS: Question Class = Internet address class

00000:   00 80 C7 D7 68 7E 08 00 2B 3F D8 0D 08 00 45 00    ....h~..+?....E.
00010:   00 36 C1 13 00 00 80 11 48 BA CE F7 49 6E CE F7    .6......H...In..
00020:   49 8C 05 66 00 35 00 22 18 C9 00 06 01 00 00 01    I..f.5."........
00030:   00 00 00 00 00 00 04 64 63 6E 77 03 63 6F 6D 00    .......dcnw.com.
00040:   00 0F 00 01                                        ....
```

The server chora.sakes.com is running the IMC and needs to find out where to send mail for a user in the dcnw.com domain. Listing 4.15 shows the packet from chora.sakes.com querying the DNS on 206.247.73.140. The Question Type is shown as Mail exchange; that is, the server is asking for the MX record for dcnw.com. Note also the section on DNS Flags: the eight bit is a "1," indicating that the DNR is asking for a recursive query. We see the effect of that request in the response from the DNS in Frame 4, which is shown in Listing 4.16.

```
LISTING 4.16 DNS MX RESPONSE

Frame Time    Src MAC Addr Dst MAC Addr Protocol
4     26.304 POP3         CHORA        DNS       0x6:Std Qry Resp. for dcnw.com.

   IP: ID = 0xD005; Proto = UDP; Len: 91
      IP: Source Address = 206.247.73.140
      IP: Destination Address = 206.247.73.110
   UDP: Src Port: DNS, (53); Dst Port: Unknown (1382); Length = 71 (0x47)
      UDP: Source Port = DNS
   DNS: 0x6:Std Qry Resp. for dcnw.com. of type Mail Xchg on class INET addr.
      DNS: Answer section: dcnw.com. of type Mail Xchg on class INET addr.
         DNS: Resource Name: dcnw.com.
         DNS: Resource Type = Mail exchange
         DNS: Resource Class = Internet address class
         DNS: Time To Live = 3600 (0xE10)
         DNS: Resource Data Length = 9 (0x9)
         DNS: Preference = 10 (0xA)
         DNS: Exchange Mailbox: pop3.dcnw.com.
      DNS: Additional Records Section: pop3.dcnw.com. of type Host Addr
         DNS: Resource Name: pop3.dcnw.com.
         DNS: Resource Type = Host Address
         DNS: Resource Class = Internet address class
         DNS: Time To Live = 3600 (0xE10)
         DNS: Resource Data Length = 4 (0x4)
         DNS: IP address = 206.247.73.140

00000:  08 00 2B 3F D8 0D 00 80 C7 D7 68 7E 08 00 45 00   ..+?......h~..E.
00010:  00 5B D0 05 00 00 80 11 39 A3 CE F7 49 8C CE F7   .[......9...I...
00020:  49 6E 00 35 05 66 00 47 4F 35 00 06 85 80 00 01   In.5.f.GO5......
00030:  00 01 00 00 00 00 01 04 64 63 6E 77 03 63 6F 6D 00   .......dcnw.com.
00040:  00 0F 00 01 C0 0C 00 0F 00 01 00 00 0E 10 00 09   ................
00050:  00 0A 04 70 6F 70 33 C0 0C C0 28 00 01 00 01 00   ...pop3...(.....
00060:  00 0E 10 00 04 CE F7 49 8C                        .......I.
```

The response from the DNS server has two parts. The first is the direct answer to the request for the MX record, indicating that the domain dcnw.com is served by the Mail server pop3.dcnw.com. However, because the DNS supported a recursive query, the DNS server realized that the DNR needed the Address record for dcnw.com's mail server as well. Consequently, the DNS response contains a section of "Additional Records," with the A record showing pop3.dcnw.com's IP address. Using that information, chora.sakes.com opens up a connection to port 25 of 206.247.73.140 to begin the SMTP transfer.

In this chapter, we have seen how SMTP systems use DNS to locate the target hosts to which to deliver mail. In Chapter 6 we will examine various ways to configure the IMC and how it works with the DNS.

References

For more information, see

- *Internet E-Mail Services,* Electronic Messaging Association, 1994
- *Domain Name Registration,* Electronic Messaging Association, 1994
- *DNS and Bind,* Albitz and Liu, O'Reilly
- *TCP/IP,* Microsoft Windows NT Server 3.5 Documentation, Microsoft Corporation, 1994
- "Internetworking with Microsoft TCP/IP on Microsoft Windows NT 3.5," Course 472, Microsoft Education and Certification
- "Implementation Details of the Microsoft LAN Manager TCP/IP Protocol," Additional Reading, *Internetworking with Microsoft TCP/IP on Microsoft Windows NT 3.5,* Course 472, Microsoft Education and Certification
- "Dynamic Host Configuration Protocol and Windows Internet Name Service, Microsoft Windows NT Server 3.5," Additional Reading, *Internetworking with Microsoft TCP/IP on Microsoft Windows NT 3.5,* Course 472, Microsoft Education and Certification
- *Internetworking with TCP/IP, Volume I Principles, Protocols, and Architecture.* Douglas E. Comer. 1991, Prentice Hall
- *Internetworking with TCP/IP, Volume II Design, Implementation, and Internals.* Douglas E. Comer. 1991, Prentice Hall
- RFC 1034 at http://ds.internic.net/rfc/rfc1034.txt
- RFC 1035 at http://ds.internic.net/rfc/rfc1035.txt

CHAPTER 5

Installing the Internet Mail Connector

In this chapter, we give basic guidelines for installing the IMC and troubleshooting some of the more common problems with installation. Although you will want to set up a custom installation for your own site eventually, beginning with the minimal installation we describe here lets you find installation problems quickly and easily and gives you a working base you can build on as you become more familiar with the IMC.

Minimal Installation

When you install Exchange Server version 4.0, you get three address types automatically: a Microsoft Mail address, an X.400 address, and a Simple Message Transfer Protocol (SMTP) address. If you install version 5.0, you get four addresses — the three listed above plus a cc:Mail address. Exchange Server creates these addresses even if you have not installed and configured the appropriate connectors to deliver mail to them.

When Exchange Server at the Athens site shown in Figure 4.1 (page 61) was first installed, we added an Exchange recipient named Chris. If you view the mailbox in the Exchange Administrator and select the E-mail Addresses tab, you see the addresses for Chris (Figure 5.1).

Figure 5.1
Exchange Addresses

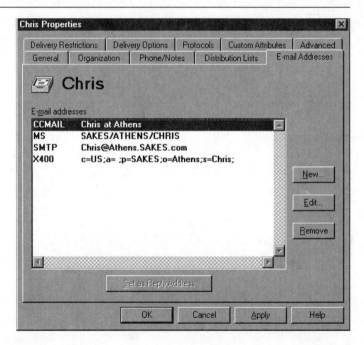

Exchange Server has created e-mail addresses for Chris independent of any connectors we have installed. For example, Chris has an SMTP address of chris@athens.sakes.com, even though we have not yet installed the Internet Mail Connector (IMC). You can configure the default address by clicking on the Configuration folder under Patmos in the Exchange Administrator and double-clicking Site Addressing, as shown in Figure 5.2.

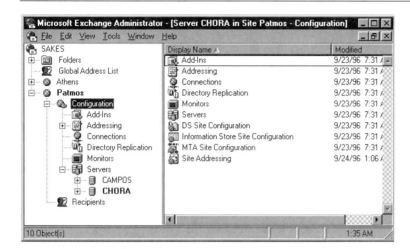

Figure 5.2
Configuring the Default Address in Exchange Server 4.0

The Site Addressing Properties dialog box contains the information for the default e-mail address spaces for the site. You can change these addresses through the Site Addressing tab, which is shown in Figure 5.3.

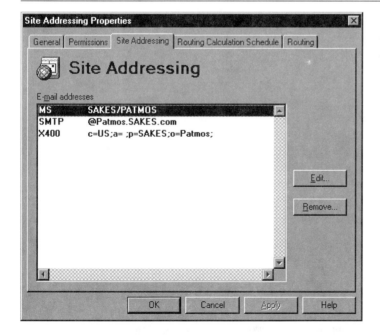

Figure 5.3
Exchange Server 4.0 Site Addressing Tab, Patmos

Because the Patmos site is running Exchange Server 4.0, no cc:Mail address type is included. In this site, the default SMTP address space for recipients is @patmos.sakes.com. For example, the user Spyros on chora.sakes.com has an address of spyros@patmos.sakes.com, and the user Nicholas on campos.sakes.com has an address of nicholas@patmos.sakes.com. The Site Addressing tab in the Athens site shows the default address spaces (Figure 5.4).

Figure 5.4

Exchange Server 4.5 Site Addressing Tab, Athens

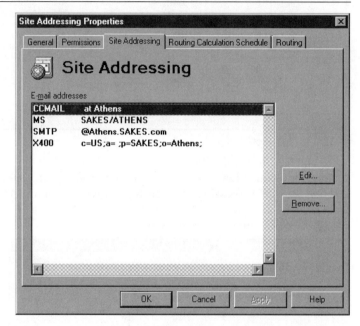

The default SMTP address space for recipients on the Athens site is @athens.sakes.com, and the user Chris on kifissia.sakes.com can be reached at chris@athens.sakes.com. Since the Athens site is currently running Exchange Server 5.0, those users also have cc:Mail addresses, unlike the Patmos recipients. You can change the default site addressing to be anything you want. For example, you might want users in the Patmos site, or even in the entire organization, to be known as @sakes.com rather than @site.sakes.com.

To get mail delivered to recipients using an SMPT address, however, we need to install and configure the IMC in the site. In Exchange 4.0, you need to do a Custom/Complete installation of the server and select the IMC. In Exchange 5.0, you do not select the connector during software installation; instead, you install the IMS by selecting New Other from the File menu and choosing Internet Mail Service to start an installation wizard. Once it is installed, you can see the IMC or the IMS by clicking on Connections for the site, as shown in Figure 5.5.

In our sample site, two servers are operating in the Patmos site, chora.sakes.com and campos.sakes.com. Although you install the IMC on a server, clicking on Connections shows site-level resources that have been installed. Consequently, in the Connections folder you will see an IMC object for all the servers on which it was installed. In our example, the IMC was installed only on chora.sakes.com, so the Configuration folder shows only one IMC (see Figure 5.6).

The dates to the right of the connector name indicate the date and time that the connector was last modified. If we had installed the IMC on campos.sakes.com as well, the Connections folder would show two connectors, as Figure 5.7 indicates. An Exchange 5.0 server would appear as Internet Mail Service rather than Internet Mail Connector. See Appendix E for further details.

Although we see two IMC objects, one for chora.sakes.com and one for campos.sakes.com, the presence of a connector in the Connections folder does not mean that the connector is configured and running, only that it has been

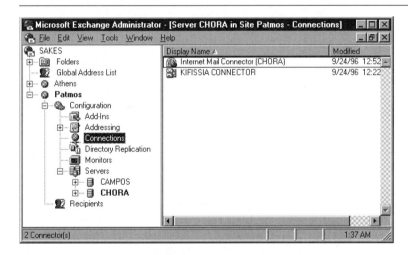

Figure 5.5

Connections on chora.sakes.com

Figure 5.6

One Internet Mail Connector in the Site

Figure 5.7

Two Internet Mail Connectors in the Site

installed. To make the connector run, you need to do a minimal configuration from Exchange Administrator and start the service in the server's Control Panel.

To configure the connector on chora.sakes.com, double-click on Internet Mail Connector (CHORA) in the Connections folder in the Exchange Administrator. You can configure the connector from any server in the site or from any desktop that has the Administrator graphical user interface (GUI) installed. When you double-click on IMC, you will get a warning message indicating that the Administrator name is blank and that you must enter one to configure the connector. When you click OK, you are presented the IMC Properties dialog box with the Internet Mail tab active. This tab is shown in Figure 5.8. If the server were running Exchange 5.0, the bold lettering would read "Internet Mail Service (CHORA)." See Appendix E for examples. You first need to click the Change button and select an Administrator for the connector.

Figure 5.8
Internet Mail Tab

In this case, we have selected the user Postmaster in the Patmos site to be the Administrator of the connector. As the designated administrator, the user Postmaster will receive messages concerning problems with SMTP mail delivery. It is generally useful to create a generic account to receive these messages, because it removes any reliance on the continued employment of a specific individual in any one capacity. The postmaster mailbox can either forward all mail to the current individual responsible for the connector, or that individual can be given access to the postmaster mailbox. In either case, the postmaster mailbox and its folders stay intact if a different employee is assigned postmaster duties.

In a basic installation, you must take one other step for SMTP mail to start flowing. You must select the Address Space tab and configure the IMC to process SMTP mail. Initially, you should select the default to process SMTP mail for all addresses, as shown in Figure 5.9.

Figure 5.9
Address Space Tab, Default

When you first bring up this tab, the list box on the left is empty. Click New Internet to create an address entry. The SMTP Properties dialog box, shown in Figure 5.10, will appear.

If you leave the E-mail domain field blank or put in an asterisk, the connector will handle mail for all e-mail domains. The cost factor is a relative number; it is relevant only if you have multiple connectors. Both of these

Figure 5.10

SMTP Properties,
General Tab

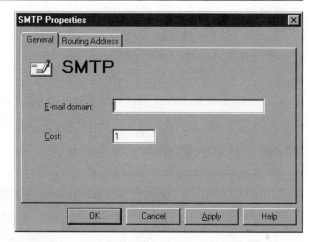

parameters will be discussed more later. If you click OK, the entry appears in the Address Space tab in Figure 5.11.

The purpose of the IMC is to route messages for specific e-mail domains. When you first start, it is easiest to indicate that the IMC will handle mail for all domains. To let the IMC handle the mail, do not enter any information in the two fields shown in Figure 5.10 and click OK. You are returned to the Address Space tab shown in Figure 5.9, with a single entry in the list box showing that the IMC on chora.sakes.com processes mail for any domain.

The IMC is now sufficiently configured to start processing mail, and you are ready to start the service in the Control Panel. When you click OK to close the Internet Mail Connector (CHORA) Properties window, you get a warning message telling you that you may not have taken all the necessary steps. The warning points out that you need to make sure that the outside world is aware that this server is now processing SMTP mail for your recipients. In other words, Domain Name Service (DNS) servers need to have a Mail Exchanger (MX) record pointing to your server. This message is very important — as we saw in Chapter 4, DNS is a vital component of the SMTP mail delivery system, and you do need to ensure that the DNS is set up correctly. However, this message is not warning you that you may have left out something in configuring the IMC on your server, and you can safely proceed.

After you have closed the IMC Properties dialog box, you need to start the service from the Control Panel, as shown in Figure 5.12.

When you first bring up the Control Panel's Services applet, the IMC is listed as requiring Manual startup. The screen also shows that IMC has not been started. You should set the IMC to start automatically, using the Exchange Service account that you use for the rest of the Exchange services, and then start

Figure 5.11
Address Space Tab

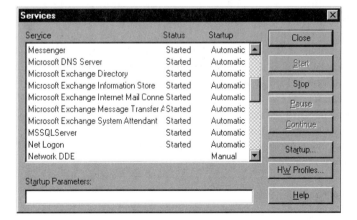

Figure 5.12
The Internet Mail Connector Service

the connector. Once the service has started, the IMC can deliver mail to SMTP recipients within and outside your organization.

Basic Troubleshooting

If you do a minimal installation and configuration of IMC, you should be able to exchange messages with Internet recipients immediately. Any problems at this stage usually can be divided into three broad categories.

- The IMC will not start
- The IMC cannot send messages
- The IMC cannot receive messages

These problems are usually caused by a few basic configuration errors that are well documented in the Microsoft Knowledge Base. Fortunately, they are also relatively easy to resolve. As an example, we'll use a simple scenario of a user on the Exchange server with the IMC installed.

The IMC Will Not Start

The following two Knowledge Base articles discuss a number of reasons why the IMC service will not run:

- "The Internet Mail Connector Fails to Start," Article ID: Q148727
- "IMC error 1067, Dr. Watson on MSEXIMC.EXE," Article ID: Q149542

The most likely cause of this problem in a new installation is an incorrectly configured Address Space. You should start your installation with the simplest configuration, using a blank space in the Address Space, as shown in Figure 5.9. This configuration lets the Internet Mail Connector send mail to all recipients and provides a basic configuration on which to build after you know your service works. If you have entered anything in this box, try removing it and see if the IMC starts.

According to Microsoft Product Support Services (PSS), another common reason why the IMC service might not start is the lack of an X.400 address for the IMC administrator. You should verify that you have not deleted the X.400 address of the mailbox.

The IMC Cannot Send Messages

If you cannot send messages through the IMC, the messages are probably getting stuck in the IMC outbound queue. That is, the messages have been received and processed by the IMC, but it cannot contact a host to deliver them. By default, they will be returned to the sender within three days with a Non-Delivery Report.

First, make sure that the IMC is physically connected to the remote host and that your TCP/IP protocol is correctly configured. From the server running the IMC, check connectivity to a known host such as ftp.microsoft.com by pinging:

```
ping ftp.microsoft.com
```

If this test works, you know that your physical connection to the Internet is correct and that the TCP/IP configuration on the IMC server is correctly configured to point to a DNS host. At this point, you should test the DNS MX and A records using nslookup with a known host, as discussed in Chapter 3; for example, your nslookup test might be similar to that shown in Figure 5.13.

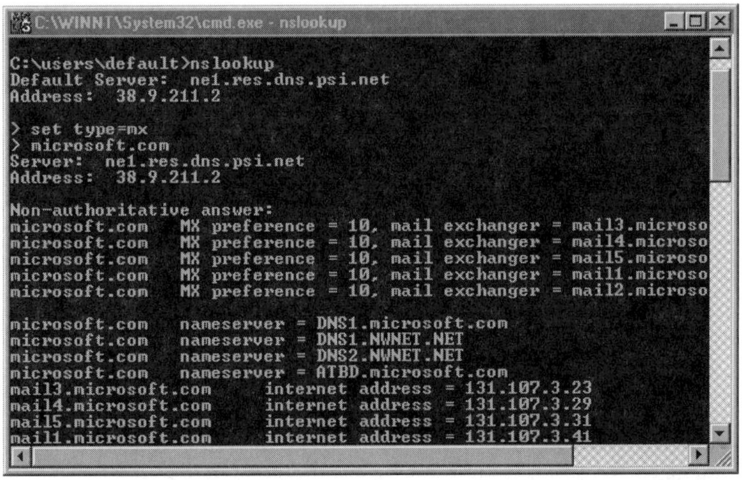

Figure 5.13
Testing DNS Records with Nslookup

In this example, Microsoft administrators stipulate that mail for users in the microsoft.com domain should be forwarded to the servers mail1.microsoft.com through mail5.microsoft.com and that these servers have IP addresses as shown above. In your case, you should run nslookup from the server running the IMC. If nslookup works from that machine, you know that the IMC should be able to deliver a message to a user at Microsoft.

If the ping and nslookup tests work but you still cannot send mail from a user on the IMC server to a recipient on the Internet, you can check for problems in a few other areas. The most likely problem is, again, a misconfiguration of the Address Space option. As before, you should start with this item blank. The second most likely cause is that you set the Transfer Mode on the

Connections property page incorrectly. Make sure that the Transfer Mode is set to process both inbound and outbound messages.

The IMC Cannot Receive Messages

Judging by the messages in the newsgroups on the Internet, the most common problem encountered when setting up the IMC is not being able to receive messages from remote users. Almost always the problem is caused by incorrect entries in the DNS. As we discussed in Chapter 4, the DNS must include an MX record associating the IMC server with your e-mail domain. You should test this record with an nslookup command to identify the MX and A records for your domain and verify that these records specify that mail for your users should be forwarded to the Internet Protocol (IP) address for your IMC host.

You should also verify that the IMC service is started. By default, the IMC is not started even after you configure the options. You must start it manually or set it to start automatically upon boot. Of course, if you are able to send outbound mail, the service must be started and working. You can verify that the IMC is correctly processing inbound mail by starting Telnet and connecting to port 25 of the IMC Server. Follow the procedure outlined in Chapter 2 for manually sending yourself a mail message to test the functionality of the service.

References

For more information, see

- **"The Internet Mail Connector Fails to Start,"** *Microsoft Knowledge Base,* **Article ID: Q148727, at**
  http://www.microsoft.com/kb/bussys/exchange/q148727.htm
- **"IMC error 1067, Dr. Watson on MSEXIMC.EXE,"** *Microsoft Knowledge Base,* **Article ID: Q149542, at**
  http://www.microsoft.com/kb/bussys/exchange/q149542.htm

CHAPTER 6

Internet Mail Connector Reference Guide

This chapter is a reference guide to the various tabs in the Internet Mail Connector (IMC) Properties dialog box. To bring up the IMC Properties dialog box, double-click on the Internet Mail Connector in the Connections window. We will discuss all eleven tabs on the dialog box in the following order:

- General
- Internet Mail
- Connections
- Queues
- MIME Types
- Delivery Restrictions

- Advanced
- Address Space
- Connected Sites
- Dial-up Connections
- Diagnostics Logging

Exchange 5.0 introduces two additional tabs, Routing and Security, which are discussed in Appendix E. In addition, the MIME Types tab has been moved to the new site-level Protocols container, though it retains the same functionality. Using these tabs, you can configure the IMC many different ways, and the following sections show you how to customize the IMC to meet your specific needs. In Chapter 7, "Connector Models," we discuss various strategies for configuring connectors within your organization and show you how to take advantage of the functionality described in this chapter. For an exhaustive discussion of each of the tabs in this dialog box, see Chapter 11, "Using the Internet Mail Connector," in the *Microsoft Exchange Server Administrator's Guide*.

The General Tab

The General tab is used only to set limits on the size of messages that the IMC handles. Figure 6.1 shows that the IMC on chora.sakes.com is configured to handle messages of any size.

Figure 6.1

The General Tab

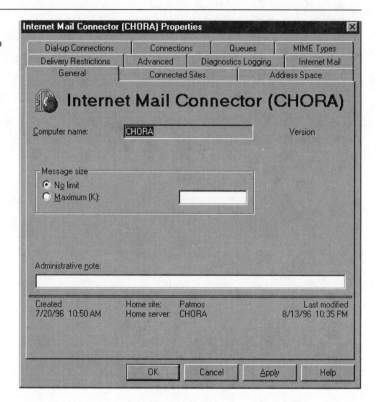

If you need to limit the size of a message that can be transported by the IMC, you can select the Maximum (K) option under Message size and enter the message size in the box to the right. You'll need to start and stop the IMC service in the Control Panel for this change to take effect. If users attempt to send messages through the IMC that exceed this size, they get a Non-Delivery Receipt (NDR).

For example, if we set the maximum to 50K and Spyros attempts to send a message to judy@dcnw.com that is 200K, he receives the following error message:

```
The following recipient(s) could not be reached:

Judy on 8/12/96 8:16:10 PM
        The content length of the message is too long for the
        recipient to take delivery
   [MSEXCH:MSExchangeMTA:Patmos:CHORA]
```

Administrators will typically limit message sizes if their Internet connection is slow or unstable. For example, if you are connected to an Internet service provider (ISP) using a 28.8 kbps dialup link that is running continuously, you might find that 2 MB messages cause the link to hang. In that case, you might limit the IMC to processing messages under 1 MB. Don't specify a limit if you are using the IMC as a site connector doing directory replication — it may prevent system messages passing through the IMC.

The General tab also shows the computer name. The name shown here is for information purposes only. You cannot change the name of the Exchange server after Exchange is installed. Finally, you can put a comment in the Administrative note section that can only be seen by administrators when looking at this screen.

The Internet Mail Tab

The Internet Mail tab, shown in Figure 6.2, has many features you will use regularly. When you first configured the IMC, you used the Internet Mail tab to identify an Administrator for the connector. Now you can use the Change button to change the identity of the Administrator, and you can use the Notifications button to specify which messages the IMC should send to the Administrator.

The Notifications dialog box, shown in Figure 6.3, appears when you click on the Notifications button in the Administrator's Mailbox section.

If you click the top option in the Notifications box, the administrator will get copies of all NDRs generated by the IMC, each of which indicates a specific type of failure. This option can generate a lot of mail to the administrator, so you might want to limit this notification to the more important NDRs. Listing 6.1 is an example of an NDR.

In this case, the sender of the message attempted to send a message to the user spiros@patmos.sakes.com. Because the user misspelled the name (with the letter "i" instead of a "y"), the sender was notified that the recipient could not be found, and the administrator indicated in Figure 6.2 got a copy of the NDR. The last line of the NDR shows the specific the IMC that generated the error message; in this case the IMC on an Exchange Server, CHORA, in the Patmos site of the SAKES organization. This information can be useful in troubleshooting if you have a large organization with many servers running the IMC.

Figure 6.2

The Internet Mail Tab

Figure 6.3

Notifications

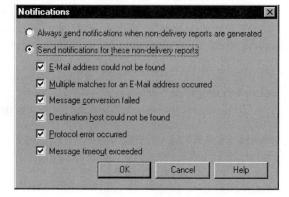

LISTING 6.1 SAMPLE NON-DELIVERY REPORT

```
Your message did not reach some or all of the intended recipients.

    To:       Spyros Sakellariadis
    Subject:  Testing IMC on Chora
    Sent:     6/22/96 11:10:46 AM

The following recipient(s) could not be reached:

    spiros@patmos.sakes.com on 6/22/96 11:10:46 AM
            Recipient Not Found
            [MSEXCH:IMC:SAKES:Patmos:CHORA]
```

NDR messages are particularly valuable for debugging communications problems with remote systems. For example, you can identify problems with gateways or encoding formats by getting copies of the NDRs. Considering that most users are not likely to pass NDR information back to the administrator, this feature ensures the administrator gets a copy and lets administrators solve problems before users become irate.

NDRs also come in handy when employees leave your company. You get notified if, for example, they subscribed to a series of list servers but had not canceled their subscriptions before leaving.

Some NDR messages are slightly less obvious.

```
Unable to deliver the message due to a communications failure
    [MSEXCH:IMC:API:IT] 3553 I refuse to talk to myself
    (loopback connection refused)
```

Another one of my favorites is

```
A mail message was not sent because of a protocol error:

550 you could say goodbye
```

Whoever said that programmers have no sense of humor?

You can specify a number of parameters for the format of the message being transmitted using the Message Content Information portion of the Internet Mail tab (Figure 6.2). The first section, on the left side of the group, lets you specify whether attachments should be encoded using MIME, uuencode, or Binhex.

We discussed MIME and uuencode — and their differences — in Chapter 2. The Binhex option under uuencode is for files exchanged with Macintosh users. The MIME or uuencode option lets you determine the default method for encoding attachments. If you select MIME and send a message with an attachment from a user Spyros on chora.sakes.com to Judy on pop3.dcnw.com, the message will be MIME encoded. Listing 6.2 shows a fragment of a trace of such a message.

In this example, the message from Spyros was routed through the IMC on chora.sakes.com. The message identifier is 01BB7C95.8A5D6B10, and the message is composed of two body parts — a single line of text and the bitmap 256color.bmp. You can see these components clearly in Listing 6.2. Because the IMC is configured to encode messages using MIME by default, the message headers include the MIME information we discussed in Chapter 2. For example, a header has been added showing that the message is encoded using MIME-Version 1.0. Also, because the IMC was unable to verify that the recipient could decode a MIME message, it added a note of warning in the header: "some or all of this message may not be legible." Following this, the ASCII text message is forwarded as 7-bit ASCII, and the attached bitmap is forwarded as a base 64 encoded body part.

LISTING 6.2 TRACE OF MESSAGE WITH MIME ATTACHMENT

```
SMTP: Data = Received: by chora.sakes.com with Microsoft Exchange (IMC
             4.0.837.3)
SMTP: Data = id <01BB7C95.8A5D6B10@chora.sakes.com>; Sun, 28 Jul 1996
             15:00:39 -0400
SMTP: Data = Message-ID:
             <c=US%a=_%p=SAKES%l=CHORA-960728190037Z-6@chora.sakes.com>
SMTP: Data = From: Spyros <spyros@patmos.sakes.com>
SMTP: Data = To: Judy <judy@dcnw.com>
SMTP: Data = Subject: Msg w/MIME attachment
SMTP: Data = Date: Sun, 28 Jul 1996 15:00:37 -0400
SMTP: Data = X-Mailer:  Microsoft Exchange Server Internet Mail Connector
SMTP: Data = MIME-Version: 1.0
SMTP: Data = Content-Type:multipart/mixed;
             boundary="----_NextPart_000_01BB7C95.8A5FB500"
SMTP: Data = This message is in MIME format. Since your mail reader does not
             understand
SMTP: Data = this format, some or all of this message may not be legible.
SMTP: Data = ---- =_NextPart_000_01BB7C95.8A5FB500
SMTP: Data = Content-Type: text/plain; charset="us-ascii"
SMTP: Data = Content-Transfer-Encoding: 7bit
SMTP: Data = >This msg has an attachment
SMTP: Data = >
SMTP: Data = ---- =_NextPart_000_01BB7C95.8A5FB500
SMTP: Data = Content-Type: application/octet-stream; name="256color.bmp"
SMTP: Data = Content-Transfer-Encoding: base64
SMTP: Data = Qk16DAAAAAAAABoDAAAMAAAAoAB4AAEACAAAAAAAAP8A/
             wD/AAAA/////wD/AP////8QGAwAAG0A
SMTP: Data = QASVMH11GBSqMK6ZEAg4JHEAAEyZSIV1IG1lLG1MQCg8MH1tJG1dGBxVJEhVLE
             hVHEhZJEjmOLKd
```

If we reconfigure the IMC to encode messages using uuencode, the data stream for our message example is very different. Listing 6.3 shows a trace of this message.

In addition to letting the user add binary attachments to messages, the Exchange client lets the user include rich-text formatting in the body of the message. Obviously, these rich-text messages must also be encoded for

```
LISTING 6.3 TRACE OF MESSAGE WITH UUENCODED ATTACHMENT
SMTP: Data = Received: by chora.sakes.com with Microsoft Exchange (IMC
             4.0.837.3)
SMTP: Data = id <01BB7C99.D57AB590@chora.sakes.com>; Sun, 28 Jul 1996
             15:31:23 -0400
SMTP: Data = Message-ID:
             <c=US%a=_%p=SAKES%l=CHORA-960728193122Z-7@chora.sakes.com>
SMTP: Data = From: Spyros <Spyros@Patmos.SAKES.com>
SMTP: Data = To: Judy <judy@dcnw.com>
SMTP: Data = Subject: Msg w/uuencode attachment
SMTP: Data = Date: Sun, 28 Jul 1996 15:31:22 -0400
SMTP: Data = X-Mailer:  Microsoft Exchange Server Internet Mail Connector
             Version
SMTP: Data = Encoding: 4 TEXT, 448 uuencode
SMTP: Data = X-MS-Attachment: 256color.bmp 0 00-00-1980 00:00
SMTP: Data = >This msg has an attachment
SMTP: Data = >
SMTP: Data = begin 600 256color.bmp
SMTP: Data = M0DUZ# `````!H#```,```H !X``$``$`" `` ```````/\`_P#`````P#`
SMTP: Data = M`/____\0& P``&T`O 25,'EU&!!2J,*!Z9$`@@@')$``$`!R$R(&)9R+:@%`(
SMTP: Data = M,'UM)&E=&!O5!$A5+$M9!$J)$$O.+*+=/'5=#$%"N4(4`-*X(72#$%'%E]+'4`
SMTP: Data = MFF0!5+$R\' BR/-9I1 R-.'FJ2)&5,(G6..,)(+&VJ-(G62.;B2-8H!'76.,95
```

transcription. If the IMC is set to encode messages using MIME, the rich-text message simply becomes a MIME body part. For example, suppose Spyros sends a message to Judy that includes rich text, as shown in Figure 6.4.

Figure 6.4
Rich Text in Message

The formatted text in Figure 6.4 is an example of rich text, which is handled differently from ASCII text. The sender of the message can specify whether the rich text is transmitted using MIME, uuencode, or stripped out entirely. To choose this option, select Properties from the File Menu, which brings up the Properties dialog box shown in Figure 6.5.

Figure 6.5
Message Properties

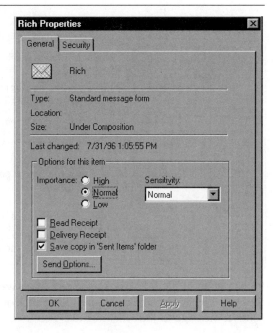

The title of the dialog box is the subject of your message plus the word "properties"; hence the title "Rich Properties" for the message shown in Figure 6.4. Click the Send Options button to bring up the available encoding options, shown in Figure 6.6.

Figure 6.6
Attachment Encoding Send Options

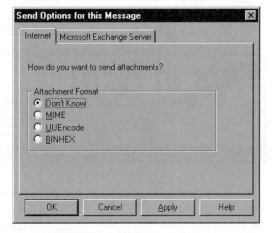

You select the encoding format for messages from this dialog box. For example, if you're sending a message to a user on a Macintosh, you can select BINHEX as the encoding method. If you select MIME and send the message, the rich text MIME body part will appear in the data stream, as shown in Listing 6.4.

Notice that the text of the message — "This is rich!" — is shown in 7-bit ASCII. The rich-text formatting is included as a new MIME body part, ms-tnef, or Transport Neutral Encoding Format, encoded with a standard base 64 encoding scheme. However, the system administrator can choose to encode outbound attachments with uuencode rather than MIME using the options in the Message Content Information group shown in Figure 6.2. If the administrator chooses uuencode, the rich text sent by this user is appended to the message as a special attachment, as shown in Listing 6.5.

LISTING 6.4 RICH TEXT ENCODED AS A MIME BODY PART

```
SMTP: Data = From: Spyros <Spyros@Patmos.SAKES.com>
SMTP: Data = To: Judy <judy@dcnw.com>
SMTP: Data = Subject: Rich
SMTP: Data = Date: Sun, 28 Jul 1996 16:19:04 -0400
SMTP: Data = X-Mailer: Microsoft Exchange Server Internet Mail Connector
SMTP: Data = MIME-Version: 1.0
SMTP: Data = Content-Type:multipart/mixed;
             boundary="- =_NextPart_000_01BB7CA0.800FEEC0"
SMTP: Data = This message is in MIME format. Since your mail reader does not
             understand
SMTP: Data = this format, some or all of this message may not be legible.
SMTP: Data = —— =_NextPart_000_01BB7CA0.800FEEC0
SMTP: Data = Content-Type: text/plain; charset="us-ascii"
SMTP: Data = Content-Transfer-Encoding: 7bit
SMTP: Data = This is rich!
SMTP: Data = —— =_NextPart_000_01BB7CA0.800FEEC0
SMTP: Data = Content-Type: application/ms-tnef
SMTP: Data = Content-Transfer-Encoding: base64
SMTP: Data = eJ8+IgcUAQaQCAAEAAAAAAABAAEAAQeQBgAIAAAA5AQAAAAAAADoAAEIgAcA
             GAAAAE1QTS5NaWNy
SMTP: Data = b3NvZnQgTWFpbC5ob3R1ADEIAQWAAwAOAAAAzAcHABwAEAATAAQAAAAdAQEggA
             MADgAAAMwHBwAc
SMTP: Data = ABAAEwAFAAAAHgEBCYABACEAAAAxMkY0ODg3Nzc3RThDRjExZOUIzRTA4MDAyQk
             JGRUI4NwA+BwEN
```

When you send a rich-text formatted message using MIME, a MIME body part is added. However, when you send a rich-text formatted message using uuencode, an attachment called WINMAIL.DAT is added to the bottom of the message with the formatting parameters. As you can see from Listing 6.5, the text of the message is still in 7-bit ASCII.

Using the options in the Message Content Information group in Figure 6.2, the system administrator can specify whether *attachments* are sent using MIME or uuencode. The Interoperability button in the Send Attachments Using group lets the administrator specify whether the user can select the

LISTING 6.5 RICH TEXT ATTACHED AS A UUENCODED FILE, WINMAIL.DAT

```
SMTP: Data = From: Spyros <Spyros@Patmos.SAKES.com>
SMTP: Data = To: Judy <judy@dcnw.com>
SMTP: Data = Subject: Rich
SMTP: Data = Date: Sun, 28 Jul 1996 16:30:33 -0400
SMTP: Data = X-Mailer:  Microsoft Exchange Server Internet Mail Connector
SMTP: Data = Encoding: 2 TEXT, 24 UUENCODE
SMTP: Data = X-MS-Attachment: WINMAIL.DAT 0 00-00-1980 00:00
SMTP: Data = This is rich!
SMTP: Data = begin 600 WINMAIL.DAT
SMTP: Data = M>)\^(B04`0:0" `$```````!``$``0`````!````!``$```````!````!`````!
SMTP: Data = M&  ```$032Y-:6-R;W-09G0@36%I;"Y;W1E`#$`(`06 `P`.``S`<`<!`````!
SMTP: Data = M$ `>`""""$%```!%%`0$@@@ , `#@```,P'!@`````1`$``!$$`"1!("#``````R
```

encoding scheme for the *body* of the message. Clicking the Interoperability button brings up the dialog box shown in Figure 6.7.

Figure 6.7

Interoperability

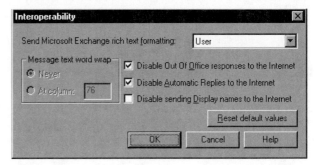

You specify the encoding procedure by selecting User, Always, or Never from the drop-down list box. If you want to force the message to go out as MIME or uuencoded, you select either Always or Never, respectively. If you select User, then the IMC will include rich text only when rich text is enabled for the recipient — that is, if the recipient is an Exchange recipient, or if the message sender has selected "Always send to this recipient in Microsoft Exchange rich-text format" in his or her Personal Address Book entry for the recipient.

Note that if rich text is enabled and messages are being sent to legacy mail systems, your users may report problems. In particular, the recipient may complain about receiving "garbage" (in reality, the attachment Winmail.dat or MIME tnef body parts in the message). To avoid this problem, the *Microsoft Exchange Server Administrator's Guide* (see "Enabling Rich Text for Outbound Messages" in Chapter 11) suggests using one of the following methods to communicate with legacy systems:

- Disable rich text for the domain of non-MAPI recipients
- Disable rich text for each custom recipient
- Disable rich text in the sender's personal address book entry for the recipient
- Disable rich text for the IMC

The Interoperability dialog box (Figure 6.7) has other important check-boxes. For example, the administrator can disable Out of Office responses to the Internet and Automatic Replies to the Internet. These features let the IMC administrator prevent users from inadvertently causing havoc on the Internet. For example, suppose that a user subscribes to several list servers on the Internet that generate dozens of messages a day. If that user creates an Out of Office rule that replies to the sender when the user goes on vacation, the list servers on the Internet will be sent a message such as "I am out of the office until August 31 basking on a Greek beach" every time the list server forwards a message to the user. As a result, the 5,000 or more other subscribers to the list server will receive this message several dozen times per day. A wise Exchange administrator will either educate the company's users or disable automatic responses to the Internet.

As we have seen, the Exchange administrator can select whether to use MIME or uuencode as the default encoding scheme. The administrator can also override this decision on a per-domain basis. To override the default encoding, click the E-Mail Domain button from the Internet Mail tab shown in Figure 6.2. Clicking the E-Mail Domain button brings up the dialog box, shown in Figure 6.8, listing domains that are exceptions to the MIME/uuencode rule specified on the Internet Mail tab.

Figure 6.8
Per Domain Override

The E-Mail Domain window is used to specify domains that need to be treated differently from the default; the default settings are not adequate to handle messages to and from these domains. To add a new domain to the list, click on the Add button, which brings up the dialog box in Figure 6.9.

Figure 6.9

Add E-Mail Domain

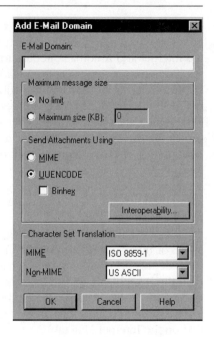

This dialog box lets you override all the default options for the domain you're going to add. In this way, the administrator can create a general policy and override it when necessary.

By using the various features we've been discussing, you could, for example, choose MIME as the default but create a list of domains for which uuencode would be used. Conversely, you could choose uuencode as the default and use MIME on a per-domain basis. At the time of publication, most recipients are still on e-mail systems that do not support MIME. Consequently, the simplest strategy would be to uuencode by default. However, with that strategy the exception list would be growing daily, and many messages would be going out unnecessarily using uuencode, taking up significantly more bandwidth than needed. The alternative is to pick MIME as the default, and rapidly try to create the list of per-domain overrides needed. As companies switch to MIME-compliant gateways, you can update the exception list.

The final parameter that can be set from the Internet Mail tab is the Enable Message Tracking option, which appears in the checkbox in the lower left-hand corner of Figure 6.2 (page 112).

Exchange implements message tracking for troubleshooting purposes. You can enable message tracking for many different components of server operation, including

- Message Transfer Agents
- Information Store
- MS Mail Connector
- Internet Mail Connector

Message tracking is enabled separately for each IMC in a site. When you enable message tracking, the information about the progress of a message through the various locations in the site is stored in a text file in \exchsrvr\tracking.log. A new log file is created daily, with the name reflecting the date on which it was created, in yyyymmdd.log format. You can read the tracking log with any ASCII editor, such as Notepad. Listing 6.6 shows a section from a tracking log file.

LISTING 6.6 TRACKING LOG 19960802.LOG

```
c=US;a= ;p=SAKES;l=KIFISSIA-960802153548Z-2  1003  1996.8.2 15:36:26
/o=SAKES/ou=Athens/cn=Configuration/cn=Connections/cn=Internet Mail
Connector (KIFISSIA)
dcnw.com  <c=US%a=_%p=SAKES%l=KIFISSIA-960802153548Z-
2@kifissia.sakes.com>[RV0CWAAC]
/o=SAKES/ou=ATHENS/cn=RECIPIENTS/cn=CHRIS  0  1013  0  0  1  judy@dcnw.com

c=US;a= ;p=SAKES;l=KIFISSIA9608021537RV0F5AAD 1004  1996.8.2 15:37:30
/o=SAKES/ou=Athens/cn=Configuration/cn=Connections/cn=Internet Mail
Connector (KIFISSIA)
/o=SAKES/ou=Athens/cn=Configuration/cn=Servers/cn=KIFISSIA/cn=Microsoft
Private MDB
<01BB8066.0838A490@POP3>[RV0F5AAD]  /o=SAKES/ou=Patmos/cn=internet/cn=Judy
0  890  0  0  1  /o=SAKES/ou=Athens/cn=Recipients/cn=Chris
```

The log is tab delimited and can be loaded into a spreadsheet such as Microsoft Excel. Each of the tabs in the log represents a field, and each line in the log (Listing 6.6 shows two lines in the 19960802.log) represents a logged event. Chapter 17 of the *Microsoft Exchange Server Administrator's Guide* contains a complete listing of all the fields and their entries, as well as a table of the various codes. Using this table, we can decipher the events relatively easily. Table 6.1 shows an analysis of the first event in Listing 6.6.

TABLE 6.1 ANALYZING AN EVENT IN THE TRACKING LOG

#	Field Name	Value	Comment
1	Message ID	c=US;a= ;p=SAKES;l=KIFISSIA-960802153548Z-2	Unique identifier
2	Event #	1003	Gateway transfer out
3	Date/Time	1996.8.2 15:36:26	Date & time
4	Gateway name	/o=SAKES/ou=Athens/cn= Configuration/cn=Connections/cn= Internet Mail Connector (KIFISSIA)	Name of connector
5	Partner name	dcnw.com	
6	Remote ID	<c=US%a=_%p=SAKES%l=KIFISSIA- 960802153548Z-2@kifissia.sakes. com>[RV0CWAAC]	Msg ID used by gateway
7	Originator	/o=SAKES/ou=ATHENS/cn= RECIPIENTS/cn=CHRIS	X.500 name of sender
8	Priority	0	0=Normal
9	Length	1013	Msg length, bytes
10	Seconds	0	not used
11	Cost	0	not used
12	Recipients	1	# of recipients
13	Recipient	judy@dcnw.com	

In this case, we have picked an event from the message tracking log as the message passes out of the IMC to the Windows NT Mail SMTP host on pop3.dcnw.com.

A detailed analysis of a large tracking log would be an exhausting task. Fortunately, Exchange Server provides a graphical tool to track messages in these in these logs. To use this tool, select Track Message from the Tools menu in the Microsoft Exchange Administrator dialog box (see Figure 6.10).

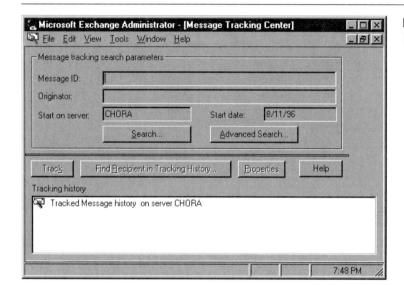

Figure 6.10
The Track Message Tool

Using this tool, you can track messages as they travel through the Exchange organization. It works by analyzing all the logs that you have enabled in the organization, and it presents the information to you in an easy-to-read report. For more information on the Tracking Facility, read Chapter 17, "Troubleshooting," in the *Microsoft Exchange Server Administrator's Guide*. In addition, we will use this tool to show the progress of a message through an extended Exchange organization in Chapter 7.

The Connections Tab

The Connections tab, shown in Figure 6.11, has four groups of parameters you can set to configure the IMC.

The Transfer Mode group, on the upper left-hand side of the screen, lets you configure the IMC to accept or reject specific inbound and outbound messages. You can even configure it not to accept any messages at all. The default

Figure 6.11

The Connections Tab

setting is Inbound & Outbound, which lets the IMC handle messages in both directions. In a small organization with only one or two servers running the IMC, you would rarely change the default. However, in large organizations that have multiple sites and servers, changing this option can be very helpful.

Using the Transfer Mode options, you can customize how traffic is routed throughout the organization and site. For example, an organization receiving a lot of information from the Internet could configure one IMC to process only outbound messages and have three or four servers process inbound messages. In this way, inbound messages are allocated a larger percentage of the computing resources; this strategy improves performance with regard to inbound messages but does not penalize the performance of the outbound messages. We will discuss strategies for using this parameter in Chapter 7, "Connector Models," in the context of sites with multiple IMCs.

The None (Flush Queues) option lets the system process queues without accepting more messages. This option is used when preparing to move or remove the IMC. Also, current versions of backup software for Windows NT (Arcada's Backup Exec and Cheyenne's Arcserve) will work for the open

Exchange databases, but they do not back up pointers in the queues. Therefore, items waiting to be processed by the IMC do not get backed up, and the integrity of the backup is not ensured. The best way to ensure a perfect backup is to flush the queues by setting the Transfer Mode to None, wait until the queues are empty, and then run the backup.

Use the Advanced button in the Transfer Mode group to specify the maximum number of connections per IMC. The Advanced dialog box is shown in Figure 6.12.

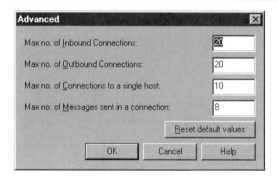

Figure 6.12
Advanced Transfer Mode

This parameter specifies the number of simultaneous connections to port 25 of the target host the IMC will use, and it specifies the number of allowable simultaneous connections to port 25 of the IMC server. For example, if you only connected to a Microsoft Mail 3.2 Simple Message Transfer Protocol (SMTP) Gateway that supports only one connection, you could change the Max no. of Connections to a single host parameter to 1. However, you should note that these settings affect the IMC as a whole, not just a single domain. Consequently, changing the setting here to a "1" affects all the domains.

Normally you would not change the default parameters; optimizing Exchange Server at this level of detail is a relatively advanced task and usually unnecessary. If you think that you can improve performance by changing these parameters, you should set up a plan that tracks performance using Windows NT's Performance Monitor, use LoadSim before and after changing the parameters, and compare the results. (Note that the Load Simulator in Exchange Server 4.0 does not have loading parameters for the IMC, so you need to develop your own simulation techniques.)

The second group of parameters in the Connections tab is the Message Delivery group located in the upper right-hand corner of the tab (see Figure 6.11). These options determine whether the IMC works with the DNS on the IMC host to identify the target hosts for sending mail, or whether the IMC blindly forwards all mail to a single SMTP server. If you want the IMC to use

the DNS for finding target mail servers for e-mail recipients, select Use Domain
Name Service. Using this option requires, of course, that you have correctly
configured TCP/IP on the IMC host itself to use DNS (see Figure 4.6) — it will
not use a DNR on any other host in your network.

If you want the IMC to forward all messages to a single host for security
or routing purposes, select the Forward all messages to host option. Also, Service Pack 2 for Exchange Server added the group's option box for dialing a
remote host and delivering all the mail to that host. You enable this feature by
checking the Dial using box and selecting a Remote Access Server (RAS) entry
from your RAS phone book for a remote SMTP host.

If you use Forward all messages to host rather than DNS, you normally
specify an IP address rather than a host name. If you do use a host name,
you need either an entry in the local hosts file on the server running the IMC
or an A record in the DNS. If you have neither, you will get a 1069 error
when you start the IMC.

As we have seen in other IMC configuration parameters, you can set a
default message delivery mechanism and override the default as needed by
using the E-Mail Domain button. Clicking this button brings up the E-Mail
Domains screen shown in Figure 6.13.

Figure 6.13

*Connections Per
Domain Override*

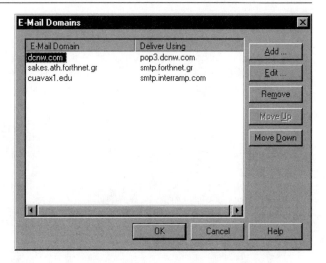

In this example, all mail is delivered using DNS to identify the mail
servers except for mail to the three e-mail domains listed: dcnw.com,
sakes.ath.forthnet.gr, and cuavax1.edu. For these three domains, the IMC
delivers the mail to the hosts shown in the right column. Use the Add button
to add another entry (Figure 6.14).

Figure 6.14
Add E-Mail Domain

If your default is to use DNS, the Add E-Mail Domain dialog box lets you add exceptions to the DNS strategy. If your default is to send all mail to a specific host, for example an e-mail server at PSINet (for more information on PSINet, see Appendix A, "Connecting with an Internet Service Provider"), the Add E-Mail Domain dialog box lets you make exceptions to that forwarding rule. As we saw earlier, Service Pack 2 added a dial-up functionality for the IMC, and you can use it in the per-domain override as well.

The third set of options you can set on the Connections tab (Figure 6.11) lets you filter incoming or outgoing messages by remote host IP address. These options are contained in the Accept or Reject Host group.

You can accept the default, which accepts messages from all hosts, or you can use the Accept or reject by host option to filter mail to or from specific hosts. This option is useful if you want to prohibit mail from a specific listserver or to a competitor. If you select the Specify Hosts button, you bring up the window shown in Figure 6.15.

In this example, we are prohibiting the IMC from processing mail to or from two hosts in the 204.241.136.0 network. You might also use this option to prohibit individuals in that network from communicating with your users for reasons of security or communications costs. You edit entries in the list by clicking the Edit button, which brings up the dialog box in Figure 6.16.

You can specify a specific host by entering its Internet Protocol (IP) address. You can also specify a group of computers if you enter the IP address of a network and a valid subnet mask.

The fourth and final group in the Connections tab (Figure 6.11) is the Connector Message Queues group, which lets you configure the way the IMC handles messages that cannot be delivered.

Figure 6.15
Specify Hosts

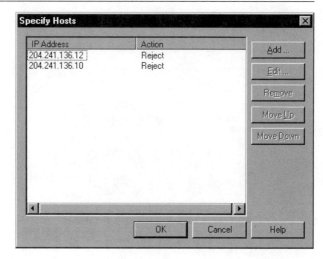

Figure 6.16
Edit Dialog Box

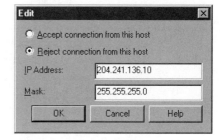

The Connector Message Queues group lets you specify the period of time that must elapse before messages are returned. The Retry interval (hrs) box lets you indicate how frequently the IMC attempts to send a message, and if you click the Message Timeouts button you can specify what the IMC should do with messages it cannot deliver. Figure 6.17 shows the Message Time-outs dialog box.

Normally, you will not need to change these values. However, in some environments, for example, where messages need to be delivered very quickly and with a high degree of reliability, you might want to reduce the time-out for urgent messages from 24 hours to 4 hours.

The Queues Tab

The Queues tab, shown in Figure 6.18, lets you see how many messages are waiting to be processed by the IMC — either inbound or outbound.

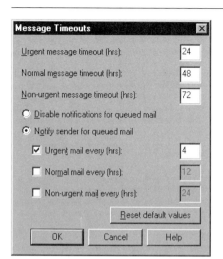

Figure 6.17
Message Timeouts

Figure 6.18
The Queues Tab

You can monitor four queues from this page, and you can select these queues using the drop-down list below the Queue Name label. The four queues are

- Inbound messages awaiting conversion
- Inbound messages awaiting delivery
- Outbound messages awaiting conversion
- Outbound messages awaiting delivery

We discussed the movement of messages in and out of these queues in Chapter 3, "IMC Overview." How long messages stay in these queues depends on the parameters you entered in the Advanced and Connections tabs.

This page is useful when users complain that a message they sent was not delivered. From this page, you would be able to determine that this message was, for example, in a queue waiting for the remote host to come back online.

Under some circumstances you might want to delete a message that is in the queue. For example, a number of messages may be waiting to go out to a host that has been taken out of service, and you want to kill the messages now rather than letting them stay in the queue until they generate non-delivery reports. To delete messages in the queue, highlight the messages and click the Delete button on this page. Sometimes, however, the messages keep reappearing in the queue, because of problems with the MTA and the IMC. If the messages reappear, it is necessary to access directly the Microsoft Exchange IMC Queues located within the Microsoft Exchange Message Store. The Microsoft Knowledge Base article Q151775, "XCON: Viewing or Deleting Messages in MTS-IN or MTS-OUT Queues," shows the steps for accessing the queues and how to delete mail from this queue using the Microsoft Exchange MDB Viewer Utility on the Exchange Server CD.

The MIME Types Tab

The IMC in Exchange Server 4.0 includes a MIME Types tab that lets you specify MIME body part types that the IMC will recognize and process. Figure 6.19 shows this tab and the default types. The IMS in Exchange 5.0 does not include this tab; instead, this tab has been moved to a new container object at the site level, the Protocols tab. To view this tab, select the Protocols container and select Properties from the File menu.

We discussed MIME in Chapter 2, "SMTP Basics," and we discussed how to specify whether the IMC should use MIME earlier in this chapter. If you do decide to use MIME, you can use the options on this tab to configure the IMC to tag body parts of outgoing messages with an appropriate MIME content

Figure 6.19
The MIME Types Tab

type, based on the extension of the attached file, and to apply the appropriate extension to incoming MIME messages.

For example, if a message includes an attachment created in Microsoft Word, the IMC can tag the body part as being of type application/msword. The recipient can then view the contents of the message using Microsoft Word. If you look at the data stream coming off the IMC when spyros@patmos.sakes.com sends judy@dcnw.com a message with a Word document, you will see the Word portion sent as a body part described as follows:

```
Content-Type: application/msword; name="homephone.doc"
Content-Transfer-Encoding: base64
```

Because the MIME Types tab includes an entry for files with a .doc extension, the IMC labels the body part as "application/msword" and encodes it with base 64 encoding. If the recipient of the message has a similar content-type registration, then the recipient's SMTP service can identify and correctly label the document.

The same is true for all the types shown in Figure 6.19. If spyros@patmos.sakes.com sends a compound document with a number of these attachments, the MIME message might contain a number of these labels. Each of the following MIME types is included in the MIME Types tab.

```
Content-Type: audio/x-wav; name="CAMERA.WAV"
Content-Transfer-Encoding: base64

Content-Type: image/jpeg; name="acropolis.jpg"
Content-Transfer-Encoding: base64

Content-Type: image/gif; name="fido.gif"
Content-Transfer-Encoding: base64
```

You can even get correctly labeled body parts for some types not included in the MIME Types tab.

```
Content-Type: application/x-zip-compressed; name="paulp15.zip"
Content-Transfer-Encoding: base64
```

In this case, the IMC correctly identified a .zip file and labeled it an "x-zip-compressed" body part even though it is not shown in the MIME Types tab. The IMC identifies such files because it natively recognizes a number of body parts that are not registered on the MIME Types tab. The .zip type is a recognized MIME type, listed in the Internet Assigned Numbers Authority (IANA) (See Table 2.5) registration list, and the IMC picks that up.

Unfortunately, however, the IMC does not recognize many of the IANA registered types, including ones registered by Microsoft. For example, the .xls type was registered by Microsoft in April 1996, but if you try to attach an Excel spreadsheet, you get the following content type.

```
Content-Type: application/octet-stream; name="Budget1996.xls"
Content-Transfer-Encoding: base64
```

The content type of "application/octet-stream" means that the IMC did not recognize the type, so it labeled the type as a generic byte (octet) stream. This message was generated with Exchange Server 4.0, Service Pack 2, and viewed using the SMS Network Monitor. Note, however, that if the recipient is using a client on a desktop with the .xls extension registered as a Microsoft Excel File Type in Windows Explorer, the attachment will probably appear with an Excel icon.

Conversely, the IMC can receive a message tagged with a content type that it recognizes. As a result, therefore, the IMC can correctly handle incoming .doc files but not .xls files. Similarly, the .mpg movie type is registered with the IANA, and can be correctly tagged by Internet Shopper's NTMail. If judy@dcnw.com sends an .mpg attachment to spyros@patmos.sakes.com, it arrives at the IMC correctly labeled as

```
Content-Type: video/mpeg; name="homemovie.mpg"
Content-Transfer-Encoding: base64
```

Unfortunately, however, the IMC does not have a MIME property type for .mpg files, even implicitly, and treats this file as a generic binary base 64 encoded object.

Don't change anything in this tab until you have tested and worked with the IMC for awhile. Later, when you need to start extending the number of MIME types that the IMC handles, you may want to add objects to the page so that the proper labeling can take place. For example, you may want to add an .xls type. Alternatively, you may have a convention in your organization that all files to clients are written in Microsoft Word, but saved with an extension .ltr. In that case, you could add a MIME type to the property page to associate the .ltr extension with Microsoft Word.

To add a new MIME type — for example, the Microsoft Word/Ltr type we just discussed — click the New button in Figure 6.19 and add the information. When you click OK, you'll see the new type in the MIME Types list, as shown in Figure 6.20.

Figure 6.20

MIME Types with .ltr Type Registered

If you send a file with the .ltr extension to someone via the IMC before adding this MIME type, the body part will be coded as an unknown type.

```
Content-Type: application/octet-stream; name="jones.ltr"
Content-Transfer-Encoding: base64
```

Once you have added it, the body part will be coded as a Microsoft Word attachment.

```
Content-Type: application/msword; name="jones.ltr"
Content-Transfer-Encoding: base64
```

Not having a MIME type registered on the sending end also causes problems if you are receiving mail in Microsoft Exchange. One sign of missing MIME types at the originator end is having attachments show up with a .dat extension. For example, an editor at Windows NT Magazine sent me a message with a Microsoft Word attachment using a shareware program called Pegasus instead of her normal Exchange client. As Figure 6.21 shows, it arrived as a .dat file, not a .doc file.

Figure 6.21

Files with a .dat Extension

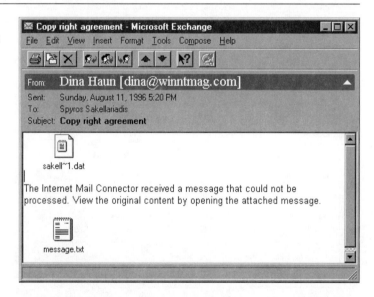

The original file, sakell~1.doc, arrived with a .dat extension. The message headers tell us what went wrong.

```
X-mailer: Pegasus Mail for Windows (v2.22)
Message-ID: <19960811201616931.AAA193@haundm.duke.com>

—Message-Boundary-6918
Content-type: Application/Octet-stream; name=sakell~1.doc; type=Unknown
Content-transfer-encoding: BASE64
```

The Microsoft Word file was not recognized when the shareware sub-mitted the message to the sender's SMTP server, so the message was labeled as an unknown document type. When it arrived, the Exchange server did not know how to process the message, so it decoded the base 64 data correctly but did not know what association to give the document. Consequently, it was given a .dat extension.

The Delivery Restrictions Tab

The Delivery Restrictions tab, shown in Figure 6.22, lets you keep individuals in your organization from using a specific IMC.

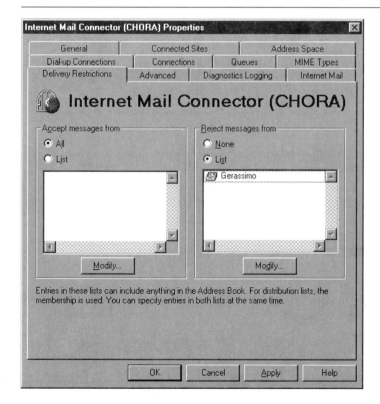

Figure 6.22

The Delivery Restrictions Tab

Figure 6.22 shows that we have configured the IMC on chora.sakes.com to accept messages from everyone except Gerassimo, a user in the Patmos site on campos.sakes.com. To add users to this "black list," select the Modify button and pick the censored users from the list of available names, as shown in Figure 6.23. Although you have to pick names from the address book, you can also pick custom recipients. The users, in other words, do not need to be local.

Figure 6.23
Modifying Delivery Restrictions

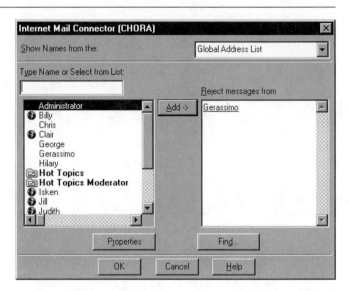

You might restrict messages from certain users for a variety of reasons — not all of them bad. For example, you might want to exclude a specific group of users from using the IMC on one particular server because they have very heavy messaging requirements. If you let them use this server's IMC, everyone else's ability to send or receive Internet mail might be adversely affected. In this case, you would create another IMC specifically for this heavy-use group and restrict everyone else from using it.

Note again that you can have two polar strategies: allow everyone, and reject by exception, or disallow everyone and allow by exception.

The Advanced Tab

The Advanced tab is shown in Figure 6.24. Initially, don't change anything on this tab. The parameters here should be changed only after you quantitatively measure system performance the Performance Monitor and the Load Simulator. For more details on monitoring performance, see the *Microsoft Exchange*

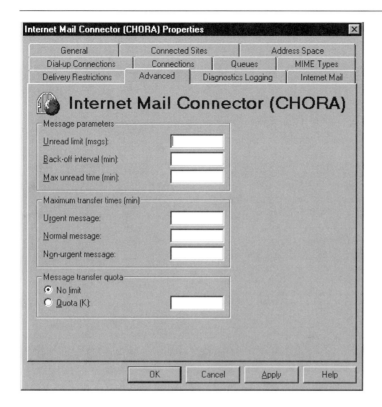

Figure 6.24
The Advanced Tab

Server Administrator's Guide and the *MS Exchange Server Support Instructor Guide* shipped on the TechNet CD.

The Address Space Tab

Figure 6.25 shows the Address Space tab. Addresses are paths messages follow when the messages leaves a site. The Address Space tab lets you designate your IMC as the message processor for specific domains. In Figure 6.25, the IMC is configured to accept mail for any e-mail domain, as we discussed at the beginning of this chapter. The Gateway Address Routing Table (GWART), which we discussed in Chapter 3, indicates that the IMC is set up this way.

Figure 6.26 shows the GWART on a server in the Athens site. In this case, the routing table on kifissia.sakes.com shows that all outbound SMTP messages are to be sent through the Connector it knows as CHORA.

Figure 6.25

The Address Space Tab

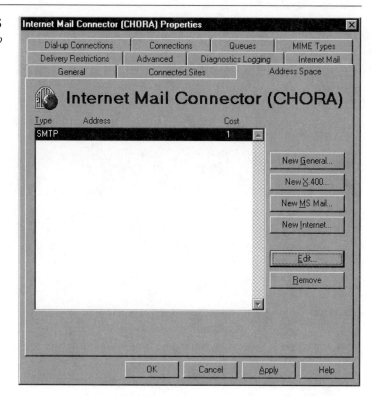

If we select the SMTP address type and click on Details, we get more information about the routing, as shown in Figure 6.27. An outbound message from a user on kifissia.sakes.com would be sent through two hops. First, it would go through the X.400 connector CHORA to the server chora.sakes.com in the Patmos site, and then it would go out the IMC (CHORA) connector.

We can illustrate the functionality of the Address Space parameters relatively easily at this stage. Suppose we change the IMC Address Space on chora.sakes.com shown in Figure 6.25 to process messages only to DCNW.COM, as shown in Figure 6.28.

To restrict the delivery of mail, enter the name of the domain in the SMTP Properties dialog box by clicking Edit. If the address you enter has a wild card either as the first character of the space or immediately after an @ (if present), the message is delivered to the IMC by the Message Transfer Agent (MTA); otherwise, it is not delivered to the IMC and the sender gets an NDR. The only exception is when the space is blank, as it was when we set up a generic IMC to handle all messages.

Figure 6.26
The GWART in the Athens Site

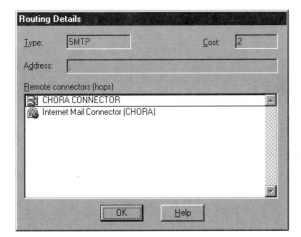

Figure 6.27
Details of the SMTP Routing

Figure 6.28
IMC (CHORA) Restricted
to DCNW.COM

In our example, two address spaces worked when we set up the network in the lab: *dcnw.com and *@dcnw.com. Conversely, the following address spaces failed, generating an NDR even for addressees in the domains you want to let through: dcnw.com, *.dcnw.com, and @*.dcnw.com.

Note that the documentation that comes with Exchange Server 4.0 is incorrect, including the discussion in the *Microsoft Exchange Server Administrator's Guide* (Appendix A, "Addressing") and the online help facility. These sources state that you simply need the Fully Qualified Domain Name (FQDN) for the address space. You need the wild card too. Note also that you need to stop and restart the MTA to reread the GWART if you change any of these addresses.

Also, we can install and configure an IMC on the kifissia.sakes.com server in the Athens site and configure it only to process messages to DUKEPRESS.COM. This setup is shown in Figure 6.29.

We now have an organization with two IMCs, one of which processes mail to DUKEPRESS.COM, the other of which processes mail to DCNW.COM. If we look at the GWART on any server, the message routing reflects this configuration. Figure 6.30 on page 142 shows the GWART on chora.sakes.com.

Figure 6.29

IMC (KIFISSIA) Restricted to DUKEPRESS.COM

The SMTP messages picked up by the MTA on chora.sakes.com will be delivered to remote hosts only if they are addressed to recipients at DUKEPRESS.COM or DCNW.COM; otherwise, they will be returned as undeliverable. If the message is to a recipient at DCNW.COM, the MTA will place it back in the information store on chora.sakes.com, where it will be picked up by the IMC (CHORA) and sent out. If the message is to a recipient at DUKEPRESS.COM, it takes two hops. By selecting the DUKEPRESS.COM line and clicking Details, you'll see the Routing Details dialog box shown in Figure 6.31.

First, the message will be sent over the X.400 connector KIFISSIA to the Athens site, and then it will be sent out through the IMC (KIFISSIA). In this way, you can control the routing of messages through the organization and even restrict the sites to which users of the network can send mail.

Note that this control does not affect inbound mail — a user on the Internet can still send mail to a valid user at either site as long as a Message Exchanger (MX) record points to an IMC. To restrict incoming messages, you use the Delivery Restrictions options or the Accept Messages from Any Hosts option discussed above.

Figure 6.30

*The GWART on
chora.sakes.com*

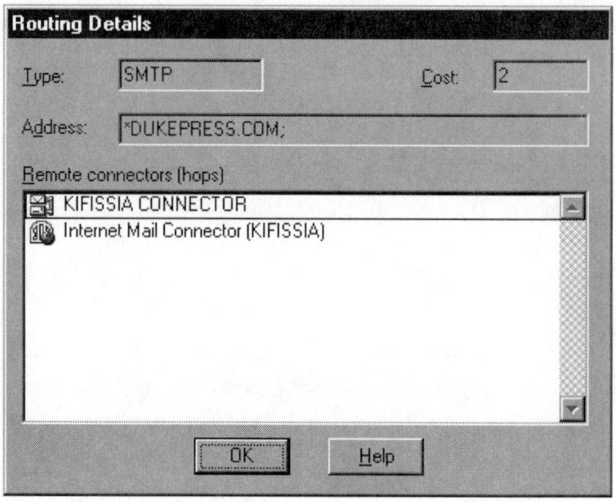

Figure 6.31

*Routing Messages to
DUKEPRESS.COM*

The Connected Sites Tab

Figure 6.32 shows the Connected Sites tab. You use this tab only to specify other Exchange sites in the same organization that will receive mail through this connector. You would use this option if you did not have a Site Connector or an X.400 connector between two sites but wanted them to be a part of the same organization. Once you connect two sites in this way, you can then set up a directory replication connector between the sites and configure/schedule directory replication as you would over an X.400 connector. We will discuss ways to use this feature in Chapter 7, "Connector Models."

Figure 6.32
The Connected Sites Tab

To add a new site, select the New button and enter the organization and site name and the FQDN of the server running the IMC at the remote site. The new site will then appear in the Connected Sites tab, as shown in Figure 6.33.

Both the Address Space and the Connected Sites tabs are used by the Directory Service to build the routing table for the MTA. If you use the IMC

Figure 6.33

A New Site Connected

only to connect sites and not to forward mail directly to the Internet, you should not have *any* entries in the Address Space tab — you should have an entry *only* in the Connected Sites tab. If you have entries in both the Address Space tab and in the Connected Sites tab, you will end up with a GWART that has many redundant and circular entries. Chapter 7 contains an extended example of how to use these features together in a large organization.

The Dial-up Connections Tab

Service Pack 2 for Exchange Server 4.0 lets Exchange Server run on Windows NT Server 4.0 and adds some functionality to the IMC. Among other features, it adds a dial-up functionality for the IMC, which lets you schedule the IMC to dial another SMTP host — for example, an Internet Service Provider (ISP) like PSINet. Figure 6.34 shows the Dial-up Connections tab.

The existing entries in the RAS phone book are listed under Available connections; typically, you will pick one that is an entry for your ISP. You can then schedule the IMC to dial the ISP using the Dial options shown in the Dial

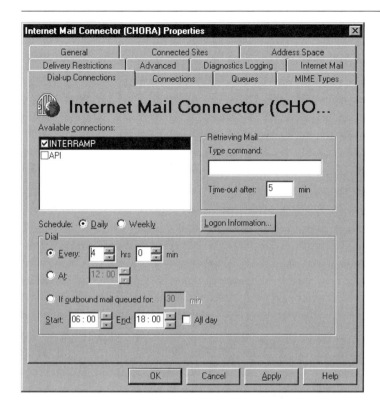

Figure 6.34
The Dial-up Connections Tab

group in Figure 6.34. The first two options let you schedule the IMC to call the ISP every few hours or at a predetermined time of the day. The third option is a dial-on-demand option, where the IMC calls the ISP only if a backlog of mail is waiting to be delivered. This feature is very useful if you want to have mail delivered soon after it is sent, or if you send mail relatively infrequently and do not want to waste cycles frequently dialing the ISP. Note, however, that if you do use the dial-on-demand option, you will not find out about incoming mail unless you have sent mail out.

The Dial-up Connections utility is also used for retrieving mail from a remote SMTP host. After you dial up the remote host and send it mail, you can ask for that host to send you any mail that has collected there. Any mail that arrives before the timeout period specified in the Retrieving Mail grouping has expired will also be sent to you. Normally, as we saw in Chapter 2, an SMTP host simply forwards mail immediately. However, some hosts can be configured to store mail temporarily and deliver it only when it receives a command from the target host. The Retrieving Mail options in the IMC include the ability to send the ISP or SMTP host this command to advise it to send you mail.

You can use the Retrieving Mail feature in the following way. First, have the DNS server for your domain show the ISP as either the primary or secondary MX host for your mail. That way, if your Exchange server is offline, mail for recipients in your domain is forwarded to the ISP, which then holds the mail and tries to deliver it to you at regular intervals. PSINet, for example, has servers that hold mail for customers if the customer's mail server is not reachable. These servers will try to forward the mail every ten minutes — for up to one week — to the customer's mail server. If your Exchange server uses the dial-up functionality in the IMC to dial PSI, any mail stored up for your domain will be sent to you automatically after PSINet's servers sense you are online. You do not need to send any command using the Type command in Figure 6.34. However, if you want PSINet to start sending you the mail immediately, you can trigger mail delivery by sending them the following command:

```
finger domain.com@mx4.smtp.psi.net
```

If your e-mail domain were patmos.sakes.com, the command would be

```
finger patmos.sakes.com@mx4.smtp.psi.net
```

In addition to a finger command, you can also send a remote shell (rsh) command to some SMTP services such as Sendmail to trigger the download. Note that you cannot send either a finger or an rsh command if the remote server is itself an Exchange server. To use the Type Command in the Dial-up tab, you need to get the specific command from your ISP.

The Diagnostics Logging Tab

Figure 6.35 shows the Diagnostics Logging tab. This tab lets you set logging options for the IMC. Events are logged to the Windows NT Application event log, and you can set the level of detail in the logs by changing the Logging Level to any Category shown in Figure 6.35. Two of the logging types, SMTP Protocol Logs and Message Archival, also generate text logs in the \imcdata\log directory.

When you install the IMC, all logging options are set to None, and you should probably keep them that way unless you have a specific need to log events; for example, if you're troubleshooting a problem. Logging increases overhead and takes up disk space. In fact, if you set a lot of the logging options to Maximum, and you have a lot of Internet traffic, your log directories can become enormous. In at least one case, we saw an Exchange server stop processing any mail because the log directories had filled the entire disk. Consequently, you should institute logging selectively and remove it when you have finished troubleshooting the problem you were tracking.

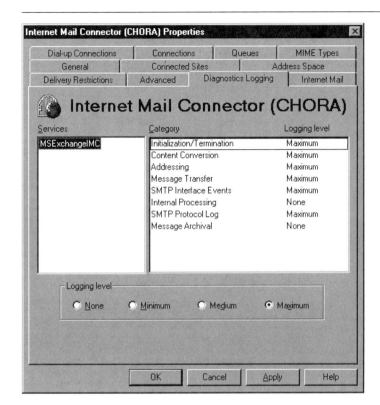

Figure 6.35
The Diagnostics Logging Tab

Appendix B of the *Microsoft Exchange Server Administrator's Guide* has a useful table, reproduced in Table 6.2, showing the functions of the different categories of logging in the IMC.

TABLE 6.2 IMC DIAGNOSTICS LOGGING	
Category	**Description**
Initialization/ Termination	Events related to starting and stopping the Internet Mail Connector
Content Conversion	Conversion of messages between MAPI and MIME, uuencode, and TNEF formats
Addressing	Address resolution, including directory searches and proxy generation
	continued

TABLE 6.2 IMC DIAGNOSTICS LOGGING, CONTINUED	
Message Transfer	Movement of messages and message queue operation
SMTP Interface Events	Interactions between SMTP hosts
Internal Processing	Operation of the Internet Mail Connector
SMTP Protocol Log	Monitoring of SMTP Connections. Setting the diagnostics logging level to Medium sends basic protocol information to text logs in \imcdata\log. Setting it to Maximum sends entire unformatted packets to the same text logs
Message Archival	Saving the text of messages. If you set the diagnostics logging level to Medium or Maximum, each message will be written to a file in imcdata\in\archive or imcdata\out\archive

To change a logging level, highlight a category and select the appropriate option button at the bottom of the screen, as shown in Figure 6.35. You need to restart the IMC after changing logging levels.

For example, to trace the movement of messages through the IMC queues, you could set the Message Transfer logging level to maximum. If you then send a few messages through the IMC in both directions, you could view the movement of the messages in the Windows NT Event Viewer in the NT Administrative Tools folder. Listing 6.7 shows the Event Viewer's Application log filtered for events with source MSExchangeIMC.

In this log, you can see that a message from Judy was received from pop3.dcnw.com and saved as a temporary file in the IMC's inbound directory, \imcdata\in. Similarly, a message from Chris was delivered to the remote SMTP server at 206.247.73.140 (pop3.dcnw.com) for a recipient in the dcnw.com domain. This level of information can obviously be helpful in troubleshooting mail delivery problems.

In addition to logging events to the Windows NT Event viewer, two of the logging categories create text files on the disk. The SMTP Protocol Log monitors SMTP connections, and setting the level to Medium or Maximum writes information to log files in the \imcdata\log directory. As you can see from Listing 6.7, setting the level to Maximum sends entire unformatted packets to the log files, which can grow very large. An example of an SMTP Protocol log file is shown in Listing 6.8.

LISTING 6.7 MESSAGE TRANSFER LOGGING

```
8/2/96   11:37:30 AM         MSExchangeIMC    Information
         Message Transfer 2002     N/A KIFISSIA
         A message from <judy@dcnw.com> in temporary file
         D:\EXCHSRVR\imcdata\in\RV0F5AAD was received from pop3.dcnw.com
         with 1 local recipients.
8/2/96   11:36:26 AM         MSExchangeIMC    Information
         Message Transfer 2001     N/A KIFISSIA
         Delivery of message
         <c=US%a=_%p=SAKES%l=KIFISSIA-960802153548Z@kifissia.sakes.com>
         from <Chris@Athens.SAKES.com> in temporary file RV0CWAAC was
         attempted to host(s) 206.247.73.140 (for dcnw.com)  with 1
         recipients delivered and 0 undeliverable.
8/2/96   11:35:55 AM         MSExchangeIMC    Information
         Message Transfer 2001     N/A KIFISSIA
         Delivery of message
         <c=US%a=_%p=SAKES%l=KIFISSIA-960802153515Z@kifissia.sakes.com>
         from <Chris@Athens.SAKES.com> in temporary file RV0BWAAB was
         attempted to host(s) 206.247.73.140 (for dcnw.com)  with 1
         recipients delivered and 0 undeliverable.
```

LISTING 6.8 SMTP PROTOCOL LOG FILE ON DISK

```
8/2/96 11:44:31 AM : A connection was accepted from pop3.dcnw.com.
8/2/96 11:44:31 AM : <<< IO: |HELO pop3.dcnw.com
8/2/96 11:44:31 AM : <<< HELO pop3.dcnw.com
8/2/96 11:44:31 AM : >>> 250 OK
8/2/96 11:44:31 AM : <<< IO: |MAIL From:<judy@dcnw.com>
8/2/96 11:44:31 AM : <<< MAIL From:<judy@dcnw.com>
8/2/96 11:44:31 AM : >>> 250 OK - mail from <judy@dcnw.com>
8/2/96 11:44:31 AM : <<< IO: |RCPT To:<chris@athens.sakes.com>
8/2/96 11:44:31 AM : <<< RCPT To:<chris@athens.sakes.com>
8/2/96 11:44:32 AM : >>> 250 OK - Recipient <chris@athens.sakes.com>
8/2/96 11:44:32 AM : <<< IO: |DATA
8/2/96 11:44:32 AM : <<< DATA
8/2/96 11:44:32 AM : >>> 354 Send data.  End with CRLF.CRLF
8/2/96 11:44:32 AM : <<< IO: |Received: from POP3 by pop3.dcnw.com (NTMail
                     3.01.03)
8/2/96 11:44:32 AM : <<< IO: |Received: by POP3 with Microsoft Mail
8/2/96 11:44:32 AM : <<< IO: |id <01BB8067.02F1F9E0@POP3>; Fri, 2 Aug 1996
                     11:37:40 -0400
8/2/96 11:44:32 AM : <<< IO: |Message-ID: <01BB8067.02F1F9E0@POP3>
8/2/96 11:44:32 AM : <<< IO: |From: Judy <judy@dcnw.com>
8/2/96 11:44:32 AM : <<< IO: |To: 'Chris' <chris@athens.sakes.com>
8/2/96 11:44:32 AM : <<< IO: |Subject: SMTP events logged
8/2/96 11:44:32 AM : <<< IO: |Date: Fri, 2 Aug 1996 11:37:38 -0400
8/2/96 11:44:32 AM : <<< IO: |MIME-Version: 1.0
8/2/96 11:44:32 AM : <<< IO: |Content-Type: text/plain; charset="us-ascii"
8/2/96 11:44:32 AM : <<< IO: |Content-Transfer-Encoding: 7bit
8/2/96 11:44:32 AM : <<< IO: |X-Info: Evaluation version at pop3.dcnw.com
8/2/96 11:44:32 AM : <<< IO: |X-Info: Internet NTMail Server
8/2/96 11:44:32 AM : <<< IO: |
8/2/96 11:44:33 AM : <<< IO: |This does too
8/2/96 11:44:33 AM : <<< IO: |.
8/2/96 11:44:33 AM : >>> 250 OK
8/2/96 11:44:33 AM : <<< IO: |QUIT
```

The information captured here is the same as we discussed in Chapter 2, "SMTP Basics," and shown in transit using a sniffer, as we discussed in Chapter 3, "IMC Basics." In the example shown above, we have captured not only the basic protocol information, but the data too. If you set the Message Archival level to Medium or Maximum, each message passing through the IMC will be written to a file in either the \imcdata\in\archive or the \imcdata\out\archive directory. The text of the message is archived in its entirety, including MIME-encoded body parts.

This feature lets you create processes that search the messages later for specific content, and it goes a long way toward satisfying some corporate and government requirements for e-mail archiving. Before you set too much in motion on this account, however, you should contact the Electronic Messaging Association in Washington, DC to get information on both privacy and archiving regulations. Exchange gives you the flexibility to enforce almost any policy that you could adopt but does not guarantee that the policy you adopt is reasonable or even in compliance with local regulations.

References

For more information, see

- **"XCON: Viewing or Deleting Messages in MTS-IN or MTS-OUT Queues,"** *Microsoft Knowledge Base,* **Article ID: Q151775, at** **http://www.microsoft.com/kb/bussys/mail/q151775.htm**
- **"MS Exchange and Mail Coexistence and Migration with LAN and Host Mail Systems," Brian Benjamin, Microsoft TechNet CD**
- **Microsoft Exchange Server Administrator's Guide**
- **Microsoft Exchange Server Concept and Planning Guide**
- **Sakellariadis, S., "E-mail Retention under NARA,"** *Messaging Magazine,* **May/June 1996, Electronic Messaging Association (EMA), Alexandria, VA**
- **Internet newsgroups on msnews.microsoft.com**
    - **microsoft.public.exchange.admin**
    - **microsoft.public.exchange.applications**
    - **microsoft.public.exchange.clients**
    - **microsoft.public.exchange.connectivity**
    - **microsoft.public.exchange.misc**
    - **microsoft.public.windowsnt.40**

CHAPTER 7

Connector Models

Microsoft uses the concept of a "domain model" to analyze and design Windows NT installations. Four such models of security strategies have been developed: the single domain model, the master domain model, the multiple master domain model, and the complete trust model. These models represent security strategies for organizations of various sizes that have specialized security and access requirements. No domain model is likely to be implemented in its pure form; rather, organizations tend to use variations.

Planning messaging connectivity in an Exchange organization has many similarities to designing a domain, and in this chapter we discuss the following four "connector models" for implementing Exchange Internet Mail Connector in an organization:

- The Single-Homed Organization
- The Multi-Homed Organization
- The Multi-Homed Site
- The Backboned Organization

Each of these four connector models represents a strategy for implementing connectivity within an Exchange organization, and each has distinct advantages and disadvantages for performance, ease of administration, and security. The simplest paradigm is the Single-Homed Organization, an Exchange organization connected to the Internet through a single connection, using a single IMC to channel all inbound and outbound SMTP traffic. Slightly more complex strategies include the Multi-Homed Organization, in which an organization uses an IMC at each Exchange site, or a Multi-Homed Site, in which an organization uses multiple IMCs at a single site. Finally, a Backboned Exchange Organization uses the Connected Sites utility in the IMC to communicate between sites in the same organization — in effect using the IMC as a form of site connector. We examine each of these four models in detail in the following sections.

Single-Homed Organization

A Single-Homed Organization has only one connection to the Internet. In the organization in Figure 7.1, the Patmos site has a physical connection to the Internet, and the IMC is installed and configured on the server chora.sakes.com. The Internet-connected site, as well as numerous other sites, can have additional servers. In our example, the Patmos site has the campos.sakes.com server, and the Athens site has the kifissia.sakes.com server. The Internet is represented by a host pop3.dcnw.com running an SMTP/POP3 server. This organization was discussed in detail in Chapters 3 and 5.

One of our clients recently installed Exchange and followed the Single-Homed Organization model. The client has offices in Virginia and New York. The Virginia office has a T1 line to the Internet, and it has a single Exchange Server supporting approximately 50 users. The New York office had a 56K line to the Internet, and it was using Sendmail on a Unix host with Eudora clients to support about 30 users. When the entire corporation moved to Exchange, the New York office installed a 256K line to the Virginia office, dropped the 56K line to the Internet, and replaced the Sendmail host with an Exchange server in the same organization as the Virginia office, but in a new site. They implemented a Site Connector over the leased line to Virginia.

Table 7.1 summarizes the main features of a Single-Homed Organization.

The Single-Homed Organization is by far the easiest to administer and the most secure of the connector models. It has only one IMC to administer, one set of parameters to configure, and one point of contact with the outside world to monitor for security breaches. However, it also represents a single point of failure: if the IMC crashes, you have no alternative path through which to receive mail.

All mail from the Internet is delivered to a single host. In the example in Figure 7.1, all mail is delivered to chora.sakes.com, which then routes mail for

Figure 7.1
Single-Homed Organization

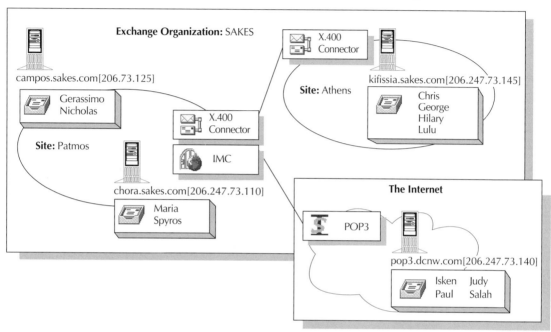

TABLE 7.1 FEATURES OF A SINGLE-HOMED ORGANIZATION

Feature	Issues
Performance	Potential bottleneck at the IMC Can improve performance for remote sites Single point of failure
Security	Highest security — only one connection to monitor and protect
Administration	Easiest to administer — only one IMC Site and X.400 Connectors need to be administered
DNS	Single MX record per site

both the Patmos and the Athens sites. At the DNS you need a Message Exchanger (MX) record for each site and an Address (A) record for chora.sakes.com.

```
patmos.sakes.com      IN    MX    10    chora.sakes.com
athens.sakes.com      IN    MX    10    chora.sakes.com
chora.sakes.com       IN    A           206.247.73.110
```

As we saw in Chapter 4, with these DNS records, any mail addressed to a user in the SAKES domain needs to be addressed to either user@patmos.sakes.com or user@athens.sakes.com. It is then delivered to chora.sakes.com, which routes it to the site and home server of the user. If we look at the e-mail address for a user in the Patmos site, for example, Spyros, we can see that his e-mail address includes the site name (Figure 7.2).

Figure 7.2
Recipient E-Mail Address

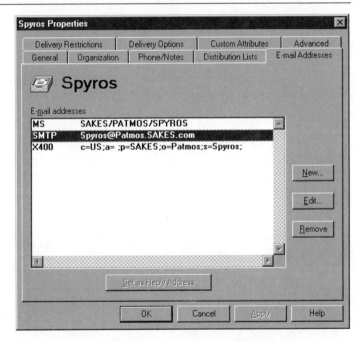

We can bring up this page in the Exchange Administrator by double-clicking on the recipient in the Recipients folder and selecting the E-mail Addresses tab. This address is the result of the default site configuration properties, as shown in Figure 7.3 for the Patmos site.

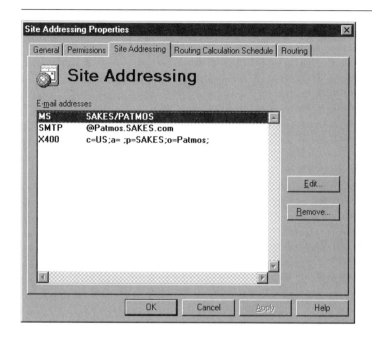

Figure 7.3

Patmos E-Mail Site Address Space

To access this screen, double-click on the Site Addressing object in the Configuration folder for the site. Any recipient in the Patmos site will have an address in the @patmos.sakes.com format by default.

If you want to have mail delivered to a single domain, such as user@sakes.com, you need to change the DNS records to the ones listed below.

```
sakes.com             IN    MX    10      chora.sakes.com
chora.sakes.com       IN    A             206.247.73.110
```

With these DNS entries, all mail addressed to user@sakes.com is forwarded to the host chora.sakes.com at 206.247.73.110.

You also need to change the Address Space information in the Site Addressing object in the Site Configuration folder to reflect the change in addressing. From Figure 7.3, highlight the SMTP entry and click the Edit button. Edit the Site Addressing screen to be like Figure 7.4.

After you edit the changes and click OK twice to return to the main Administrator screen, you will be asked whether you want to propagate this address change down to all the recipients in the site. If you answer OK, Exchange will initiate a process to change to all the recipients' e-mail addresses. For example, Spyros's e-mail address would now look like Figure 7.5. Thus, Spyros would be able to receive messages addressed to him as spyros@sakes.com, not spyros@patmos.sakes.com.

Figure 7.4

Patmos E-Mail Site Address Space, Modified

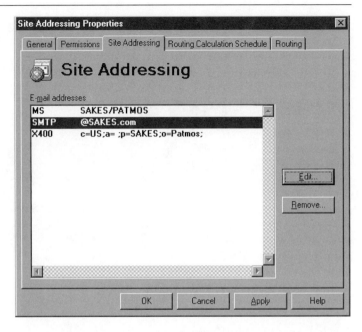

Figure 7.5

Spyros's E-Mail Address, Modified

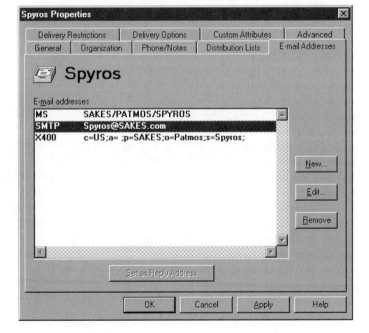

Performance in a Single-Homed Organization is influenced by a number of factors. You are obviously using more processing power and a higher percentage of your available network bandwidth if you only have one IMC running over one physical connection, as opposed to two or more connectors running over multiple physical connections. However, consider our client with offices in Virginia and New York. The performance of the mail system in New York was improved by routing the mail through a higher-bandwidth pipeline to Virginia. If they had decided to install a second IMC in New York and route their mail through the existing 56K line to the Internet, the performance would have been significantly less. Of course, if the T1 to the Internet from the Virginia office had been saturated already, they might have been better off staying with their own dedicated link. Fortunately, the Virginia T1 line had relatively little traffic.

The Single-Homed Organization is probably best for companies with only a few sites and fewer than 500 employees. The most important parameter to monitor is the percentage of utilization on the network bandwidth at the physical connection to the Internet. If your utilization is relatively low and is not markedly affected by the mail system, this connector model is adequate.

The most important parameters to measure within Exchange are the average number of messages in the IMC queues and the average number of bytes passing through the IMC per hour. As we saw in Chapter 6, the number of messages in the queues can be seen from the Queues tab in the IMC dialog box. Figure 3.7, in Chapter 3, reproduced here as Figure 7.6, shows an example of the Queues tab with a number of messages pending delivery.

To gather statistics about the average number of messages in the queues and the current throughput, you need to configure the Windows NT Performance Monitor and monitor several of the Exchange counters. Appendix B contains instructions on how to use the Performance Monitor.

In general, you want to make sure that the number of messages in the IMC queues is not continuously growing. You will see times when messages build up in the queue, but you want to see the IMC bring the number back down relatively quickly. You might also want to monitor the average time messages are in the queue to ensure they don't reside there for extended periods. If any message is in the queue for more than a few hours, you may want to examine the situation further.

In Exchange Server 4.0, a utility on the TechNet CD can make the inbound routing of messages in a Single-Homed Organization more efficient. In that release, no user interface in the IMC Administrator program defined the rerouting, so the rerouting had to be done by configuring entries in the registry. The beta releases of Exchange 5.0 included rerouting as an integral portion of Exchange Server, and it is likely that the release version will contain a graphical tool for administering it. Unfortunately, when this book went to press, the interface was not available.

Figure 7.6

Messages in the IMC Queue

The TechNet IMC Sample Extension dynamic-link library (DLL) lets the server running IMC grab inbound messages from SMTP hosts and selectively reroute those messages to other SMTP hosts before they are processed by the IMC. This off-loads work from the IMC and the MTA in the site and lets the IMC act as a smart host that can route messages to other SMTP hosts without processing the contents of the messages first. It modifies only the envelope headers, not the message contents.

Multi-Homed Organization

The Single-Homed Organization model can suffer from performance problems because it can bottleneck SMTP traffic. A Multi-Homed Organization model alleviates this problem by using multiple servers servicing mail en route to or from the Internet. Figure 7.7 shows an example of a Multi-Homed Organization, with two sites and one IMC per site.

Figure 7.7
Multi-Homed Organization

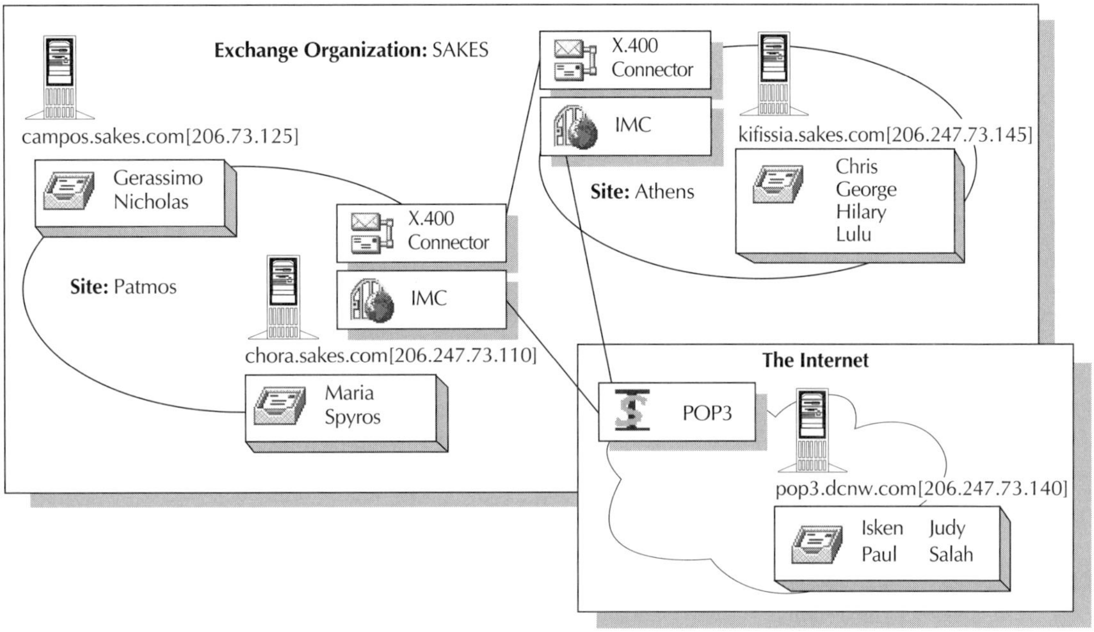

In this example, the organization has two physical connections to the Internet, one from each site. An IMC is configured on a server in each site, and a Site Connector or an X.400 Connector is configured between the two sites. The configuration details of such a site were discussed in Chapter 6 to illustrate ways to use the Address Space tab in the IMC dialog box.

Table 7.2 summarizes the features of a Multi-Homed Organization.

TABLE 7.2 FEATURES OF A MULTI-HOMED ORGANIZATION	
Features	**Issues**
Performance	Best performance for remote sites No single point of failure
Security	Lowest security — multiple remote connections to monitor and protect

continued

TABLE 7.2 FEATURES, CONTINUED	
Features	**Issues**
Administration	Hardest to administer — multiple remote IMCs Site and X.400 Connectors still need to be administered
DNS	Multiple DNS MX records need to be maintained

The Multi-Homed Organization is more complex to administer than a Single-Homed Organization. Not only do you have have multiple connectors to administer, but also you must make sure that the routing tables in each site are aware of the alternative paths to the Internet, that the MX records in the DNS are pointing to the correct computers, and so on.

Mail from the Internet is delivered to several hosts. In the example shown in Figure 7.2, mail for user@patmos.sakes.com is delivered to chora.sakes.com, and mail for user@athens.sakes.com is delivered to kifissia.sakes.com. Unlike the organization shown in Figure 7.1, the MTA on chora.sakes.com does not need to route mail to users in the Athens site because the mail arrives directly at the correct site. At the DNS you need an MX record for each site and an A record for both chora.sakes.com and kifissia.sakes.com.

```
patmos.sakes.com      IN   MX    10      chora.sakes.com
athens.sakes.com      IN   MX    10      kifissia.sakes.com
chora.sakes.com       IN   A             206.247.73.110
kifissia.sakes.com    IN   A             206.247.73.145
```

Using these DNS records, any mail addressed to a user in the SAKES domain again needs to be addressed to either user@patmos.sakes.com or user@athens.sakes.com. It would then be delivered to the correct server.

Arranging for mail to be delivered to user@sakes.com is more difficult in the Multi-Homed Organization than it is in the Single-Homed Organization. In a Single-Homed Organization, all mail arrives at one location, and the MTA on that Exchange server can route mail to the correct server based on the recipient's unique Exchange address. In a Multi-Homed Organization, mail is delivered by remote SMTP hosts to numerous locations, and the remote hosts don't know which site a recipient is on without a site name in the e-mail address.

Bearing this in mind, one option is to use the multiple IMCs as back-up delivery mechanisms. For example, you could change the DNS records to the following:

```
sakes.com              IN   MX   10   chora.sakes.com
sakes.com              IN   MX   20   kifissia.sakes.com
chora.sakes.com        IN   A         206.247.73.110
kifissia.sakes.com     IN   A         206.247.73.145
```

If you are running the primary DNS for the sakes.com domain, you would change these records at that DNS host; if you are having your ISP manage the DNS entries for your domain, you would pass these changes to the ISP's technical contact for your domain. Once the DNS records reflect the changes shown here, remote hosts will deliver all mail for user@sakes.com to chora.sakes.com, and chora.sakes.com can route the mail appropriately. If chora.sakes.com becomes unavailable, the remote hosts will deliver mail to kifissia.sakes.com as a backup. Although this setup does not achieve the performance gains desired from going to a Multi-Homed Organization for inbound mail, it does remove the single point of failure. In addition, you still have the multiple IMCs for outbound mail, which has a performance benefit.

The Multi-Homed Organization has much better performance than a Single-Homed Organization, assuming that all the sites have approximately equal bandwidth to the Internet. Also, in a Multi-Homed Organization, messages between Exchange clients and Internet recipients do not travel over the site connectors between the sites, easing the burden on the physical link between the sites, allowing much faster mail delivery, and a more direct routing of mail.

In the example shown in Figure 7.7, mail from Chris in the Athens site to Judy on the Internet can go directly to her SMTP/POP3 server, pop3.dcnw.com, without first traveling over the X.400 connector to chora.sakes.com. Also, the Internet mail system no longer has a single point of failure, because the Gateway Address Routing Table (GWART) in each site would route outbound mail through the other site in case of failure.

The Multi-Homed Organization has a number of disadvantages. Maintaining the different servers can be quite complex, and routing mail to user@sakes.com as opposed to user@patmos.sakes.com can be a problem. A more serious disadvantage is security. By allowing two or more physical connections to the Internet, you have several links that need to be protected and monitored for intruders and suspicious activity, representing an increase in cost for both labor and equipment. If you use some of the advanced IMC configuration options described in Chapter 6, such as the filtering by host or recipient, you must also make sure that you are not providing back doors to people by neglecting to apply the appropriate restrictions in both locations.

If you do find that performance reasons force you to migrate from a Single-Homed Organization to a Multi-Homed Organization, you should set up a rigorous testing policy. At the very least, you should create a script that has both test messages that should get through to the Internet as well as test messages that should not. You should then run your test scenario with all the connectors in your organization operating and again with each connector turned off, one at a time. You want to make sure that only the messages that are supposed to be delivered get to their destination, regardless of whether all your IMCs are working. Make sure you also test the situation with all IMCs working but with your site connectors disabled.

In large organizations, the IMC setup is exclusive for each domain. Duplicating the configuration manually on the different connectors is very laborious and, therefore, prone to error. The TechNet CD has a tool called the IMC Configuration Restorer that automates the process of copying the IMC configuration information to another IMC. It saves and restores the following information:

- Per-domain routes
- Per-domain content encoding
- Security exception list (accept/reject by host)
- Multipurpose Internet Mail Extensions (MIME) types

Using this tool, you can set up a Multi-Homed Organization much more efficiently.

Multi-Homed Site

To speed up mail delivery in situations with heavy traffic to and from the Internet, we can install multiple IMCs in a single site but only one IMC per server in the site. Figure 7.8 shows an example of a Multi-Homed Site.

Unlike a Multi-Homed Organization, in which each different site has its own physical connections to the Internet and its own server configured with the IMC, a Multi-Homed Site has multiple IMCs in the same site. Whether the site has a single physical pipe to the Internet or multiple connections is irrelevant to the configuration of the site's IMCs. Obviously, though, the more physical connections, the greater the available bandwidth. To focus our discussion exclusively on the features of a Multi-Homed Site we removed — in comparison to Figure 7.7 — the IMC from the kifissia.sakes.com server in the Athens site. In an enterprise environment, however, we would normally see a number of Multi-Homed Sites within a Multi-Homed Organization.

The IMCs on the different servers in a site can be configured differently. In the example shown in Figure 7.8, we have the IMC on both chora.sakes.com and campos.sakes.com in the Patmos site, and as we saw in Chapter 6, we can configure these in different ways. Chapter 11 of the *Microsoft Exchange Server Administrator's Guide* contains the following guidelines for configuring multiple IMCs in a single site:

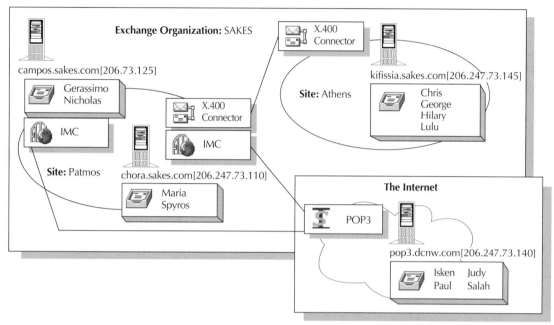

Figure 7.8
Multi-Homed Site

- If the amount of mail to specific domains on the SMTP messaging system can be divided, consider configuring each IMC to process mail only for specific domains.
- Assign a cost to each IMC. This cost will partially determine IMC throughput and can be used to optimize IMC performance.
- If incoming and outgoing mail to the SMTP messaging system is balanced, consider configuring one IMC to process incoming messages and other IMCs to process outgoing messages.

Improved performance is the primary reason for using multiple IMCs in a single site. Simply put, performance improves if you split up the processing of mail traffic. The procedures for configuring the IMCs this way were covered in Chapter 6 in the sections on the Address Space and Connections tabs.

If you do need the increased performance of multiple IMCs in a single site, you need to address how to configure the different connectors. First, you need to add entries in the DNS to route inbound mail correctly. For example, if you have the two connectors shown in Figure 7.8, you might add the following entries in the DNS:

```
patmos.sakes.com        IN    MX    10       chora.sakes.com
athens.sakes.com        IN    MX    10       chora.sakes.com
patmos.sakes.com        IN    MX    20       campos.sakes.com
athens.sakes.com        IN    MX    20       campos.sakes.com
```

The A records remain the same as in the previous example. In this case, mail to either site is delivered by the remote SMTP mailers first to chora.sakes.com and then to campos.sakes.com if chora.sakes.com is unavailable. The MTA on the servers would consult the GWART to determine where to deliver the mail and send messages addressed to users in the Athens site to kifissia.sakes.com over the internal X.400 connector or site connector.

Alternatively, you can set up the DNS as follows:

```
patmos.sakes.com        IN    MX    10       chora.sakes.com
athens.sakes.com        IN    MX    10       campos.sakes.com
patmos.sakes.com        IN    MX    20       campos.sakes.com
athens.sakes.com        IN    MX    20       chora.sakes.com
```

Mail routing is significantly different here. Mail for users in the Patmos site gets delivered as before to chora.sakes.com or campos.sakes.com if chora.sakes.com fails. However, mail for users in the Athens site gets delivered to campos.sakes.com first and chora.sakes.com second. This setup changes the traffic patterns significantly, and you need to understand the implications of these changes for your bandwidth utilization and server performance.

In both these scenarios, we have allowed the IMC to process both inbound and outbound mail. In Chapter 6 we saw that you can configure the IMC's transfer mode to allow it to process both inbound and outbound mail, or just mail in just one direction (see Figure 6.11, Transfer Mode). To get the best performance in the Multi-Homed Site in our example, you can configure the IMC on campos.sakes.com to deliver outbound mail only and configure the IMC on chora.sakes.com to receive inbound mail only. The DNS entries would change as follows:

```
patmos.sakes.com        IN    MX    10       chora.sakes.com
athens.sakes.com        IN    MX    10       chora.sakes.com
```

In this case, we have removed the MX record for campos.sakes.com because it is configured only to process outbound mail. We can imagine a number of scenarios where this might be useful. For example, if you were deluged by inbound mail, the IMC on chora.sakes.com might become saturated, and its performance would suffer. Outbound mail performance would not be affected, though, because it is routed through campos.sakes.com.

A final configuration option would be to give different users privileges on different connectors. For example, you could configure the IMC on campos.sakes.com to process outbound mail to any recipient but limit its use to senior executives. You could configure another server with an IMC to deliver mail only to a limited set of e-mail domains, but have the server open to all employees in the organization.

Backboned Organization

Having a site connector or an X.400 connector between two Exchange sites may not be feasible in certain environments. For example, in the case of a small satellite office with very little traffic to the home office, installing a leased line between the sites or contracting with a public X.400 carrier may be prohibitively expensive. One option would be to connect the two sites with a Dynamic RAS connector; another would be to use the IMC to backbone the two sites.

Using the IMC's Connected Sites facility, you can connect two Exchange sites and move both messaging and directory replication to the Internet. In effect, you are creating a form of site connector, backboning over SMTP. Figure 7.9 shows an example of a Multi-Homed organization that uses the IMC as the connector between two sites.

Figure 7.9
Backboned Organization

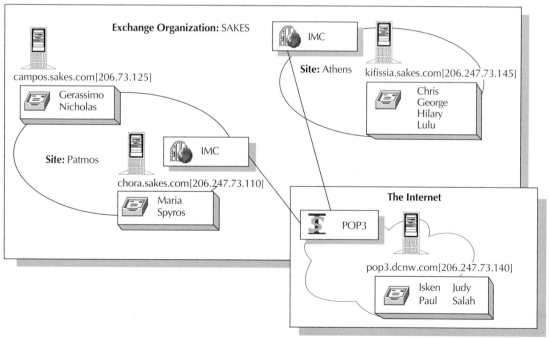

In this example, the X.400 connector between the Athens and Patmos sites shown in Figures 7.1 and 7.8 has been removed, and the Athens site has installed a connection to the Internet. If you use the IMC's Connected Sites tab in the IMC Properties dialog box (see Chapter 6, Figure 6.32), you can set up directory replication and messaging between the two sites.

We will treat the organization shown in Figure 7.9 as a Multi-Homed Organization, and set up the DNS records as follows:

```
patmos.sakes.com      IN    MX    10      chora.sakes.com
athens.sakes.com      IN    MX    10      kifissia.sakes.com
```

In this case, all mail for users in the Patmos site is delivered to chora.sakes.com in the Patmos site, and mail for users in the Athens site is delivered to kifissia.sakes.com. The only difference between this implementation and that of a standard Multi-Homed Organization relates to the internal administration of the IMCs and the lack of a Site Connector or X.400 Connector. If you opt for this setup, you must be careful, though: if you set up directory replication over the IMC, do not set a limit on the size of the messages that can be sent through the connector. If you do, you might prohibit delivery of system messages used during replication, and the databases would be inconsistent.

Chapter 8 of the *Exchange Server Concepts and Planning Guide* gives an extended example of how the Connected Sites and Addresses options work together. Figure 7.10 shows the example from the Concepts and Planning Guide redrawn and modified to be consistent with our SAKES organization examples.

In this organization, we have a private Internet Protocol (IP) network with dedicated lines between the sites and only one pipe to the Internet. Exchange is set up with an X.400 connector between the Rhodos and Athens sites and an IMC connecting Australia to Athens and Athens to Patmos. The Internet connection is provided by a second IMC in the Patmos site. The goal is to route all messages between organization recipients and Internet recipients through the connector on the server Chora.sakes.com. To have Internet mail for SAKES recipients routed through Chora.sakes.com, we need to configure the DNS for all four sites. The MX records in the DNS would be as follows:

```
patmos.sakes.com      IN    MX    10      chora.sakes.com
athens.sakes.com      IN    MX    10      chora.sakes.com
rhodos.sakes.com      IN    MX    10      chora.sakes.com
australia.sakes.com   IN    MX    10      chora.sakes.com
```

Figure 7.10
Extended SAKES Organization

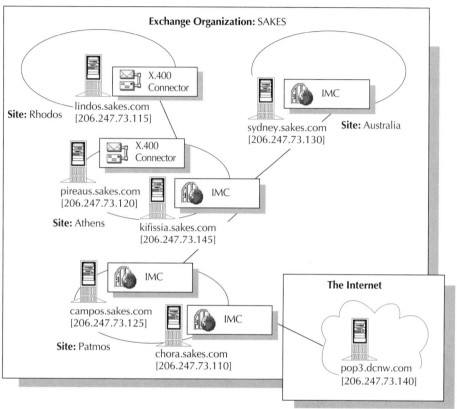

A remote SMTP host sending mail to a recipient anywhere in the SAKES.COM domain would connect only to Chora.sakes.com. In turn, Chora.sakes.com would do a lookup on the proxy SMTP address and resolve it into an internal unique Exchange Distinguished Name (DN) and route it to the appropriate server. To deliver mail between sites, the IMC's Connected Sites tab in the IMC Properties dialog box must be configured for each connector used to reach another Exchange site, as shown in Table 7.3.

TABLE 7.3 CONNECTED SITES PROPERTIES FOR EXTENDED SAKES ORGANIZATION

Site	Connector	Organization	Site	Routing address
Patmos	IMC (CAMPOS)	SAKES	Athens	SMTP:*athens.sakes.com
Patmos	IMC (CHORA)	na	na	na
Athens	IMC (KIFISSIA)	SAKES	Australia	SMTP:*australia.sakes.com
Athens	IMC (KIFISSIA)	SAKES	Patmos	SMTP:*patmos.sakes.com
Australia	IMC (SYDNEY)	SAKES	Athens	SMTP:*athens.sakes.com

For example, the Connected Sites tab for the IMC (CAMPOS) is shown in Figure 7.11.

Figure 7.11

IMC (CAMPOS) Connected Sites Tab

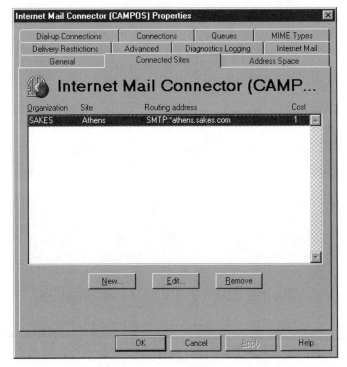

Similarly, the IMC (CHORA) Connected Sites tab is shown in Figure 7.12.

Figure 7.12
IMC (CHORA) Connected Sites Tab

Figures 7.11 and 7.12 implement the configuration shown in Table 7.3. The Connected Sites tabs for the IMCs in the Athens and Australia sites would be similarly configured. In Table 7.3, we configured the Connected Sites options so that each server with an IMC is aware of the server on the other side of the connector. This setup allows, for example, mail originating in the Athens site to be delivered either to the Australia site or the Patmos site over the IMC configured on kifissia.sakes.com.

To set up Directory Replication among the Australia, Athens, and Patmos sites, we need to create Directory Replication Connectors on the IMCs at each of these sites. At each site we need to reference only the one server in the adjacent site, rather than all the other sites. For example, in the Patmos site we only need to reference kifissia.sakes.com rather than sydney.sakes.com in the Australia site, because the directory objects for the Australia site are already replicated to the Athens site, and the Patmos site would get the information from Athens.

Figure 7.13 sets up the Directory Replication connector in the Patmos site to transmit directory objects to and from the Athens site. To create a Directory Replication Connector using the Exchange Administrator, highlight the Directory Replication folder in the site and select New Other/Directory Replication Connector from the File Menu. Enter the name of a server in the adjacent site and click OK, and the Directory Replication Connector properties window will come up (Figure 7.13 shows the Patmos-Athens connection).

Figure 7.13

*Directory Replication
Connector in Patmos Site*

In the Athens site, you create Directory Replication Connectors in a similar way, one to each of the other sites.

Only the IMC on chora.sakes.com will be delivering mail to the Internet, so it is the only IMC that needs an Address Space. The Address Space needs to be configured to deliver mail to all domains, as shown in Table 7.4.

TABLE 7.4 ADDRESS SPACES FOR EXTENDED SAKES ORGANIZATION			
Site	**Connector**	**Type**	**Address**
Patmos	IMC (CAMPOS)	na	na
Patmos	IMC (CHORA)	SMTP	*
Athens	IMC (KIFISSIA)	na	na
Australia	IMC (SYDNEY)	na	na

The Address Space tab for the IMC (CHORA) is shown in Figure 7.14. Similarly, the Address Space tab for the IMC (CAMPOS) is shown in Figure 7.15.

Figure 7.14
IMC (CHORA) Address Space Tab

Figure 7.15
IMC (CAMPOS) Address
Space Tab

Address Space tabs for the other IMCs are similar to the IMC (CAMPOS) configuration. Based upon this set of address spaces, mail is routed through the organization to the IMC on chora.sakes.com for delivery to remote recipients. If you set up the Connected Sites and Address Spaces in this way, the GWART at each site reflects the proper path. For example, the GWART in the Australia site, shown in Figure 7.16, routes a message through three hops.

If we look at the Routing Details, Figure 7.17, for messages to the Internet (shown in Figure 7.16 as an *), we see the connectors that deliver the messages.

For example, mail from a user in the Australia site to judy@dcnw.com is routed first to the IMC (SYDNEY) on sydney.sakes.com. This routing takes place because the GWART entry in the Australia site shows the IMC on sydney.sakes.com as the first hop on the journey. This GWART entry was created by the Connected Sites entry in the IMC on sydney.sakes.com. The IMC on sydney.sakes.com carries the message to the IMC on kifissia.sakes.com in the Athens site. Once the message has reached kifissia.sakes.com, the MTA there consults the GWART in the Athens site and determines that the message should be forwarded through the IMC (KIFISSIA) to campos.sakes.com in the Patmos

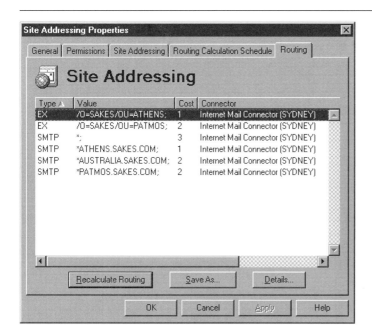

Figure 7.16
Australia GWART

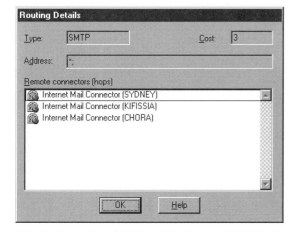

Figure 7.17
Australia GWART Details

site. This GWART entry was created by the Connected Sites entry in the IMC on kifissia.sakes.com. Finally, once the message has reached campos.sakes.com, the MTA there consults the GWART in the Patmos site and determines that the message should be forwarded to the IMC (CHORA) connected to the Internet and finally to the host for the dcnw.com domain. This final GWART entry was created by the Address Space entry in the IMC on chora.sakes.com.

If Judy replies to the message from the user in the Australia site, the MX records shown above for this extended organization route all the mail back to chora.sakes.com. The MTA on chora.sakes.com hands it off to the connector on campos.sakes.com, which transfers it to the connector on kifissia.sakes.com and finally to sydney.sakes.com.

Site	IMC	Message Delivery Options
Patmos	IMC (CHORA)	Use domain name service (DNS)
Patmos	IMC (CAMPOS)	Forward all messages to host 206.247.73.145 (kifissia.sakes.com)
Athens	IMC (KIFISSIA)	Forward all messages to host 206.247.73.125 (campos.sakes.com) Per domain override for Australia - Forward all messages to host 206.247.73.130 (sydney.sakes.com)
Australia	IMC (SYDNEY)	Forward all messages to host 206.247.73.145 (kifissia.sakes.com)

TABLE 7.5 MESSAGE DELIVERY OPTIONS

Configuring the Connected Sites and the Address Space options rebuilds the GWARTs, which are used by the MTAs in the organization to identify routes for the messages. To complete the configuration, we need to configure the message delivery options for the IMC servers. Only the IMC on chora.sakes.com should use DNS; all others should forward mail to their relevant adjacent host, as shown in Table 7.5.

For example, the Connection tab of the IMC (CHORA) in Figure 7.18 shows the Message Delivery options configuration.

Figure 7.18
IMC (CHORA) Message Delivery Options

The Connections tab of the IMC (CAMPOS) is shown in Figure 7.19.

Figures 7.18 and 7.19 show the IMCs in the Patmos site configured per the specifications in Table 7.5. As before, you should use either the IP address for the host or its host name, but not both. Using the IP address would be more efficient. After these options are set up, we can send messages between any user in the organization and a user on the Internet. For example, we can send a message from a user Carol in Australia to judy@dcnw.com.

Figure 7.19

IMC (CAMPOS) Message
Delivery Options

Message Tracking

If we turn on message tracking for all the MTAs and IMCs, we can see the progress of this message, as shown in Figure 7.20.

Figure 7.20 shows the message was submitted by Carol and picked up by the MTA on SYDNEY (shown by the MTA symbol). Because the message was addressed to a remote recipient, the MTA consulted the GWART in the Australia site, shown in Figure 7.12, and routed the message to the IMC (SYDNEY) for transfer to the Athens site. Figure 7.21 shows this message arriving in Athens.

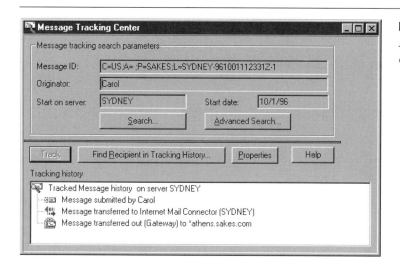

Figure 7.20
Message Tracking on SYDNEY

Figure 7.21
Message Tracking on KIFISSIA

The message is temporarily stored in the Private Information Store on the server KIFISSIA, and the MTA picks it up, consults the GWART, and redelivers it to the IMC. The IMC transfers it to the PATMOS site, where we pick it up on the CAMPOS server, as shown in Figure 7.22.

Figure 7.22
Message Tracking on CAMPOS

Again, the message is temporarily stored in the database and then picked up by the MTA on CAMPOS. After consulting the GWART in the PATMOS site, the MTA transfers the message to the MTA on CHORA because CHORA contains an IMC configured for Internet delivery. Figure 7.23 shows the message picked up by CHORA.

Figure 7.23

Message Tracking on CHORA

In the final step, the message is transferred to the IMC for delivery to the remote host dcnw.com.

Summary

In this chapter we examined a number of possible strategies for implementing connectivity in an Exchange organization. Fortunately, it is not critical that you choose the correct strategy for your entire organization before you implement your first IMC. Unlike the process of setting up an Exchange Organization itself, wherein you need to make decisions about names and boundaries that will be with you forever, the process of implementing Internet connectivity is very flexible. You can bring up and take down connectors almost at will, experimenting until you have found a strategy that works well for your organization in its current form. As the organization changes over time, you can modify the location and configuration of the IMCs to meet the new requirements without being hampered by your previous IMC design.

As soon as you install your first IMC in your organization, all your users will have Internet connectivity. The routing tables in all the organization's sites will be updated through the process of directory replication across your existing Site and X.400 connectors. At this stage, you will have a Single-Homed Organization. Add a second IMC in the same site, and you'll have a Multi-Homed Site; add a second IMC in a different site, and you have a Multi-Homed Organization. In either case, the process of directory replication again will take care of updating the routing tables in each site, and the message traffic patterns will change accordingly. If you feel that the new patterns are inefficient, you can deinstall one of the IMCs, and the routing tables will automatically revert to their previous states.

Provided that you leave at least one IMC installed and you take care to implement the appropriate IMC and DNS changes, the worst that can happen is that mail delivery is slow as it gets rerouted through the organization. With this in mind, you should experiment with the various IMC setups discussed in this chapter to see which best fits your current needs. The best IMC setup may well be the one that has evolved through experimentation rather than planning.

The decision about where to place and how to configure the IMCs in an organization depends on a number of factors:

- Physical network topology
- Network bandwidth
- Location of users
- Message traffic patterns
- Connection costs

In Appendix C, we discuss monitoring the performance of the IMC using the Windows NT Performance Monitor. You should use the Performance Monitor regularly to assess the performance of any connector and work out a procedure for assessing the performance of your IMC connectivity as a whole. Even though all your IMCs are performing well, connectivity might not be optimal for all users. For example, you may have configured the address spaces and connected sites in such a way that a message from an Exchange user is routed internally through twenty hops just to go out an IMC that it could have reached in two hops. To measure and assess the effectiveness of your overall strategy, you need to use all the tools that come with Exchange Server, including the Performance Monitors for the MTAs, the Server and Link Monitors, and the message tracking facility. If you do use all these tools on a regular basis, you should be able to easily optimize message traffic patterns within your organization. The challenge is to do enough traffic analysis to enable you to anticipate changes in time to prevent bottlenecks and other message delivery problems. Exchange Server comes with the tools you need — the rest is up to you!

APPENDIX A

Connecting with an Internet Service Provider

You need three items to set up your organization with Exchange-Internet connectivity:

- A valid domain name
- Two Domain Name Service (DNS) servers
- A physical connection to the Internet

You can get each of these yourself or you can contract with an Internet service provider (ISP) that has them.

To get your domain name, you can apply directly to InterNIC, the organization that manages domains on the Internet in the United States. You can get instructions from InterNIC at http://ds1.internic.net/ds/dspg01.html, the InterNIC's Directory and Database Services page. Essentially, you fill out a form on the Web, specifying the domain name you want and giving information about who will administer it. After you submit the form, you get an e-mail message with an ASCII version of the official registration form contained in the body of the message. You then e-mail this form to the registration body. If the registration is approved, you get an e-mail message indicating that the name will be registered in one business day. A day later, you can do a WHOIS on the Internet and find the name registered. (You frequently hear a disclaimer that the volume of registrations causes the registration process to take up to ten business days. On the other hand, registration for the two domains used in this book, SAKES.COM and DCNW.COM, took one day each.)

Obviously, if you are going to register a domain name electronically, you need to have access to the Internet already (but from a different domain, or through an ISP). If you do not have access to the Internet, you can contract with an ISP to register your domain, or you can register using hard-copy forms and the U.S. Postal Service.

The main problem with registering a domain name on your own (without an ISP) is that the form you fill out requires two DNS servers to contain information about your domain before InterNIC will register your name. If InterNIC cannot verify the two DNS servers when they process your application, the registration form will not be accepted.

As we discussed in Chapter 2, DNS plays a major part in Simple Message Transfer Protocol (SMTP) messaging: it enables SMTP hosts to identify remote hosts for delivering mail. To register a domain name, none of the Resource Records (for example, the Start of Authority (SOA), Name Server (NS), Mail Exchanger (MX) or Address (A) records) must in the database at the time of registration, but the DNS does have to be up and running.

As we discussed in Chapter 4, it is relatively simple to set up a DNS server in Windows NT Server. The usual problem, however, is that small organizations are unlikely to have two servers with the capacity to run DNS, and they do not want the associated maintenance costs. If you do have the capacity, then adding the MX and A records is relatively simple.

Instead of doing this work yourself, typically you would contract with an Internet Service Provider (ISP) to register your domain, get an IP address for your network, and establish a physical connection to the Internet. You then connect to the ISP through a dial-up Point-to-Point Protocol (PPP) connection or leased line. You can use the ISP's DNS if you do not want to run your own. PSINet is a large nationwide ISP, and in this appendix we will discuss how you would work with them, as an example, to set up your Exchange-Internet connectivity.

Figure A.1 is excerpted from PSINet's Web site at http://www.psi.com. Online quotations for their services are available from this site.

PSINet provides a wide variety of Internet solutions; we are concerned only with those relating to the three items mentioned at the beginning of the chapter. For a fee, PSINet will manage the registration process and run DNS servers for your organization. It provides a number of options for connecting to the Internet, ranging from inexpensive dial-up solutions for small businesses to high-speed connections for large volume accounts. The two main options we're interested in are the LanDial and the InterFrame services.

PSINet describes its on-demand services as the ideal solutions "for small companies and branch offices that need full Internet access for their local area networks (LANs) but are not yet ready for a full-time dedicated connection." Two types of on-demand service are available: LAN-Dial, which offers modem

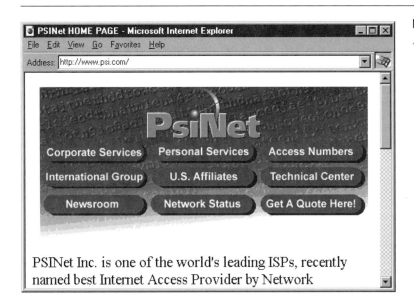

Figure A.1
PSINet's Web Site

connections at 14.4/28.8 kbps, and LAN-ISDN, which offers integrated service digital network (ISDN) connections at 64/128 kbps.

The choice between modem and ISDN communications depends upon price and your bandwidth needs. Both of these services could be used with Exchange Internet Mail Connector's (IMC's) Dial-Up Connection facility described in Chapter 6, which lets you dial up PSINet on a regular basis to send and retrieve mail. In 1996 in the Washington, DC, area, the approximate cost for this type of connection was $50 per month for the telephone service and about $150 per month for the ISP's dial-up service. *Inc. Magazine* (No. 3, 1996, p. 35) estimates the nationwide average cost per month of a line connection to be $20 – $60 and the average cost of an ISP service to be $20 – $40.

The Dial-Up facility in the IMC requires that the Exchange server be set up with a modem and Remote Access Service (RAS), as shown in Figure A.2. In this case, RAS is used exclusively for the IMC and you are not providing any other Internet connectivity to your LAN clients.

Figure A.2

*Connecting with PSINet
Using the IMC Dial-Up
Connection*

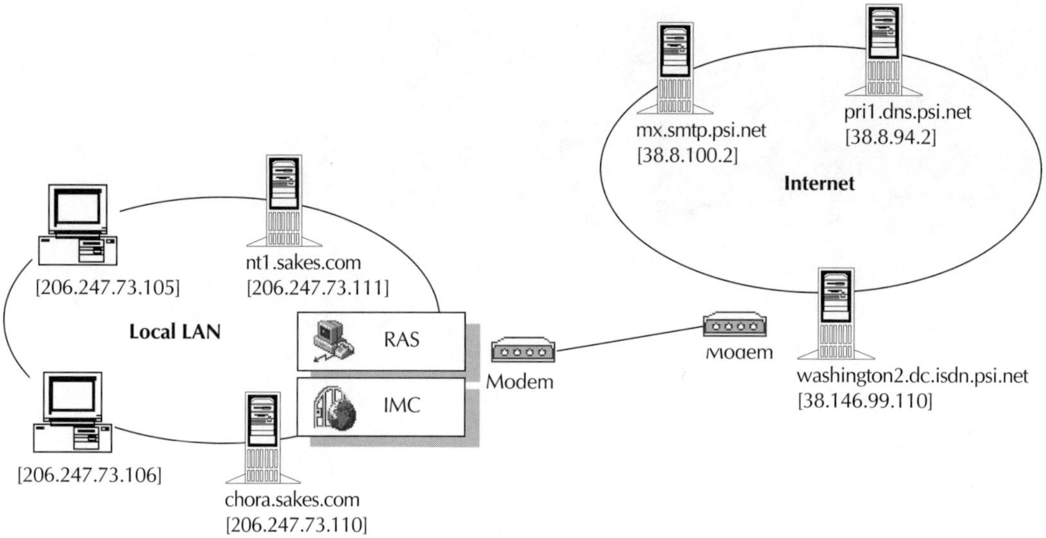

If you do want to provide Internet access to your desktops and still want to use a RAS connection from a Windows NT server instead of buying a router, you need to do two things. First, you need to configure a Windows NT server on your network (not necessarily the Exchange server) as an IP router over RAS. Second, you need to work out a way to keep the ISP or the telephone company from dropping the line during extended periods of inactivity. Figure A.3 shows a typical configuration of this type.

It is relatively simple to configure the Windows NT server as an Internet Protocol (IP) router over a RAS Point to Point (PPP) connection. The procedure is described in the Windows NT Resource Kit, and you can get additional details in an article by Ed Tittel and Mary Madden in *Windows NT Magazine* ("Easy Access to the Internet," July 1996). Both of these documents, however, do not give you enough detail if you have only a Class-C network address. Appendix B gives the step-by-step instructions for setting up a Windows NT router in that case.

If you have a dial-up connection to your ISP, you will find that the ISP or telephone company may drop your connection after a period of inactivity. You can keep the line up by creating a batch file or a service that pings a

Figure A.3

Connecting with PSINet Using a Windows NT Router

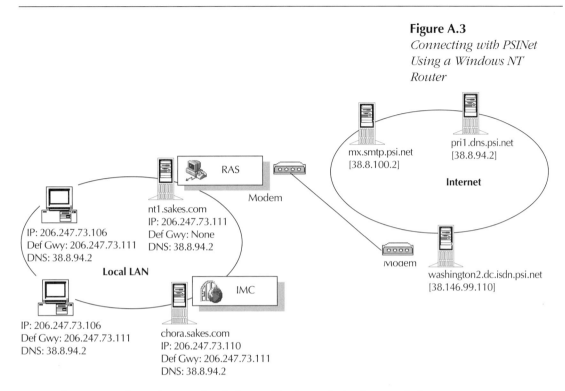

mx.smtp.psi.net
[38.8.100.2]

pri1.dns.psi.net
[38.8.94.2]

Internet

RAS

Modem

nt1.sakes.com
IP: 206.247.73.111
Def Gwy: None
DNS: 38.8.94.2

IP: 206.247.73.106
Def Gwy: 206.247.73.111
DNS: 38.8.94.2

Local LAN

Modem

washington2.dc.isdn.psi.net
[38.146.99.110]

IMC

IP: 206.247.73.106
Def Gwy: 206.247.73.111
DNS: 38.8.94.2

chora.sakes.com
IP: 206.247.73.110
Def Gwy: 206.247.73.111
DNS: 38.8.94.2

remote host every five minutes, simulating traffic through the line at all times. Another way to keep your line is to get a product such as the shareware Tardis, which sets the clock on your system based on a timeserver on the Internet. You can set up this program to check the time every five minutes. You should, of course consult the ISP and the phone company about whether they charge an extra fee for continuous service!

PSINet's Interframe service is the next step up from a dial-up service and gives you connectivity at speeds of 56 kbps and up. This setup requires that you buy a router, a communications device (CSU/DSU), and have the telephone company install a special line to your facility. Figure A.4 shows a typical setup.

Your network is connected to a dedicated IP router, which itself is connected to a specialized communications device called a CSU/DSU. The IP router needs at least one Ethernet (typically) interface for your LAN, and one wide area network (WAN) interface for connecting to the CSU/DSU. Which CSU/DSU you buy depends upon the speed and type of line you lease from the telephone company; for example, a 56 kbps or 256 kbps Frame Relay (as you would need for PSINet's Interframe service) or a T1 line. In the example shown in Figure A.4, the local LAN is on the 206.247.73.0 network, and your IP router routes all packets for remote hosts to its interface to the CSU/DSU.

Figure A.4

*Connecting with PSINet
Using a Router and
CSU/DSU*

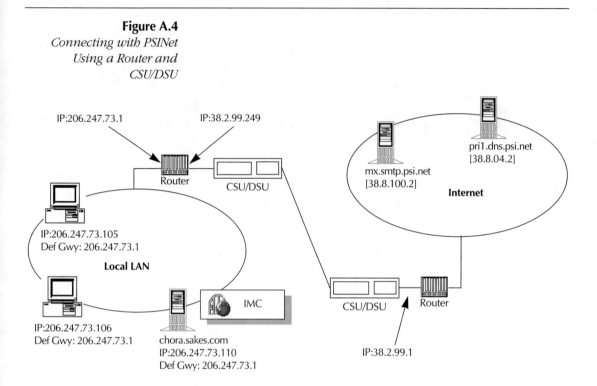

In the configuration shown in Figure A.4, Internet connectivity from the desktop is continuous and at a higher speed than it would be if you used Windows NT as a router. The disadvantage of this configuration over the previous one, however, is cost. First, the 1996 cost for the router and the CSU/DSU is approximately $2,000. Second, the monthly cost (Washington, DC area, 1996) for this type of connection is about $120 to the telephone company and about $350 to the ISP for a 56 kbps connection service. In contrast, *Inc. Magazine* (No. 3, 1996, p.35) estimates the nationwide average monthly cost of a 56 kbps line connection to be $70 and the average cost of the ISP service to be $250. Faster connections are available, but they are significantly more expensive.

For more information, see

- PSINet Literature
- PSINet Web site, at http://www.psi.com
- Tittel, E. and Madden, M., "Easy Access to the Internet," *Windows NT Magazine*, pp. 107–110, July 1996

References

APPENDIX B

Using Windows NT as a Router to Connect a Class C Network to an ISP

This appendix describes how to connect systems on a local area network (LAN) to an Internet Service Provider (ISP) using a Windows NT server with a modem as the router.

Much of the information in this appendix is contained in the Windows NT 3.5 Resource Kit, Volume 2, Chapter 22, "Remote Access Service and the Internet." The procedures and information are basically the same for Windows NT 4.0 and may also be reprinted in the NT 4.0 Resource Kit when it is available. The example presented here shows how to set it up using a LAN-Dial account from PSINet; different services will require modifications to this setup.

When you get a LAN-Dial account with PSINet, it typically registers your domain name, assigns you an IP address, and gives you some basic information. For example, it might give you the following information, plus a password:

Account ID:	LD0000
Assigned IP address:	206.247.73.1
Domain name:	sakes.com
IP Address of POP:	38.146.99.110
DNS Servers:	38.8.94.2, 38.8.95.2
Phone No.:	(202) 408-3199

Using the IP addresses shown in this book, you might configure your
LAN as shown in Figure A.2 in Appendix A. On your LAN, the desktops should
be configured with Transport Control Protocol/Internet Protocol (TCP/IP), and
the default gateway should be the Windows NT system acting as a router. On
the NT system acting as a router, and that system alone, configure TCP/IP to
have no default gateway. Table B.1 presents a sample configuration.

TABLE B.1 IP CONFIGURATION		
Workstation	**Desktop client**	**Windows NT router**
IP address	206.247.73.105	206.247.73.111
Subnet address	255.255.255.0	255.255.255.0
Default gateway	206.247.73.111	Leave blank

To set up the Remote Access Service (RAS) server for dial-out connectivity,
you create a phone book entry for the PSINet Point of Presence (POP) using the
phone number PSINet provides. Exactly how you configure the RAS entry
depends upon the ISP. PSINet's requirement for the connection requires you to
configure the RAS entry as follows:

• Select PPP as the server type
• Select TCP/IP as a network protocol
• Disable LCP extensions
• Disable header compression
• Enable software compression
• Enable any authentication, including clear text
• Disable "Server assigned IP address" and enter the IP address given to you
  above; e.g., 206.247.73.1
• Enter the IP addresses of the ISP's DNS servers
• Enable "Using default gateway on remote network"
• Leave the "Authenticate using current user name" option unchecked.

When you start RAS, you should enter the ISP-assigned account ID as the User
Name and the assigned password as the password. Do not enter a Domain Name.

Once connected, open a DOS window on the RAS server and try the following tests:

- Ping the IP address of a known host at the ISP. For example, if your ISP is PSINet, you might ping 38.9.211.2, which is one of their DNS servers. It should work. If it does not, RAS is not properly set up. If it does work, you have the PPP properly set up.
- Then ping the IP address of a known host outside the ISP's domain. For example, you might ping 198.105.232.2, one of the IP addresses for Microsoft's FTP servers. If it does not work, call your ISP.
- Ping the name of a known host; for example, ftp.microsoft.com. If it does not work, you probably entered an incorrect DNS server address. Correct the address and try again.

To configure the RAS server as an IP router, run the Registry Editor and go to the following key:

```
\HKEY_LOCAL_MACHINE\SYSTEM\CurrentControlSet\Services\Tcpip\Parameters
```

Add the following key:

```
IPEnableRouter (REG_DWORD)=1
```

Documentation on this key is in the TCP/IP Transport Entries, Part 1, of the Windows NT Resource Kit. In addition, you can search the TechNet CD for further documentation. The October CD has seven articles describing its use.

In addition, you need to go to the key

```
HKEY_LOCAL_MACHINE\System\CurrentControlSet\Services\RasArp\Parameters
```

and add or modify the following key:

```
DisableOtherSrcPackets (REG_DWORD)=0
```

Note that the Windows NT 3.5 Resource Kit has a misprint on page 420; the key should be set to 0, not to 1 as stated in the Resource Kit.

You have one last item to configure if you have been assigned a single Class-C network address by your ISP. For the RAS box to act as a router, it must know that any IP packets it receives destined for your local subnet (206.247.73.0 in the example above) should be sent to its NIC (206.247.73.111 in the example) and that any packets it receives destined for anywhere else should be sent to the RAS interface (206.247.73.1 in the example). However, when you bring up RAS, it obliterates the current routing table and you need to rebuild the routes. You might assume the routing table is lost because you are attempting to route within a single Class-C address with no subnetting;

whatever the cause, we used the following solution for about a year with good results.

Before dialing the POP, open a DOS window on the RAS server and type **ROUTE PRINT**. You will see entries for the NIC card, the loopback (127.0.0.0), and a few other items that we can ignore. Now dial the ISP and retype **ROUTE PRINT**. You will probably see two entries for your local LAN (206.247.73.0 in the example) showing that packets should be sent first (Metric = 1) to the RAS interface (206.247.73.1, i.e., PSI), and second (Metric=2) to the NIC (206.247.73.111; i.e., your LAN). This procedure causes problems, and you need to delete the entry and rebuild it. First dial the POP. Then, from the DOS window, type:

```
route delete 206.247.73.0
route add 206.247.73.0 mask 255.255.255.0 206.247.73.111
```

This input needs to be modified, of course, for your real Class-C address. These changes make sure that any packets for the LAN received by the RAS box are redirected to the NIC on the server; that is, to your local LAN. It is convenient to put this information in a batch file and execute the batch file to dial and correct the routing table. The following batch file does the trick:

```
rasdial psi <your LAN DIAL account number> <your LAN DIAL password>
route delete 206.247.73.0
route add 206.247.73.0 mask 255.255.255.0 206.247.73.111
```

You might even want to schedule this batch file so that it executes periodically in case your line is dropped. Table B.2 shows the routing table that worked on our Windows NT server for close to two years.

TABLE B.2 ROUTING TABLE ON RAS ROUTER				
Network Address	Netmask	Gateway Address	Interface	Metric
0.0.0.0	0.0.0.0	206.247.73.1	206.247.73.1	1
127.0.0.0	255.0.0.0	127.0.0.1	127.0.0.1	1
206.247.73.0	255.255.255.0	206.247.73.111	206.247.73.111	1
206.247.73.1	255.255.255.255	127.0.0.1	127.0.0.1	1

continued

TABLE B.2 ROUTING TABLE ON RAS ROUTER, CONTINUED

Network Address	Netmask	Gateway Address	Interface	Metric
206.247.73.111	255.255.255.255	127.0.0.1	127.0.0.1	1
206.247.73.255	255.255.255.255	206.247.73.111	206.247.73.111	1
224.0.0.0	224.0.0.0	206.247.73.1	206.247.73.1	1
224.0.0.0	224.0.0.0	206.247.73.111	206.247.73.111	1
255.255.255.255	255.255.255.255	206.247.73.111	206.247.73.111	1

At this point, you should be able to go to any desktop and ping ftp.microsoft.com by name.

For more information, see

References

- **Windows NT Resource Kit, Appendix**
- **Tittel, E. and Madden, M., "Easy Access to the Internet,"** *Windows NT Magazine*, **pp. 107–110, July 1996**
- **"How to Configure Windows NT as a Remote IP Router,"** *Microsoft Knowledge Base*, **Article Q123024**
- **"Cannot Ping Across Router After Connecting as a RAS Client,"** *Microsoft Knowledge Base*, **Article Q128647**

APPENDIX C

Monitoring the Internet Mail Connector with the Windows NT Performance Monitor

Exchange Server exports many objects that you can view in the Windows NT Performance Monitor. Figure C.1 shows the top-level objects that you can monitor.

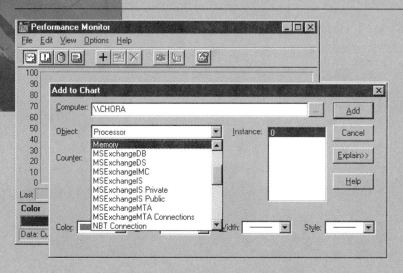

Figure C.1
Exchange Objects in the Windows NT Performance Monitor

Each of these objects has many different counters. For example, Figure C.2 shows that the Exchange Internet Mail Connector object has numerous counters. Listing C.1 contains the counters you can monitor for the IMC.

Figure C.2

Exchange Internet Mail Connector Object

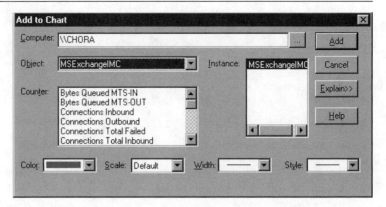

LISTING C.1 EXCHANGE OBJECTS EXPORTED TO THE WINDOWS NT PERFORMANCE MONITOR

- Bytes Queued MTS-IN
- Bytes Queued MTS-OUT
- Connections Inbound
- Connections Outbound
- Connections Total Failed
- Connections Total Inbound
- Connections Total Outbound
- Connections Total Rejected
- Inbound Bytes Total
- Inbound Messages Total
- Messages Entering MTS-IN

- Messages Entering MTS-OUT
- Messages Leaving MTS-OUT
- NDRs Total Inbound
- NDRs Total Outbound
- Outbound Bytes Total
- Outbound Messages Total
- Queued Inbound
- Queued MTS-IN
- Queued MTS-OUT
- Queued Outbound

You can find a brief description of each of these counters in the Performance Monitor online help. In addition, we have talked about many of these items throughout this book. For example, in Chapters 3 and 5 we discussed the flow of a message through the system and the different queues an outbound message passes through between the Information Store and its final delivery to a remote host. You can view the progress of such a message by using the message tracking facility of Exchange and by viewing the diagnostics logs.

The purpose of Windows NT's Performance Monitor is to let you gauge the performance of the system as a whole and, in our case, the performance of the Exchange server. That is, we can use the Performance Monitor to gather statistics about the performance of the Exchange server as it is currently configured.

When you install Exchange, eight preconfigured workspaces of the Performance Monitor are added to the Exchange group in the Start menu (or Program Manager); three of these workspaces relate specifically to the IMC. These workspaces measure different aspects of the IMC's performance, and they have a different combination of the counters shown in Listing C.1. For example, Figure C.3 shows the Queues workspace.

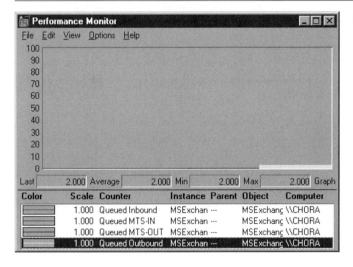

Figure C.3
Queues

The Performance Monitor has been preconfigured with the following four counters:

- Queued Inbound
- Queued MTS-IN

- Queued MTS-OUT
- Queued Outbound

These counters, which measure the number of messages in the inbound and outbound queues for the IMC, are helpful if you want to see whether messages are building up in one of the specific queues or if you want to track the number of messages passing through. You can view the current state of a queue in the Exchange Administrator tool itself, as we saw in Chapters 3 and 5, but the Performance Monitor adds a logging and temporal dimension to the other information.

Also, the Performance Monitor lets you set alerts that will notify you if a condition you are monitoring occurs. For example, if you suspect you have a faulty connection to the Internet, you can be alerted if the number of messages in the outbound queue builds up to preset number.

The second preconfigured workspace of the Performance Monitor, Statistics, shows gross statistics about the IMC. Figure C.4 shows the statistics workspace.

Figure C.4

Statistics

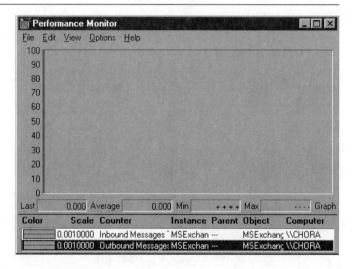

This workspace only shows two counters:

- Inbound Messages Total
- Outbound Messages Total

This feature monitors the performance of the connector and determines the volume of messages being processed. It is useful for determining if your users are using the facility and for comparing the load on different IMCs within your organization. For example, you might find that the number of messages flowing through this connector is very high compared to another connector; you might want to reconfigure the IMCs to process the load more evenly.

The third preconfigured workspace of the Window NT Performance Monitor, Traffic, gives you more information on the traffic through the IMC. Figure C.5 shows the Traffic workspace.

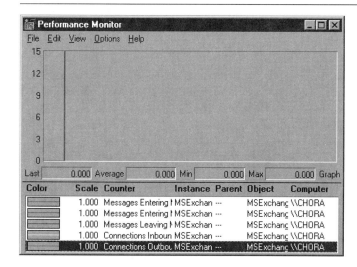

Figure C.5
Traffic

This workspace monitors five counters:

- Messages Entering MTS-IN
- Messages Entering MTS-OUT
- Messages Leaving MTS-OUT
- Connections Inbound
- Connections Outbound

Whereas the Statistics workspace gives you overall data and the Queues workspace gives you a picture of what is built up in the various queues, the Traffic workspace tells you about the progress of messages on either side of the IMC. For example, messages in the MTS queues are waiting to get picked up by the IMC or have been given to the MTA by the IMC. Analyzing these counters lets you assess the performance of the IMC relative to your needs and to the rest of your system. If the queue to the IMC has built up, either from the MTA or from a remote host, it might indicate that the IMC is a bottleneck in the system.

To use the Performance Monitor effectively, you need to monitor carefully chosen counters over a period of time or under a specific load. You can then change various hardware or software configurations and compare the performance of the system before the change and after to assess whether your actions improved the situation. Although a complete tutorial on the use of the Performance Monitor is beyond the scope of this book, we cannot overestimate the value of being thoroughly familiar with the use of this diagnostic tool.

In the following paragraphs, we cover the basic procedures for using the Performance Monitor in the very narrow context of the Exchange IMC; readers needing more information are encouraged to take the Microsoft Educational Services certified courses on Windows NT.

In this appendix, we're using the Performance Monitor to get a picture of our system's performance so we can determine if the IMC is a bottleneck in the system. We create this picture by setting up a chart and a log in the Performance Monitor and selecting objects to monitor. Fortunately, as we saw above, we can use three preconfigured monitors as a starting point. For now, we concentrate on the Traffic monitor, though the procedures would be the same for the other two monitors.

If we open up the Traffic monitor from the Start menu or Program Manager, we get the screen shown in Figure C.6.

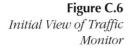

Figure C.6
Initial View of Traffic Monitor

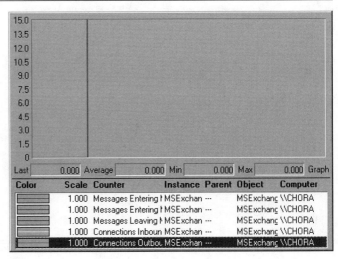

Notice that the title and menu bars are missing. Under normal circumstances, you would leave it this way; however, if you want a more precise configuration, you need to bring up the menu bar. To do so, double-click anywhere on the window, which gives you the screen shown previously in Figure C.5.

The chart presents real-time information about the performance of the IMC. For reference purposes, you will want to log this information to a file on a disk, using the following steps:

- From the View menu, choose Log.
- From the Edit menu, choose Add to Log. You will see the Add To Log dialog box, which contains all the objects you can monitor.
- In the Objects box, select MSExchangeIMC and choose Add. Click on Done.
- From the Options menu, choose Log. The Log Options dialog box appears, letting you choose the file name to store the data and an interval for polling the activity, as shown in Figure C.7.

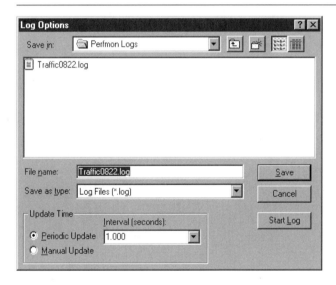

Figure C.7
Log Options Dialog Box

- Enter a file name, such as Traffic0822.log. Choosing a name that includes the date that the log is started is helpful for archiving purposes.
- Enter an interval for polling. The default is every 15 seconds, which is probably adequate for daily operations. If you want to test the log and view more activity, change it to every second. Do not forget to change it back after you are satisfied the log captures the information you want. When a

log starts, all the counters for the IMC are captured to disk, so this log file can become very large.

- Click the Start Log button.

- Create some activity by sending mail through the IMC. Unfortunately, the Load Simulator tool on the Exchange Server CD does not allow you to configure custom recipients to generate test traffic, so you will need to create the message traffic manually. You can see how large the log is getting from the File Size box in the Performance Monitor, shown in Figure C.8. When the log has reached at least 100K in size, stop the activity and view the log.

Figure C.8

Logging Activity

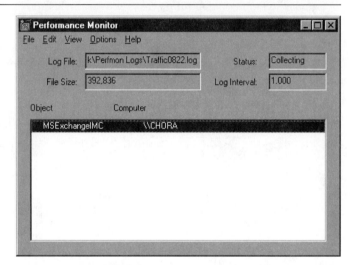

- From the Options menu choose Log, then from the Log Options dialog box choose Stop Log.

Now that we have captured the data, we need to view the logged information, which we can do using the following steps:

1. From the View menu, choose Chart. You will see the preconfigured monitor for Traffic analysis.

2. From the Options menu, choose Data From.

3. Select the log file you created above (Traffic0822.log in our case). Notice that the specific counters from the Traffic analysis monitor have disappeared. You now need to add them.

4. From the Edit menu, choose Add to Chart.

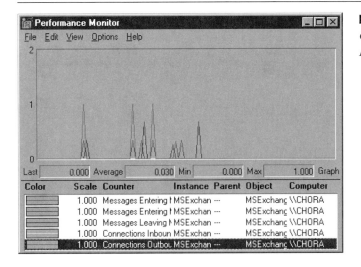

Figure C.9
Chart with Data from Log File

5. In the Counter box, select all the counters that were in the Traffic analysis monitor and click Add to Chart. Click Done, and the chart displays the data collected in your log.

6. Change the scale of the chart if necessary. From the Options menu, choose Chart.

7. In the Chart Options dialog box, enter an appropriate number for the Vertical Maximum, so that the data spans most of the Y axis. Click OK to return to the chart.

At this point, you should see the logged data in your chart. Using these procedures, we sent a few messages in both directions through the IMC, which produced the chart shown in Figure C.9.

Looking at the log file, we can see the various traffic patterns and have information to do a traffic analysis on the IMC. Hopefully, this information will let you detect any patterns and anticipate any problems in your system.

Use the following steps to create a report from the collected data:

1. From the View menu, choose Report. If you did not do steps 2 and 3 above, you need to do them now.

2. From the Edit menu, choose Add to Report

3. Select the counters for the Traffic monitor, from step 5 above.

4. Choose Done.

Figure C.10 shows a sample report.

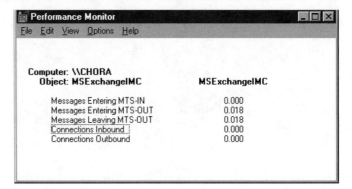

Finally, you should examine the procedures for creating alerts with the Performance Monitor, and you should also take advantage of the extended functionality available through some of the utilities on the TechNet CDs. For example, the Command Line Mail Sender (sendmail.exe) is a utility that comes on the TechNet CD or with Microsoft Exchange Resource Kit that can be combined with the Performance Monitor to send a message to a predetermined user when a specific alert is triggered. You could use this feature to send a message to the administrator if the messages in the IMC queues exceed a specified amount or if the average resident time of a message in the queue exceeds a set limit. The full syntax of the Sendmail command is as follows:

```
SENDMAIL -u profile name -p password -r recipient(s) [-c copy
recipient(s)] [-s subject] [-m message] [-f file attachment(s)] [-v] [-?]
```

To have a message sent to the administrator that says "The IMC queue is bogging down," follow these steps:

1. Run the Srvany.exe utility in the Windows NT Resource Kit to set up Performance Monitor to run as a service.

2. Add an alert that starts when the IMC queue has more than 20 messages.

3. In the Alert Send window, run the Command Line Mail Sender by typing the following in the Run Program on Alert box:

```
SENDMAIL -u administrator -p -r administrator -s "IMC ServerAlert" -m
"The IMC Queue is bogging down"
```

When the alert is started, the Sendmail.exe utility logs on to Exchange as the administrator profile and sends a message to the Administrator with the subject "IMC ServerAlert" and the message body "The IMC Queue is bogging down."

For a full description of the use of the Sendmail utility, see "Using the Command Line Mail Sender" in the Microsoft Exchange Resource Kit. In addition, check the article in the Microsoft Knowledge Base, "Using the SENDMAIL.EXE Utility with the AT Scheduler," Q151670.

For more information, see **References**

- **Windows NT Server System Guide**
- **"Supporting Microsoft Windows NT Server 3.51," Course 659, Microsoft Educational Services.**
- **"Using the SENDMAIL.EXE Utility with the AT Scheduler,"** *Microsoft Knowledge Base,* **Article ID: Q151670.**
- **"Using the Command Line Mail Sender" in the Microsoft Exchange Resource Kit.**

APPENDIX D

Internet Shopper Ltd.'s NTMail

Throughout this book we have used Microsoft Exchange Server to communicate with SMTP/POP3 hosts on the Internet. In our lab, we have used an SMTP/POP3 server from Internet Shopper Ltd. called NTMail. For more information on NTMail, visit Internet Shopper's Web site, shown in Figure D.1.

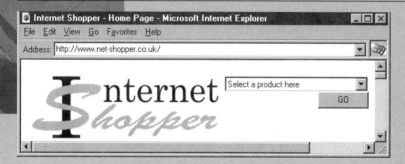

Figure D.1
http://www.net-shopper.co.uk/

You can download the entire product and a temporary key that lets you use it until the end of the current month. Each month you can download a new key, or you can purchase a permanent key from Internet Shopper Ltd. Internet Shopper revises the software on a regular basis; the version and license used in this book were kindly provided by Internet Shopper.

NTMail runs on Windows NT (Intel and Alpha platforms) and is very simple to set up and administer. Consequently, our lab was able to emulate the Internet with a single machine, pop3.dcnw.com, running Windows NT 4.0, DNS, and NTMail. All the interactive Telnet sessions, as well as the IMC examples, used this product.

Once you have downloaded the product and a key, run Setup. The setup procedure adds several icons to the Control Panel; we are concerned with only the NTMail icon, which lets you configure and run NTMail. To start the server, bring up the NTMail Control Panel application and select the Key tab, as shown in Figure D.2.

Figure D.2

*Entering the Activation
Key for NTMail*

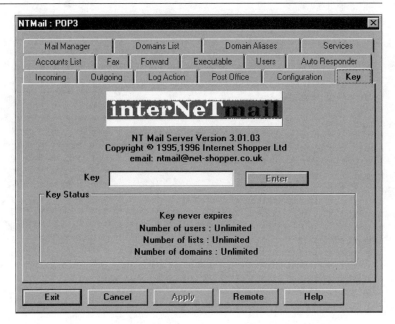

Once you have entered the key you downloaded and the product is installed and functional, you need to specify the e-mail domain names (not an NT Domain, of course) that the server hosts, which you do from the Incoming tab shown in Figure D.3. In this case, the server is providing POP3 and SMTP service only for the DCNW.COM domain.

Finally, you need to add some mailboxes from the Accounts List. You can also add users from another icon in the control panel, the NTMailUsers icon tab, as shown in Figure D.4.

For our examples, we only need to add an account for Judy (judy@dcnw.com). If you are using NTMail to test your Exchange connectivity, you will need a license for as many users as you plan to add here. Under most circumstances, two or three users are sufficient for testing purposes.

NTMail is a very good product that has a number of uses in the Exchange environment. In this book we used it for testing connectivity and demonstrating interoperability with Exchange Server. If you read the various Internet newsgroups on mail, you will find people using it in conjunction with Exchange Server for operations such as forwarding services or querying POP3 accounts periodically and forwarding the mail to the Exchange SMTP service. It is definitely worth considering for your environment.

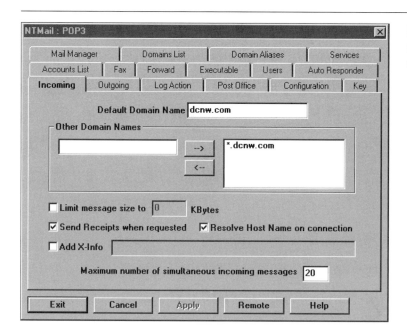

Figure D.3
*Configuring Domains
in NTMail*

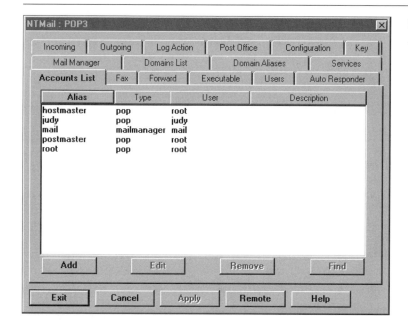

Figure D.4
Adding Accounts to NTMail

References

For more information, see

- **Internet Shopper Ltd.'s Web site, at http://www.net-shopper.co.uk/**

APPENDIX E

Exchange Server 5.0

There are several differences between the Internet Mail Connector in Exchange 4.0 and Exchange 5.0. The most obvious difference is the name change to the Internet Mail Service (IMS), as you can see in Figure E.1.

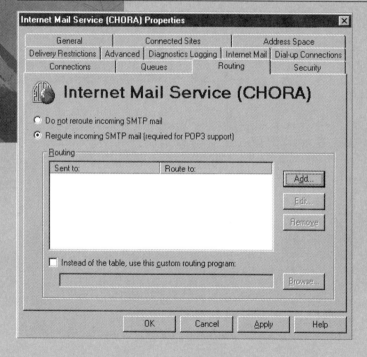

Figure E.1
Internet Mail Service

The IMS is implemented natively to the server and is installed with the Internet Mail Wizard by choosing New Other from the File menu. The wizard makes installing the IMS much simpler and eliminates a number of the problems experienced by Exchange 4.0 users. The native implementation is said to result in faster performance, though we have not yet seen any benchmark test results.

Besides these changes, the IMS differs from the IMC in three ways: the IMS generally provides more support for RFCs, it includes new routing features, and it supports new security features. We will consider each of these differences in greater detail.

RFC Support

The IMS supports more Internet RFCs than the IMC, including

- RFC 1870, SMTP Service Extension for Message Size Declaration
- RFC 1891, SMTP Service Extension for Delivery Status Notifications

As well as supporting more RFCs, Exchange Server 5.0 supports additional functionality in RFCs 1521 and 1522 regarding MIME (see Chapter 2) and includes additional character sets.

The press release for Exchange Server 5.0 describes the function of some of these new features very well. Discussing RFC 1870, the press release (available at http://www.microsoft.com/exchange/inetmail.htm) indicates:

> Many products today have provided a way for the Administrator to enforce the size of messages they wish to send or receive from their hosts. Microsoft Exchange Server does this today. The problem with this approach has been that there is no way to communicate the limit to the sending host before the message transfer is initiated. Hence messages are rejected after a certain amount of data has been transferred, tying up system resources unnecessarily. RFC 1870 allows the receiving host to indicate the maximum size of a message they can accept, and therefore other conforming hosts will not send any data on the wire if this size is exceeded. This is a recommended protocol, and any SMTP message host should implement it fully in order to manage Internet bandwidth.

For example, in Chapter 6 we discussed the process for limiting the size of messages that can be transferred by the gateway (see Figure 6.9). In Exchange Server 5.0, the process for negotiating a message used by the server lets it reject a message before getting even the first byte, *provided that* the originating mail server also supports RFC 1870.

Discussing RFC 1891, the press release points out that:

> Historically on the Internet there was no way to verify if a message had been received or read at its destination. While a few products tried to implement this capability using non-standard methods, not every host supported these methods so the result was uneven. Using RFC 1891, Exchange Server provides the ability to request a delivery status notification for any recipient on a message. Email users will get delivery status notification across the Internet from other Exchange Server 5.0 host, or from other messaging systems that support this standard.

Lack of delivery receipts for Internet messages has long been a complaint of users, and Exchange Server 5.0 supports the new standards that make delivery receipts possible. Note again, however, that these receipts will be received only if the recipient's mail system supports the RFC as well. Some of the additional fields specified in RFC 1891 are not supported yet.

Routing Tab

As indicated in Chapter 6, Exchange Server 5.0 has added a couple of tabs to the property pages for the Internet Mail Connector/Service. The first of these two is the routing tab, as shown in Figure E.1, above. In Chapter 7, we mentioned that Exchange Server 4.0 included an extension DLL that lets the server act as a mail relay agent for routing messages to other domains (see page 158). This routing capability is integrated into the IMS in Exchange Server 5.0 and is configured through the routing tab. If you have a domain for which you need to route mail, click on Add from the window in Figure E.1 and add the domain name to the Routing Table Entry dialog box, as shown in Figure E.2.

Figure E.2
Adding a Routing Table Entry

In this case, we have indicated that any mail received for a recipient in the sakellariadis.com domain should not be processed by the connector in the usual way; rather, it should be rerouted immediately to whatever host handles mail for the sakes.com domain. When you click OK, this entry appears in the list in the Routing tab (Figure E.3).

Figure E.3
Routing Tab with Entry

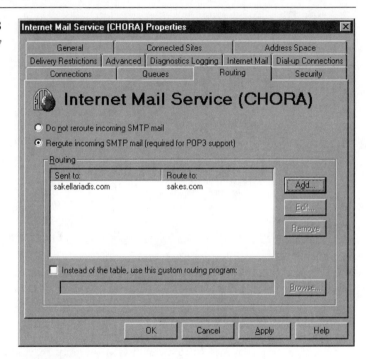

Thus, the Routing tab enables the Internet Mail Service to act as a smart host that can route messages between the Internet and other SMTP hosts without the need to define custom recipients in Exchange Server. For incoming mail, the Help file has a very useful table, reproduced here as Table E.1, that explains the use of this feature.

For example, if you want Exchange Server to be the single point of entry into your organization and you have mail recipients on a third-party system (for example, a Unix host running Sendmail), you could use the Routing tab to route mail to that system. Without this feature, to keep the incoming mail from being rejected, you would need to either do a directory synchronization between the Exchange organization and the third-party system or add custom recipients manually into the Exchange Global Address List.

TABLE E.1 INCOMING MAIL AND THE ROUTER

Option	Description
Do not reroute incoming SMTP mail	Only messages addressed to recipients listed in the Microsoft Exchange Server Global Address List are delivered. All other mail is returned with a non-delivery report (NDR).
Reroute incoming SMTP mail (required for POP3 support)	Incoming mail is rerouted according to the entries in the Routing property page.

Security Tab

The second new tab in the IMS is the Security tab (Figure E.4).

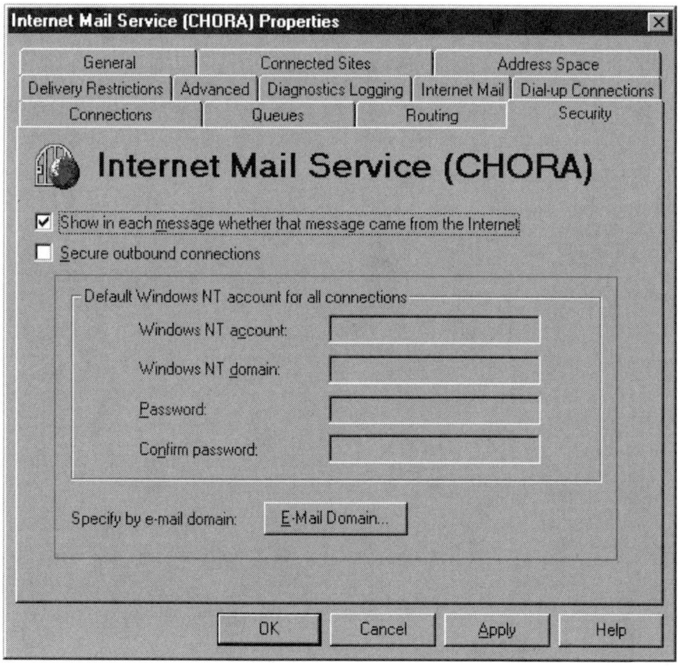

Figure E.4
Security Tab

One of the biggest concerns about the Internet is security, and Exchange Server 5.0 gives you several mechanisms by which to protect SMTP messages sent over the Internet. The Microsoft press release expresses the concern in this way:

> One of the single biggest concerns on the Internet is security. Most if not all SMTP communications occur in the clear, since there was no agreed upon mechanism to encrypt the session. This is still an area of concern on the Internet, and a number of people are thinking about the right solutions. Realizing that our customers need this functionality today, we have implemented support within the SMTP framework to encrypt sessions between consenting hosts.

The Security tab in the Internet Mail Service lets you specify two related features that increase the security between consenting hosts.

The first feature, "Show in each message whether that message comes from the Internet," is a header that Exchange Server 5.0 adds to messages passing through the connector, compliant with the various RFCs for the Header fields for SMTP messages. You can see this header by manually viewing the headers (if you are looking at the message through a sniffer, for example) or using the Exchange 5.0 client. The header of the message will then show whether the message traveled through the IMS in its journey from the sender to the recipient. This information could be of value to the recipient, because the possibility always exists that the message was tampered with or viewed *en route*.

The second feature, Secure Outbound Connections, lets the Exchange administrator limit the IMS to talking to remote connectors in Windows NT sites over trusted connections. For example, if you are connecting remote sites of the same organization via the IMS, this feature lets you ensure that a hostile agent is not impersonating (spoofing) the identity of the remote site.

The security feature that concerns many users of Internet mail in general is that messages are transmitted in 7-bit ASCII, so that most text messages are entirely legible to any unintended recipient of the message. Starting with version 4.0, Exchange Server includes a security feature called the Key Management server that lets users send mail that is encrypted over the wire but only to users within the same organization (that is, to users who have the same Key Management server). Exchange Server 5.0 lets you send encrypted messages to users in different organizations.

When you implement Advanced Security in an Exchange organization, the user can encrypt or digitally sign a message simply by clicking on an icon in the toolbar or by selecting Encrypt (Seal) from the Tools menu. The recipient of an encrypted message sees a lock icon by the message in the Inbox and can only decrypt and read the message if that recipient is the actual intended recipient of the message. Recipients demonstrate their identity by their network login and by entering a private key/password into a decryption dialog box that comes up when they try to read the message. Any unintended recipients of the message cannot read the message.

The end-user process for encrypting and decrypting messages sent with the Exchange client is very user friendly, and the messages themselves are encrypted using CAST 40, DES (56), or CAST 60 algorithms. Note, however, that the purpose of the process is to encrypt messages sent over the Internet to users only in Exchange organizations.

Exchange Server 5.0 provides one more facility to secure SMTP messages sent over the Internet, in the form of encrypting messages downloaded with the POP3 protocol. If you enable POP3 support for a mailbox, you have the option of allowing three types of authentication:

- Basic
- Windows NT Challenge/Response
- Secure Sockets Layer (SSL)

If you pick the SSL method of authentication for the mailbox, all POP3 sessions will encrypt both the authentication session and all subsequent data traveling over the wire. This feature provides, therefore, an encrypted and secure method for transmitting SMTP messages from a server to a client.

BIBLIOGRAPHY

World Wide Web Sites

- ds.internic.net/rfc
- www.cis.ohio-state.edu/text/faq/usenet/mail/mime-faq/part3/faq.html
- www.psi.com
- www.net-shopper.co.uk
- domen.uninett.no/~hta/x400/ (Index to X.400 Web Pages)
- domen.uninett.no/~hta/x400/standards.html (The X.400 Standards)
- www.itu.ch/itudoc/itu-t/rec/x/x200-499.html (ITU-TS. Series X Recommendations: X.200 to X.499)
- andrew2.andrew.cmu.edu/cyrus/email/standards-X400.html (X.400 Protocol Resources)
- www.to.icl.fi/mhstands.html (Message Handling System)

Public Usenet Newsgroups

- comp.mail.mime
- microsoft.public.mail.connectivity
- microsoft.public.exchange.connectivity
- microsoft.public.messaging.misc
- info.ietf.smtp
- microsoft.public.mail.connectivity
- microsoft.public.exchange.clients
- microsoft.public.messaging.misc
- info.ietf.smtp
- comp.protocols.iso.x400

Newsgroups on msnews.microsoft.com

- microsoft.public.exchange.admin
- microsoft.public.exchange.applications
- microsoft.public.exchange.clients
- microsoft.public.exchange.connectivity
- microsoft.public.exchange.misc
- microsoft.public.windowsnt.40

Microsoft Educational Services Courses

- "Implementing Microsoft Mail 3.2," Course 341, Microsoft Educational Services.
- "MS Exchange Server Support Instructor Guide," Product Support Services Worldwide Training, January 2, 1996, Microsoft TechNet CD.
- "Fundamentals of Microsoft Exchange Server 4.0," Course 730, Microsoft Education and Certification.
- "Internetworking with Microsoft TCP/IP on Microsoft Windows NT 3.5," Course 472, Microsoft Education and Certification.
- "Supporting Microsoft Windows NT Server 3.5," Course 659, Microsoft Educational Services.
- "Supporting Systems Management Server 1.1," Course 646, Microsoft Education and Certification.

Microsoft Product Documentation

- Windows NT Server 3.51
- Windows NT Server 4.0
- Microsoft Mail 3.x
- Microsoft Exchange Server 4.0
- Microsoft Systems Management Server 1.1

Microsoft Knowledge Base Articles

- "Appendix A: Introduction to Messaging Standards," *Microsoft Mail Resource Kit*, Microsoft TechNet CD.

- "MS Exchange Server: Using Industry Standards for Greater Compatibility," *Microsoft TechNet CD*, Technical Notes.

- "MS Exchange Server Planning and Optimization Guide," *Microsoft TechNet CD*, Technical Notes.

- "MS Exchange and Mail Coexistence and Migration with LAN and Host Mail Systems," Brian Benjamin, *Microsoft TechNet CD*.

- "X400: How MTAs Initiate and Communicate," *Microsoft Knowledge Base,* Article ID: Q86988; at http://www.microsoft.com/kb/bussys/mail/q86988.htm.

- "XCON: Viewing or Deleting Messages in MTS-IN or MTS-OUT Queues," *Microsoft Knowledge Base,* Article ID: Q151775; at http://www.microsoft.com/kb/bussys/mail/q151775.htm.

- "X400: Documentation Index for X.400 and X.25 Protocols," *Microsoft Knowledge Base,* Article ID: Q86961.

- "How to Configure Windows NT as a Remote IP Router," *Microsoft Knowledge Base*, Article Q123024.

- "Cannot Ping Across Router After Connecting as a RAS Client," *Microsoft Knowledge Base*, Article Q128647.

Digital Equipment Corporation Articles

- "MAILbus400 Message Transfer Agent: Introduction and Glossary," Digital Equipment Corporation, 1194. Order Number: AA-Q89LA-TE.

- "MAILbus400 Message Transfer Agent: Planning and Setup," Digital Equipment Corporation, 1194. Order Number: AA-Q89MB-TE.

- "DEC X.500 Directory Service: Management," Digital Equipment Corporation, 1194. Order Number: AA-QEVEB-TE.

Electronic Messaging Association Publications

- *Internet E-Mail Services*, Electronic Messaging Association, 1994.

- *Externally Defined Body Parts (Body Part 15); Issues and Recommendations*, Electronic Messaging Association, 1994.

- *Directory Attribute Mapping Guide*, Electronic Messaging Association, 1995.

Other Articles and Books

- Sakellariadis, S., "Migrating from MS Mail 3.2/SMTP to MS Exchange Server," *Windows NT Magazine*, pp. 66-73, April 1996.
- Betanov, C., *Introduction to X.400,* Artech House Publishers, 1996.
- *CCITT Recommendations X.400-X.430,* 1984 (commonly called the "Red Book").
- *CCITT/ISO Recommendations X.400-X.420,* 1988 ("Blue Book").
- *Domain Name Registration*, Electronic Messaging Association, 1994.
- Albitz & Liu, *DNS and Bind,* O'Reilly, 1996.
- Comer, D. E., *Internetworking with TCP/IP, Volume I: Principles, Protocols, and Architecture*, Prentice Hall, 1991.
- Comer, D. E., *Internetworking with TCP/IP, Volume II: Design, Implementation, and Internals,* Prentice Hall, 1991.
- Custer, H., *Inside Windows NT,* Microsoft Press, 1992, pp. 315-319.
- Windows NT Resource Kit, Appendix C.
- Tittel, E. and Madden, M., "Easy Access to the Internet," *Windows NT Magazine,* pp. 107–110, July 1996.

INDEX

New Books in the Duke Press Library

MIGRATING TO WINDOWS NT 4.0

By Sean Daily

A comprehensive yet concise guide to the significant changes users will encounter as they make the move to Windows NT 4.0. Includes a wealth of tips and techniques. 9 chapters, 450 pages.

POWERING YOUR WEB SITE WITH WINDOWS NT SERVER

By Nik Simpson

Explores the tools necessary to establish a presence on the Internet or on an internal corporate intranet using WWW technology and Windows NT Server. 500 pages. CD included.

MICROSOFT EXCHANGE UP & RUNNING

By Bill Kilcullen

A practical guide to incorporating the Exchange model. This book is the link between technical manuals and everyday concerns faced by professionals charged with the task of implementing and managing a complex messaging system. 300 pages. CD included.

THE MICROSOFT EXCHANGE USER'S HANDBOOK

By Sue Mosher

A must-have, complete guide for users who need to know how to set up and use all the features of the Microsoft Exchange client product. 600 pages. CD included.

THE ADMINISTRATOR'S GUIDE TO MICROSOFT SQL SERVER 6.5

By Kevin Cox and William Jones

Delivers expert technical advice, practical management guidelines, and an in-depth look at the database administration aspects of the Microsoft SQL Server 6.5 product. 450 pages.

DEVELOPING YOUR AS/400 INTERNET STRATEGY

By Alan Arnold

Addresses the issues unique to deploying your AS/400 on the Internet. Includes procedures for configuring AS/400 TCP/IP and information about which client and server technologies the AS/400 supports natively. Don't put precious corporate data and systems in harm's way. Arnold shows you how to reconcile the AS/400 security-conscious mindset with the less secure philosophy of the Internet community. This enterprise-class tutorial evaluates the AS/400 as an Internet server and teaches you how to design, program, and manage your Web home page. 225 pages.

THE TECHNOLOGY GUIDE TO ACCOUNTING SOFTWARE
A Handbook for Evaluating Vendor Applications

By Stewart McKie

Are you involved in recommending or selecting financial software for your department or company? Whether you are a CFO, an IS professional, or a practicing accountant, if the answer is Yes, then this book is must reading! It is designed to help managers evaluate accounting software, with an emphasis on the issues in a client/server environment. McKie cuts the marketing hype and provides a range of useful checklists for shortlisting products to evaluate in more detail. More than 50 vendors are profiled, and a resource guide and a glossary are included. 225 pages.

Also Published by *NEWS/400* and Duke Press

THE A TO Z OF EDI

By Nahid M. Jilovec

Electronic Data Interchange (EDI) can help reduce administrative costs, accelerate information processing, ensure data accuracy, and streamline business procedures. Here's a comprehensive guide to EDI to help in planning, startup, and implementation. The author reveals all the benefits, challenges, standards, and implementation secrets gained through extensive experience. She shows how to evaluate your business procedures, select special hardware and software, establish communications requirements and standards, address audit issues, and employ the legal support necessary for EDI activities. 263 pages.

APPLICATION DEVELOPER'S HANDBOOK FOR THE AS/400

Edited by Mike Otey, a **NEWS/400** *technical editor*

Explains how to effectively use the AS/400 to build reliable, flexible, and efficient business applications. Contains RPG/400 and CL coding examples and tips, and provides both step-by-step instructions and handy reference material. Includes diskette. 768 pages, 48 chapters.

AS/400 DISK SAVING TIPS & TECHNIQUES

By James R. Plunkett

Want specific help for cleaning up and maintaining your disks? Here are more than 50 tips, plus design techniques for minimizing your disk usage. Each tip is completely explained with the "symptom," the problem, and the technique or code you need to correct it. 72 pages.

AS/400 SUBFILES IN RPG

On the AS/400, subfiles are powerful and easy to use, and with this book you can start working with subfiles in just a few hours — no need to wade through page after page of technical jargon. You'll start with the concept behind subfiles, then discover how easy they are to program. The book contains all of the DDS subfile keywords announced in V2R3 of OS/400. Five complete RPG subfile programs are included, and the book comes complete with a 3.5" PC diskette containing all those programs plus DDS. The book is an updated version of the popular *Programming Subfiles in RPG/400*. 200 pages, 4 chapters.

C FOR RPG PROGRAMMERS

By Jennifer Hamilton, a **NEWS/400** *author*

Written from the perspective of an RPG programmer, this book includes side-by-side coding examples written in both C and RPG clear identification of unique C constructs, and a comparison of RPG op-codes to equivalent C concepts. Includes many tips and examples covering the use of C/400. 292 pages, 23 chapters.

CL BY EXAMPLE

By Virgil Green

CL by Example gives programmers and operators more than 850 pages of practical information you can use in your day-to-day job. It's full of application examples, tips, and techniques, along with a sprinkling of humor. The examples will speed you through the learning curve to help you become a more proficient, more productive CL programmer. 864 pages, 12 chapters.

CLIENT ACCESS TOKEN-RING CONNECTIVITY

By Chris Patterson

Attaching PCs to AS/400s via a Token-Ring can become a complicated subject — when things go wrong, an understanding of PCs, the Token-Ring, and OS/400 is often required. *Client Access Token-Ring Connectivity* details all that is required in these areas to successfully maintain and troubleshoot a Token-Ring network. The first half of the book introduces the Token-Ring and describes the Client Access communications architecture, the Token-Ring connection from both the PC side and the AS/400 side, and the Client Access applications. The second half provides a useful guide to Token-Ring management, strategies for Token-Ring error identification and recovery, and tactics for resolving Client Access error messages. 125 pages, 10 chapters.

COMMON-SENSE C
Advice and warnings for C and C++ programmers

By Paul Conte, a **NEWS/400** *technical editor*

C programming language has its risks; this book shows how C programmers get themselves into trouble, includes tips to help you avoid C's pitfalls, and suggests how to manage C and C++ application development. 100 pages, 9 chapters.

CONTROL LANGUAGE PROGRAMMING FOR THE AS/400

By Bryan Meyers and Dan Riehl, **NEWS/400** *technical editors*

This comprehensive CL programming textbook offers students up-to-the-minute knowledge of the skills they will need in today's MIS environment. Progresses methodically from CL basics to more complex processes and concepts, guiding readers toward a professional grasp of CL programming techniques and style. 512 pages, 25 chapters.

DDS BY EXAMPLE

By R S Tipton

DDS by Example provides detailed coverage of the creation of physical files, field reference files, logical files, display files, and printer files. It includes more than 300 real-life examples, including examples of physical files, simple logical files, multi-format logical files, dynamic selection options, coding subfiles, handling overrides, creating online help, creating reports, and coding windows. 360 pages, 4 chapters.

DDS PROGRAMMING FOR DISPLAY & PRINTER FILES

By James Coolbaugh

Offers a thorough, straightforward explanation of how to use Data Description Specifications (DDS) to program display files and printer files. Covers basic to complex tasks using DDS functions. The author uses DDS programming examples for CL and RPG extensively throughout the book, and you can put these examples to use immediately. Focuses on topics such as general screen presentations, the A specification, defining data on the screen, record-format and field definitions, defining data fields, using indicators, data and text attributes, cursor and keyboard control, editing data, validity checking, response keywords, and function keys. A complimentary diskette includes all the source code presented in the book. 446 pages, 13 chapters.

DATABASE DESIGN AND PROGRAMMING FOR DB2/400

By Paul Conte

This textbook is the comprehensive guide for creating flexible and efficient application databases in DB2/400. The author shows you everything you need to know about physical and logical file DDS, SQL/400, and RPG IV and COBOL/400 database programming. Clear explanations illustrated by a wealth of examples, including complete RPG IV and COBOL/400 programs, demonstrate efficient database programming and error handling with both DDS and SQL/400. Each programming chapter includes a specific list of "Coding Suggestions" that will help you write faster and more maintainable code. In addition, the author provides an extensive section on practical database design for DB2/400. This is the most complete guide to DB2/400 design and programming available anywhere. Approx. 772 pages, 19 chapters.

DESKTOP GUIDE TO THE S/36

By Mel Beckman, Gary Kratzer, and Roger Pence, **NEWS/400** *technical editors*

This definitive S/36 survival manual includes practical techniques to supercharge your S/36, including ready-to-use information for maximum system performance tuning, effective application development, and smart Disk Data Management. Includes a review of two popular Unix-based S/36 work-alike migration alternatives. Diskette contains ready-to-run utilities to help you save machine time and implement power programming techniques such as External Program Calls. 387 pages, 21 chapters.

THE ESSENTIAL GUIDE TO CLIENT ACCESS FOR DOS EXTENDED

By John Enck, Robert E. Anderson, and Michael Otey

The Essential Guide to Client Access for DOS Extended contains key insights and need-to-know technical information about Client Access for DOS Extended, IBM's strategic AS/400 product for DOS and Windows client/server connectivity. This book provides background information about the history and architecture of Client Access for DOS Extended; fundamental information about how to install and configure Client Access; and advanced information about integrating Client Access with other types of networks, managing how Client Access for DOS Extended operates under Windows, and developing client/server applications with Client Access. Written by industry experts based on their personal and professional experiences with Client Access, this book can help you avoid time-consuming pitfalls that litter the path of AS/400 client/server computing. 430 pages, 12 chapters.

ILE: A FIRST LOOK

By George Farr and Shailan Topiwala

This book begins by showing the differences between ILE and its predecessors, then goes on to explain the essentials of an ILE program — using concepts such as modules, binding, service programs, and binding directories. You'll discover how ILE program activation works and how ILE works with its predecessor environments. The book covers the new APIs and new debugging facilities and explains the benefits of ILE's new exception-handling model. You also get answers to the most commonly asked questions about ILE. 183 pages, 9 chapters.

IMPLEMENTING AS/400 SECURITY, SECOND EDITION

A practical guide to implementing, evaluating, and auditing your AS/400 security strategy

By Wayne Madden, a **NEWS/400** *technical editor*

Concise and practical, this second edition brings together in one place the fundamental AS/400 security tools and experience-based recommendations that you need and also includes specifics on the latest security enhancements available in OS/400 Version 3 Release 1. Completely updated from the first edition, this is the only source for the latest information about how to protect your system against attack from its increasing exposure to hackers. 389 pages, 16 chapters.

INSIDE THE AS/400
An in-depth look at the AS/400's design, architecture, and history
By Frank G. Soltis

The inside story every AS/400 developer has been waiting for, told by Dr. Frank G. Soltis, IBM's AS/400 chief architect. Never before has IBM provided an in-depth look at the AS/400's design, architecture, and history. This authoritative book does just that — and also looks at some of the people behind the scenes who created this revolutionary system for you. Whether you are an executive looking for a high-level overview or a "bit-twiddling techie" who wants all the details, *Inside the AS/400* demystifies this system, shedding light on how it came to be, how it can do the things it does, and what its future may hold — especially in light of its new PowerPC RISC processors. 475 pages, 12 chapters.

INTRODUCTION TO AS/400 SYSTEM OPERATIONS
by Patrice Gapen and Heidi Rothenbuehler

Here's the textbook that covers what you need to know to become a successful AS/400 system operator. System operators typically help users resolve problems, manage printed reports, and perform regularly scheduled procedures. *Introduction to AS/400 System Operations* introduces a broad range of topics, including system architecture; DB2/400 and Query; user interface and Operational Assistant; managing jobs and printed reports; backup and restore; system configuration and networks; performance; security; and Client Access (PC Support).

      The information presented here covers typical daily, weekly, and monthly AS/400 operations using V3R1M0 of the OS/400 operating system. You can benefit from this book even if you have only a very basic knowledge of the AS/400. If you know how to sign on to the AS/400, and how to use the function keys, you're ready for the material in this book. 234 pages, 10 chapters.

AN INTRODUCTION TO COMMUNICATIONS FOR THE AS/400, SECOND EDITION
By John Enck and Ruggero Adinolfi

This second edition has been revised to address the sweeping communications changes introduced with V3R1 of OS/400. As a result, this book now covers the broad range of AS/400 communications technology topics, ranging from Ethernet to X.25, and from APPN to AnyNet. The book presents an introduction to data communications and then covers communications fundamentals, types of networks, OSI, SNA, APPN, networking roles, the AS/400 as host and server, TCP/IP, and the AS/400-DEC connection. 210 pages, 13 chapters.

JIM SLOAN'S CL TIPS & TECHNIQUES
By Jim Sloan, developer of QUSRTOOL's TAA Tools

Written for those who understand CL, this book draws from Jim Sloan's knowledge and experience as a developer for the S/38 and the AS/400, and his creation of QUSRTOOL's TAA tools, to give you tips that can help you write better CL programs and become more productive. Includes more than 200 field-tested techniques, plus exercises to help you understand and apply many of the techniques presented. 564 pages, 30 chapters.

MASTERING AS/400 PERFORMANCE
by Alan Arnold, Charly Jones, Jim Stewart, and Rick Turner

If you want more from your AS/400 — faster interactive response time, more batch jobs completed on time, and maximum use of your expensive resources — this book is for you. In *Mastering AS/400 Performance*, the experts tell you how to measure, evaluate, and tune your AS/400's performance. From the authors' experience in the field, they give you techniques for improving performance beyond simply buying additional hardware. Learn the techniques, gain the insight, and help your company profit from the experience of the top AS/400 performance professionals in the country. 259 pages, 14 chapters.

MASTERING THE AS/400

A practical, hands-on guide

By Jerry Fottral

This introductory textbook to AS/400 concepts and facilities has a utilitarian approach that stresses student participation. A natural prerequisite to programming and database management courses, it emphasizes mastery of system/user interface, member-object-library relationship, utilization of CL commands, and basic database and program development utilities. Also includes labs focusing on essential topics such as printer spooling; library lists; creating and maintaining physical files; using logical files; using CL and DDS; working in the PDM environment; and using SEU, DFU, Query, and SDA. 484 pages, 12 chapters.

OBJECT-ORIENTED PROGRAMMING FOR AS/400 PROGRAMMERS

By Jennifer Hamilton, a **NEWS/400** *author*

Explains basic OOP concepts such as classes and inheritance in simple, easy-to-understand terminology. The OS/400 object-oriented architecture serves as the basis for the discussion throughout, and concepts presented are reinforced through an introduction to the C++ object-oriented programming language, using examples based on the OS/400 object model. 114 pages, 14 chapters.

PERFORMANCE PROGRAMMING — MAKING RPG SIZZLE

By Mike Dawson, CDP

Mike Dawson spent more than two years preparing this book — evaluating programming options, comparing techniques, and establishing benchmarks on thousands of programs. "Using the techniques in this book," he says, "I have made program after program run 30%, 40%, even 50% faster." To help you do the same, Mike gives you code and benchmark results for initializing and clearing arrays, performing string manipulation, using validation arrays with look-up techniques, using arrays in arithmetic routines, and a lot more. 257 pages, 8 chapters.

POWER TOOLS FOR THE AS/400, VOLUMES I AND II

Edited by Frederick L. Dick and Dan Riehl

NEWS 3X/400's Power Tools for the AS/400 is a two-volume reference series for people who work with the AS/400. *Volume I* (originally titled *AS/400 Power Tools*) is a collection of the best tools, tips, and techniques published in *NEWS/34-38* (pre-August 1988) and *NEWS 3X/400* (August 1988 through October 1991) that are applicable to the AS/400. *Volume II* extends this original collection by including material that appeared through 1994. Each book includes a diskette that provides load-and-go code for easy-to-use solutions to many everyday problems. *Volume I*: 709 pages, 24 chapters; *Volume II*: 702 pages, 14 chapters.

PROGRAMMING IN RPG IV

By Judy Yaeger, Ph.D., a **NEWS/400** *technical editor*

This textbook provides a strong foundation in the essentials of business programming, featuring the newest version of the RPG language: RPG IV. Focusing on real-world problems and down-to-earth solutions using the latest techniques and features of RPG, this book provides everything you need to know to write a well-designed RPG IV program. Each chapter includes informative, easy-to-read explanations and examples as well as a section of thought-provoking questions, exercises, and programming assignments. Four appendices and a handy, comprehensive glossary support the topics presented throughout the book. An instructor's kit is available. 450 pages, 13 chapters.

PROGRAMMING IN RPG/400, SECOND EDITION

By Judy Yaeger, Ph.D., a **NEWS/400** *technical editor*

This second edition refines and extends the comprehensive instructional material contained in the original textbook and features a new section that introduces externally described printer files, a new chapter that highlights the fundamentals of RPG IV, and a new appendix that correlates the key concepts from each chapter with their RPG IV counterparts. Includes everything you need to learn how to write a well-designed RPG program, from the most basic to the more complex, and each chapter includes a section of questions, exercises, and programming assignments that reinforce the knowledge you have gained from the chapter and strengthen the groundwork for succeeding chapters. An instructor's kit is available. 464 pages, 14 chapters.

PROGRAMMING SUBFILES IN COBOL/400
By Jerry Goldson

Learn how to program subfiles in COBOL/400 in a matter of hours! This powerful and flexible programming technique no longer needs to elude you. You can begin programming with subfiles the same day you get the book. You don't have to wade through page after page, chapter after chapter of rules and parameters and keywords. Instead, you get solid, helpful information and working examples that you can apply to your application programs right away. 204 pages, 5 chapters.

THE QUINTESSENTIAL GUIDE TO PC SUPPORT
By John Enck, Robert E. Anderson, Michael Otey, and Michael Ryan

This comprehensive book about IBM's AS/400 PC Support connectivity product defines the architecture of PC Support and its role in midrange networks, describes PC Support's installation and configuration procedures, and shows you how you can configure and use PC Support to solve real-life problems. 345 pages, 11 chapters.

RPG ERROR HANDLING TECHNIQUE
Bulletproofing Your Applications

By Russell Popeil

RPG Error Handling Technique teaches you the skills you need to use the powerful tools provided by OS/400 and RPG to handle almost any error from within your programs. The book explains the INFSR, INFDS, PSSR, and SDS in programming terms, with examples that show you how all these tools work together and which tools are most appropriate for which kind of error or exception situation. It continues by presenting a robust suite of error/exception handling techniques within RPG programs. Each technique is explained in an application setting, using both RPG III and RPG IV code. 164 pages, 5 chapters.

RPG IV BY EXAMPLE
By George Farr and Shailan Topiwala

RPG IV by Example addresses the needs and concerns of RPG programmers at any level of experience. The focus is on RPG IV in a practical context that lets AS/400 professionals quickly grasp what's new without dwelling on the old. Beginning with an overview of RPG IV specifications, the authors prepare the way for examining all the features of the new version of the language. The chapters that follow explore RPG IV further with practical, easy-to-use applications. 500 pages, 15 chapters.

RPG IV JUMP START, SECOND EDITION
Moving ahead with the new RPG

By Bryan Meyers, a **NEWS/400** *technical editor*

In this second edition of *RPG IV Jump Start*, Bryan Meyers has added coverage for new releases of the RPG IV compiler (V3R2, V3R6, and V3R7) and amplified the coverage of RPG IV's participation in the integrated language environment (ILE). As in the first edition, he covers RPG IV's changed and new specifications and data types. He presents the new RPG from the perspective of a programmer who already knows the old RPG, pointing out the differences between the two and demonstrating how to take advantage of the new syntax and function. 204 pages, 16 chapters.

RPG/400 INTERACTIVE TEMPLATE TECHNIQUE

By Carson Soule, CDP, CCP, CSP

Here's an updated version of Carson Soule's *Interactive RPG/400 Programming*. The book shows you time-saving, program-sharpening concepts behind the template approach, and includes all the code you need to build one perfect program after another. These templates include code for cursor-sensitive prompting in DDS, for handling messages in resident RPG programs, for using the CLEAR opcode to eliminate hard-coded field initialization, and much more. There's even a new select template with a pop-up window. 258 pages, 10 chapters.

S/36 POWER TOOLS

Edited by Chuck Lundgren, a **NEWS/400** *technical editor*

Winner of an STC Award of Achievement in 1992, this book contains five years' worth of articles, tips, and programs published in *NEWS 3X/400* from 1986 to October 1990, including more than 280 programs and procedures. Extensively cross-referenced for fast and easy problem solving, and complete with diskette containing all the programming code. 738 pages, 20 chapters.

STARTER KIT FOR THE AS/400, SECOND EDITION

An indispensable guide for novice to intermediate AS/400 programmers and system operators

By Wayne Madden, a **NEWS/400** *technical editor*
with contributions by Bryan Meyers, Andrew Smith, and Peter Rowley

This second edition contains updates of the material in the first edition and incorporates new material to enhance its value as a resource to help you learn important basic concepts and nuances of the AS/400 system. New material focuses on installing a new release, working with PTFs, AS/400 message handling, working with and securing printed output, using operational assistant to manage disk space, job scheduling, save and restore basics, and more basic CL programming concepts. Optional diskette available. 429 pages, 33 chapters.

SUBFILE TECHNIQUE FOR RPG/400 PROGRAMMERS

By Jonathan Yergin, CDP, and Wayne Madden

Here's the code you need for a complete library of shell subfile programs: RPG/400 code, DDS, CL, and sample data files. There's even an example for programming windows. You even get some "whiz bang" techniques that add punch to your applications. This book explains the code in simple, straightforward style and tells you when each technique should be used for best results. 326 pages, 11 chapters, 3.5" PC diskette included.

TECHNICAL REFERENCE SERIES

Edited by Bryan Meyers, a **NEWS/400** *technical editor*

Written by experts — such as John Enck, Bryan Meyers, Julian Monypenny, Roger Pence, Dan Riehl — these unique desktop guides put the latest AS/400 applications and techniques at your fingertips. These "just-do-it" books (featuring wire-o binding to open flat at every page) are priced so you can keep your personal set handy. Optional online Windows help diskette available for each book.

Desktop Guide to CL Programming

By Bryan Meyers, a **NEWS/400** *technical editor*

This first book of the **NEWS/400** *Technical Reference Series* is packed with easy-to-find notes, short explanations, practical tips, answers to most of your everyday questions about CL, and CL code segments you can use in your own CL programming. Complete "short reference" lists every command and explains the most-often-used ones, along with names of the files they use and the MONMSG messages to use with them. 205 pages, 36 chapters.

Desktop Guide to AS/400 Programmers' Tools

By Dan Riehl, a **NEWS/400** *technical editor*

This second book of the **NEWS/400** *Technical Reference Series* gives you the "how-to" behind all the tools included in *Application Development ToolSet/400* (ADTS/400), IBM's Licensed Program Product for Version 3 of OS/400; includes Source Entry Utility (SEU), Programming Development Manager (PDM), Screen Design Aid (SDA), Report Layout Utility (RLU), File Compare/Merge Utility (FCMU), and Interactive Source Debugger. Highlights topics and functions specific to Version 3 of OS/400. 266 pages, 30 chapters.

Desktop Guide to DDS

By James Coolbaugh

This third book of the **NEWS/400** *Technical Reference Series* provides a complete reference to all DDS keywords for physical, logical, display, printer, and ICF files. Each keyword is briefly explained, with syntax rules and examples showing how to code the keyword. All basic and pertinent information is provided for quick and easy access. While this guide explains every parameter for a keyword, it doesn't explain every possible exception that might exist. Rather, the guide includes the basics about what each keyword is designed to accomplish. The *Desktop Guide to DDS* is designed to give quick, "at your fingertips" information about every keyword — with this in hand, you won't need to refer to IBM's bulky *DDS Reference* manual. 132 pages, 5 major sections.

Desktop Guide to RPG/400

By Roger Pence and Julian Monypenny, **NEWS/400** *technical editors*

This fourth book in the *Technical Reference Series* provides a variety of RPG templates, subroutines, and copy modules, sprinkled with evangelical advice that will help you write robust and effective RPG/400 programs. Highlights of the information provided include string-handling routines, numeric editing routines, date routines, error-handling modules, tips for using OS/400 APIs with RPG/400, and interactive programming techniques. For all types of RPG projects, this book's tested and ready-to-run building blocks will easily snap into your RPG. The programming solutions provided here would otherwise take you days or even weeks to write and test. 211 pages, 28 chapters.

Desktop Guide to Creating CL Commands

By Lynn Nelson

In this most recent book in the *Technical Reference Series*, author Lynn Nelson shows you how to create your own CL commands with the same functionality and power as the IBM commands you use every day, including automatic parameter editing, all the function keys, F4 prompt for values, expanding lists of values, and conditional prompting. After you have read this book, you can write macros for the operations you do over and over every day or write application commands that prompt users for essential information. Whether you're in operations or programming, don't miss this opportunity to enhance your career-building skills. 164 pages, 14 chapters.

UNDERSTANDING BAR CODES

By James R. Plunkett

One of the most important waves of technology sweeping American industry is the use of bar coding to capture and track data. The wave is powered by two needs: the need to gather information in a more accurate and timely manner and the need to track that information once it is gathered. Bar coding meets these needs and provides creative and cost-effective solutions for many applications. With so many leading-edge technologies, it can be difficult for IS professionals to keep up with the concepts and applications they need to make solid decisions. This book gives you an overview of bar code technology including a discussion of the bar codes themselves, the hardware that supports bar coding, how and when to justify and then implement a bar code application, plus examples of many different applications and how bar coding can be used to solve problems. 70 pages.

USING QUERY/400

By Patrice Gapen and Catherine Stoughton

This textbook, designed for any AS/400 user from student to professional with or without prior programming knowledge, presents Query as an easy and fast tool for creating reports and files from AS/400 databases. Topics are ordered from simple to complex and emphasize hands-on AS/400 use; they include defining database files to Query, selecting and sequencing fields, generating new numeric and character fields, sorting within Query, joining database files, defining custom headings, creating new database files, and more. Instructor's kit available. 92 pages, 10 chapters.

USING VISUAL BASIC WITH CLIENT ACCESS APIs

By Ron Jones

This book is for programmers who want to develop client/server solutions on the AS/400 and the personal computer. Whether you are a VB novice or a VB expert, you will gain by reading this book because it provides a thorough overview of the principles and requirements for programming in Windows using VB. Companion diskettes contain source code for all the programming projects referenced in the book, as well as for numerous other utilities and programs. All the projects are compatible with Windows 95 and VB 4.0. 680 pages, 13 chapters.

FOR A COMPLETE CATALOG OR TO PLACE AN ORDER, CONTACT

NEWS/400 and Duke Press

Duke Communications International
221 E. 29th Street • Loveland, CO 80538-2727
(800) 621-1544 • (970) 663-4700 • Fax: (970) 669-3016
or shop our Web site: **www.dukepress.com**

Subscribe Now
No Risk!

Subscribe now to *Windows NT Magazine* and save over 32% off the newsstand price for a year!

Windows NT Magazine is the leading publication for IS professionals and other technical decision makers using the Windows NT operating system. *Windows NT Magazine* delivers helpful strategies for migration, enterprise networking, interoperability, and software development on Windows NT.

Try it at no risk –
Satisfaction guaranteed!